From Haven to Home

350 Years of Jewish Life in America

שפּיין וועט געווינען די קריעג!

איהר קומט אהער צו געפינען פרייהייט.

יעצט מוזט איהר העלפען זיא צו בעשיצען

מיר מוזען די עלליים פערזארגען מיט ווייץ.

לאזט קיין זאך ניט גיין אין ניוועץ

יוניטעד סטייטס שפּיין פערוואלטונג.

From Haven to Home

350 Years of Jewish Life in America

Editor:

Michael W. Grunberger

Contributors:

Hasia Diner

Leonard Dinnerstein

Eli N. Evans

Eli Faber

Deborah Dash Moore

Pamela S. Nadell

Peggy K. Pearlstein

Jonathan D. Sarna

Jeffrey Shandler

Jack Wertheimer

Stephen J. Whitfield

George Braziller, Inc.
In Association with the
Library of Congress

From Haven to Home:
350 Years of Jewish Life in America
*was made possible by a generous grant
from the Abby and Emily Rapoport
Trust Fund in the Library of Congress.*

———————————————

For the Library of Congress
W. Ralph Eubanks, Director of Publishing
Iris B. Newsom, Editor
Aimee Hess, Editorial Assistant
Antonio Alcalá, Designer

*For information,
please address the publisher:*
George Braziller, Inc.
*171 Madison Avenue
New York, NY 10016*

Cover (detail) and frontispiece:
This World War I poster, published by the U.S. Food Administration, appeals in Yiddish to the patriotic spirit and gratitude of the new arrivals to America. Its message reads: "Food Will Win the War! You came here seeking freedom, now you must help to preserve it. We must provide the Allies with wheat. Let Nothing Go To Waste!" Versions of this poster were issued in English and Italian as well.

Charles Edward Chambers, Shpeyz Vet Gevinen di Krieg! *(Food Will Win the War!), [New York], 1917. Prints and Photographs Division.*

Contents:
Shown here is the Inspection Room on Ellis Island, where new immigrants were interviewed by inspectors after passing a medical examination.

Detroit Publishing Company, *[Inspection room, Ellis Island, New York, New York], New York, circa 1912. Prints and Photographs Division.*

Library of Congress Cataloging-in-Publication Data

*From haven to home : 350 years of Jewish life in America / editor, Michael W.
Grunberger ; contributors, Hasia Diner ...[et al.].
p. cm.
Includes bibliographical references and index.*
ISBN 0-8076-1537-4 *(hardback)*
*1. Jews—United States—History. 2. Jews—United States—Emigration and immigra-
tion. 3. Jews—United States—Politics and government. 4. United States—History—
Civil War, 1861-1865—Jews. 5. Judaism—United States—History. 6. Jews in public
life—United States. 7. Antisemitism—United States—History. 8. United States—
Ethnic relations.
I. Grunberger, Michael W. II. Diner, Hasia R. III. Title.
E184.35.F76 2004
973'.04924—dc22   2004014574*

Printed in China

This volume is
dedicated to the
memory of
Abraham J. Karp
(1921-2003)—
rabbi, teacher,
collector of Hebraica,
and scholar of the
American Jewish
experience par
excellence—whose
bibliographic
tour-de-force,
*From the Ends
of the Earth*,
introduced America
to the unparalleled
collection of
Judaic treasures
preserved and made
available at the
Library of Congress.

Contents

T his volume accompanies a Library of Congress exhibition, *From Haven to Home: 350 Years of Jewish Life in America,* which opens in the Library's Thomas Jefferson Building on September 9, 2004. The exhibition marks the anniversary of the arrival in New Amsterdam of twenty-three Jews fleeing Recife (Brazil), which passed from Dutch to Portuguese rule in 1654. It is to this singular event that today's American Jewish community, robust in achievement far beyond its modest size, traces its beginnings.

The Library's collections, which currently include more than 125 million items, are rich in materials that document the history of America's Jewish community. Housed in the Library of Congress are letters from American Presidents Washington, Madison, Jefferson, and Lincoln, among others, to prominent American Jews of their day; comprehensive collections of printed books and newspapers published in the United States by and about America's Jews; and materials in multiple formats—prints, photographs, recordings, and motion pictures—all testifying to a deeply sympathetic, intensely creative, and continuously reciprocal relationship between America and its Jewish community.

It is precisely this enduring relationship that is explored by the distinguished group of historians whose essays are included in this companion volume to the exhibition. The essays

---

The Declaration of Independence *is Arthur Szyk's homage to America, his adopted land. Considered by many to be one of the twentieth century's finest miniaturists, Szyk was born to Jewish parents in Lodz, Poland, and, in 1940, emigrated to the United States where he became a citizen in 1948. This work, which was unveiled at a special ceremony on July 4, 1950, in New Canaan, Connecticut, is an exuberant expression of American patriotism using exquisitely rendered miniatures depicting historical vignettes and iconic symbols drawn from early American history.*

Arthur Szyk, Declaration of Independence, *1950. Prints and Photographs Division. Courtesy of Alexandra Bracie.*

offered here present insightful contributions to our understanding of the complexities of American Jewish history, helping us to grasp the uniqueness of the American Jewish experience while at the same time framing this experience within the overall context of American history and culture.

In mounting this exhibition, the Library of Congress has worked closely with its partners on the Commission to Commemorate 350 Years of American Jewish History: the American Jewish Archives, the American Jewish Historical Society, and the National Archives and Records Administration. The Commission's work, which represents an unprecedented collaboration between national repositories, was recognized by the U.S. Congress in a Concurrent Resolution passed on November 21, 2003. We gratefully acknowledge the Commission's assistance and thank the Commission members for their generous loans of documents and artifacts that have greatly enriched the exhibition. We are pleased that our collaboration will result in a version of this exhibition that will travel to New York, Cincinnati, and Los Angeles.

It is with deep and abiding gratitude that we acknowledge the extraordinary generosity of Mr. and Mrs. Bernard Rapoport, steadfast friends and supporters of the Library of Congress. The Library programs and events marking this anniversary—the exhibition, this companion volume, as well as a series of supplementary public programs were all made possible by a generous grant from the Abby and Emily Rapoport Trust Fund in the Library of Congress, a fund established by the Rapoports to support the Judaic programs of the Library and named in honor of their two granddaughters.

On November 24, 2003, as this book and exhibition were nearing completion, Rabbi Abraham J. Karp, a leading scholar of American Jewish history and a great friend of the Library of Congress, died in New York City. His 1991 masterwork, *From the Ends of the Earth: Judaic Treasures of the Library of Congress*, introduced the American people to the remarkable collection of Judaica and Hebraica housed in this nation's library; in a very real sense, this exhibition and catalog may be seen as a continuation of his great work. Rabbi Karp's deep erudition and galvanizing enthusiasm will be sorely missed by friends of learning and booklore the world over.

James H. Billington
The Librarian of Congress

I n September of 1654, a boatload of impoverished Jews fleeing from Recife, Brazil, landed on the shores of New Amsterdam seeking refuge. American Jewry formally marked this historical episode in 1905 and, in doing so, America's role as a great *haven* for Jewry became the focal point of this first national commemoration. The occasion celebrated the fact that 250 years had passed since Jews had won permission "to live and reside" in the New Netherlands.

A yearlong American Jewish Tercentenary was commemorated fifty years later (1954-1955) with a nationwide series of events and observances focusing on the theme "Man's Opportunities and Responsibilities Under Freedom." This universalistic motif clearly expressed U.S. Jewry's sense of being at *home* in America. The academic study of American Jewry was still in its infancy on that occasion, but the Tercentenary successfully underscored the importance of preserving and reconstructing the history of Jewish life in the American nation.

Another half-century has now passed, and from September 2004 through the fall of 2005 the American nation will observe the 350th anniversary of Jewish communal life in North America. Years from now, when historians compare and contrast the evolving character and content of these three historical commemorations, they will undoubtedly take note of one particular development that clearly distinguishes the 350th anniversary from its two predecessors:

In 1905, at the 250th anniversary of Jewish settlement in America, and again in 1954 at the 300th anniversary, commemorative medals were struck to mark the occasions. The 250th anniversary medal was presented to President Theodore Roosevelt "in recognition of his humane endeavors on behalf of the Jews oppressed in other lands." It was designed by Isidor Konti.

Isidor Konti (designer), 250th Commemorative Medal, 1905. Courtesy of the HUC Skirball Cultural Center Museum Collection, Los Angeles, California. Photography by Susan Eisenstein.

The medal issued to commemorate the 300th anniversary of Jewish settlement in America bore the inscription: "Man's Opportunities and Responsibilities Under Freedom." The medal was issued in both gold and bronze finishes and was used for special presentations at tercentenary functions. The 300th anniversary medal was designed by Nancy Dryfoos.

Nancy Dryfoos (designer), Tercentenary Commemorative Medal, 1954. Hebraic Section.

the establishment of the Congressionally recognized "Commission for Commemorating 350 Years of American Jewish History."

The "Commission" consists of four national research institutions whose large collections provide the public with access to the records that document the history of American Jewry: The Jacob Rader Marcus Center of the American Jewish Archives (AJA), the American Jewish Historical Society (AJHS), the Library of Congress (LC), and the National Archives and Records Administration (NARA). This historic partnership marks the first time in the nation's history that a collaboration of this kind has taken place in a common effort to advance our understanding of the American Jewish experience. In a sense, it marks the "coming of age" of American Jewish history, and in its own way serves as a powerful demonstration of how American culture has dramatically affected the character of Jewish life on these shores even as American Jewry has significantly influenced the overall character of the United States.

Commission members Greg Bradsher (NARA), Michael Feldberg (AJHS), and Michael Grunberger (LC) join me in acknowledging the fine support of James H. Billington, Librarian of Congress, and Governor John Carlin, Archivist of the United States, without whom this historic collaboration could not have come into being.

In his *Memoirs of American Jews, 1775–1865,* Jacob Rader Marcus (1896–1995), the "Dean of American Jewish Historians," observed that "American Jewish history is the story of *all* that happened to the Jew as an American." The Commission for Commemorating 350 Years of American Jewish History salutes the Library of Congress for retelling that story by means of a remarkable exhibit—*From Haven to Home*—and the illuminating essays published in this exhibit catalog.

Gary P. Zola, Chair
The Commission for Commemorating
350 Years of American Jewish History
&
Executive Director
The Jacob Rader Marcus Center of the
American Jewish Archives

THE GENUINE
WORKS
OF
FLAVIUS JOSEPHUS,
THE
JEWISH HISTORIAN.

Tranflated from the ORIGINAL GREEK, according to *Havercamp*'s accurate EDITION.

CONTAINING

Twenty Books of the *JEWISH* ANTIQUITIES,

WITH THE

APPENDIX, or LIFE of *JOSEPHUS,* written by himfelf:

Seven Books of the *JEWISH* WAR:

AND

Two Books againft *APION.*

ILLUSTRATED

With new PLANS and DESCRIPTIONS of the TABERNACLE of *Mofes;* and of the TEMPLES of *Solomon, Zorobabel, Herod,* and *Ezekiel;* and with correct MAPS of *Judea* and *Jerufalem.*

Together with

Proper Notes, Obfervations, Contents, Parallel Texts of Scripture, five compleat Indexes, and the true Chronology of the feveral Hiftories adjufted in the Margin.

To this BOOK are prefixed eight DISSERTATIONS, *viz.*

I. The Teftimonies of *Jofephus* vindicated.
II. The Copy of the Old Teftament made ufe of by *Jofephus,* proved to be that which was collected by *Nehemiah.*
III. Concerning God's Command to *Abraham,* to offer up *Ifaac* his Son for a Sacrifice.
IV. A large Enquiry into the true Chronology of *Jofephus.*
V. An Extract out of *Jofephus*'s Exhortation to the *Greeks,* concerning *Hades,* and the Refurrection of the Dead.

VI. Proofs that this Exhortation is genuine; and was no other than a Homily of *Jofephus*'s, when he was Bifhop of *Jerufalem.*
VII. A Demonftration that *Tacitus,* the *Roman* Hiftorian, took his Hiftory of the *Jews* out of *Jofephus.*
VIII. A Differtation of *Cellarius*'s againft *Harduin;* in Vindication of *Jofephus*'s Hiftory of the Family of *Herod* from Coins. Tranflated into *Englifh.*

With an ACCOUNT of the *Jewifh* Coins, Weights, and Meafures.

By *WILLIAM WHISTON,* M.A.
Some time Profeffor of the Mathematicks in the Univerfity of *Cambridge.*

LONDON,
Printed by W. BOWYER for the AUTHOR: and are to be fold by JOHN WHISTON, Bookfeller, at Mr. *Boyle*'s Head: *Fleetftreet.* MDCCXXXVII.

Introduction

Michael W. Grunberger

This book accompanies an exhibition of American Judaica mounted by the Library of Congress to commemorate the beginnings of American Jewish life in 1654, when twenty-three Jewish refugees from Recife, Brazil, landed in New Amsterdam. The exhibition, *From Haven to Home: 350 Years of Jewish Life in America*, features items from the collections of the Library of Congress, as well as a selection of materials from other repositories, including the Library's partners on the Commission to Celebrate 350 Years of American Jewish History: the American Jewish Archives, the American Jewish Historical Society, and the National Archives and Records Administration.

Judaica has been part of the collections of the Library of Congress since its earliest days. In 1815, Thomas Jefferson's collection of 6,487 volumes arrived in the Capitol, forming the core of a newly reconstituted congressional library, replacing the one that was burned by British troops the year before. Among Jefferson's books were a handful of notable Judaic titles, including William Whiston's translation of *The Genuine Works of Flavius Josephus, the Jewish Historian*, which was published in London in 1737. Josephus, a leader of the first-century Jewish rebellion against Rome, was captured and exiled to Rome. There he wrote *The Jewish Wars* and *Antiquities of the Jews*—works of enduring popularity that have appeared in many printed editions and translations to this day. It is likely that Josephus's account of the Jewish rebellion in 66 CE against Rome—the imperial power of its day—

A leader of the Jewish rebellion against Rome (68 CE), Flavius Josephus surrendered and became a pensioner of the Roman Emperor Vespasian. This translation of Josephus's account of the first-century Jewish rebellion against Rome may have served as inspiration for the author of the Declaration of Independence. It survives from Jefferson's personal library.

Flavius Josephus, The Genuine Works of Flavius Josephus, the Jewish Historian *.... (London, 1737). Jefferson Collection, Rare Book and Special Collections Division.*

בראשית

LIBER GENESIS.

CAPUT I. א

Deus creat cœlum et terram.

א בְּרֵאשִׁית בָּרָא אֱלֹהִים אֵת הַשָּׁמַיִם וְאֵת הָאָרֶץ:
2 וְהָאָרֶץ הָיְתָה תֹהוּ וָבֹהוּ וְחֹשֶׁךְ עַל־פְּנֵי תְהוֹם וְרוּחַ

Creat lucem, ac distinguit inter lucem et tenebras.

3 אֱלֹהִים מְרַחֶפֶת עַל פְּנֵי הַמָּיִם: וַיֹּאמֶר אֱלֹהִים יְהִי
4 אוֹר וַיְהִי אוֹר: וַיַּרְא אֱלֹהִים אֶת הָאוֹר כִּי טוֹב וַיַּבְדֵּל
5 אֱלֹהִים בֵּין הָאוֹר וּבֵין הַחֹשֶׁךְ: וַיִּקְרָא אֱלֹהִים
לָאוֹר יוֹם וְלַחֹשֶׁךְ קָרָא לַיְלָה וַיְהִי עֶרֶב וַיְהִי בֹקֶר יוֹם
אֶחָד:
פ

6 Creat expansum, et separat aquas aquis inferiores a superioribus.

6 וַיֹּאמֶר אֱלֹהִים יְהִי רָקִיעַ בְּתוֹךְ הַמָּיִם וִיהִי מַבְדִּיל בֵּין
7 מַיִם לָמָיִם: וַיַּעַשׂ אֱלֹהִים אֶת הָרָקִיעַ וַיַּבְדֵּל בֵּין הַמַּיִם
אֲשֶׁר מִתַּחַת לָרָקִיעַ וּבֵין הַמַּיִם אֲשֶׁר מֵעַל לָרָקִיעַ וַיְהִי
8 כֵן: וַיִּקְרָא אֱלֹהִים לָרָקִיעַ שָׁמָיִם וַיְהִי עֶרֶב וַיְהִי בֹקֶר
יוֹם שֵׁנִי:
פ

9 Aquæ confluunt in unum locum. Terra apparet et producit fructus.

9 וַיֹּאמֶר אֱלֹהִים יִקָּווּ הַמַּיִם מִתַּחַת הַשָּׁמַיִם אֶל מָקוֹם
10 אֶחָד וְתֵרָאֶה הַיַּבָּשָׁה וַיְהִי כֵן: וַיִּקְרָא אֱלֹהִים לַיַּבָּשָׁה
אֶרֶץ וּלְמִקְוֵה הַמַּיִם קָרָא יַמִּים וַיַּרְא אֱלֹהִים כִּי טוֹב:
11 וַיֹּאמֶר אֱלֹהִים תַּדְשֵׁא הָאָרֶץ דֶּשֶׁא עֵשֶׂב מַזְרִיעַ זֶרַע עֵץ
פְּרִי עֹשֶׂה פְּרִי לְמִינוֹ אֲשֶׁר זַרְעוֹ בוֹ עַל הָאָרֶץ וַיְהִי כֵן:
12 וַתּוֹצֵא הָאָרֶץ דֶּשֶׁא עֵשֶׂב מַזְרִיעַ זֶרַע לְמִינֵהוּ וְעֵץ עֹשֶׂה
13 פְּרִי אֲשֶׁר זַרְעוֹ בוֹ לְמִינֵהוּ וַיַּרְא אֱלֹהִים כִּי טוֹב: וַיְהִי
עֶרֶב וַיְהִי בֹקֶר יוֹם שְׁלִישִׁי:
פ

14 Deus creat luminaria in expanso.

14 וַיֹּאמֶר אֱלֹהִים יְהִי מְאֹרֹת בִּרְקִיעַ הַשָּׁמַיִם לְהַבְדִּיל בֵּין
הַיּוֹם וּבֵין הַלָּיְלָה וְהָיוּ לְאֹתֹת וּלְמוֹעֲדִים וּלְיָמִים וְשָׁנִים:
15 וְהָיוּ לִמְאוֹרֹת בִּרְקִיעַ הַשָּׁמַיִם לְהָאִיר עַל הָאָרֶץ וַיְהִי
16 כֵן: וַיַּעַשׂ אֱלֹהִים אֶת שְׁנֵי הַמְּאֹרֹת הַגְּדֹלִים אֶת
הַמָּאוֹר הַגָּדֹל לְמֶמְשֶׁלֶת הַיּוֹם וְאֶת הַמָּאוֹר הַקָּטֹן
17 לְמֶמְשֶׁלֶת הַלַּיְלָה וְאֵת הַכּוֹכָבִים: וַיִּתֵּן אֹתָם אֱלֹהִים
18 בִּרְקִיעַ הַשָּׁמַיִם לְהָאִיר עַל הָאָרֶץ: וְלִמְשֹׁל בַּיּוֹם
וּבַלַּיְלָה

A

The first complete Hebrew Bible in America appeared in a two-volume edition published in Philadelphia in 1814. Unlike the Amsterdam edition upon which it is based, this printing lacks vowel points. It is opened here to the first page of Beresheet *(Genesis).*

Biblia Hebraica, *2 vols. (Philadelphia, 1814). Hebraic Section.*

had a special resonance for the author of the Declaration of Independence. Other noteworthy Judaic titles in Jefferson's collection included a Latin translation of the *Baba Kamma* tractate of the Mishnah (a compendium of Jewish law and lore compiled circa 200 CE), published in Leyden in 1637, and a 1677 work on the grammar of the Hebrew language by the philosopher Baruch Spinoza, which appeared in Amsterdam as the fifth volume of his *Opera Posthuma* (Posthumous Works).

The origins of the Library of Congress's Hebraic collection may be traced to Jacob H. Schiff's gifts in 1912 and 1914 that enabled the Library to purchase nearly ten thousand Judaic books, manuscripts, pamphlets, and broadsides, from the private collection of noted bookseller and bibliographer, Ephraim Deinard. In the years following these initial gifts, the Library developed and expanded its Hebraic and Judaic holdings to include a wide range of research materials in Hebrew and related languages. Today, the Hebraic Section holds more than 170,000 items in Hebrew, Yiddish, Ladino, Judeo-Arabic, Judeo-Persian, Aramaic, Syriac, Coptic, Ge'ez, Amharic, and Tigrina. The Library's collection is especially strong in American Judaica, featuring a wide range of materials issued in the United States in multiple languages—primarily but not exclusively in English, Yiddish, and Hebrew—and in various formats, including printed books, manuscripts, pamphlets, microforms, broadsides, sheet music, maps, prints, photographs, films, and sound recordings. Unique to the Hebraic Section is a collection of some twelve hundred Yiddish play scripts submitted to the Library of Congress for copyright registration from the late nineteenth century until the midtwentieth century. A good number of the plays represented in this singular collection of typed, printed, and handwritten scripts were performed on the American Yiddish stage in the first half of the twentieth century.

Counted among the Hebraic treasures held in the national library is the first Hebrew Bible printed in America, a two-volume edition of the *Biblia Hebraica* (Hebrew Bible) that appeared in Philadelphia in 1814. The Bible, which was based upon an earlier Amsterdam edition, received the backing of both Jewish leaders as well as Christian clergymen, reflecting both an early instance of interfaith cooperation and a period of religious renewal that emphasized Bible study in its original language.

Of special interest is the first American haggadah, which appeared in 1837 in New York City. The haggadah, the quintessential Jewish prayer book for the home, recounts the story of the Exodus from Egypt and is recited at the festive meal of Passover. It is one of Judaism's most popular works, with more than four thousand editions of the Passover haggadah having been published to date in hundreds of cities and towns throughout the world. Solomon Jackson, the publisher of the 1837 edition of the haggadah, labeled it the "First American Edition," a point of such pride and significance that he mentioned it prominently on its English title page. By identifying it as "the first," Jackson signaled his confidence that more editions would be sure to follow to meet American Jewry's growing needs. For Jackson, this "First American Edition" reflected his own personal transformation from a sojourner in a place of temporary haven to a citizen at home in the United States of America.

The view of America as both a haven and a home reflects this country's extraordinary hospitality to the civilizations and cultures of the diverse groups of Jewish immigrants who, over the centuries, made America their home. For America's Jews, the "golden door" swung wide open, and the twin blessings of freedom and opportunity encouraged and rewarded active participation in society-at-large. But persistent challenges to group survival have also been a consequence of this unprecedented freedom, and, in response to these pressures, new modes of group affiliation and identification emerged. The essays in this companion volume, written by leading specialists in the field of American Jewish history, do much to illuminate our understanding of the American Jewish experience by addressing its singular nature within the broader context of American religious, social, political, and cultural life.

In "Prologue to American Jewish History: The Jews of America from 1654 to 1820," Eli Faber describes America's nascent Jewish communities and their struggles to address the challenges to group survival presented by an open and free society. Eli N. Evans, in "The War Between Jewish Brothers in America," chronicles the participation of Jews on both sides of the Civil War, with a particular focus on individuals such as Confederate statesman Judah Benjamin, the activist Levy sisters, and Isachar Zacharie, podiatrist, confidante, and personal emissary of President Lincoln. "A Century of Migration, 1820–1924," by Hasia Diner, identifies the European roots and characteristics of each of the migrations that over the course of a century transformed and strengthened both America and its Jewish community. In "The Crucial Decades," Deborah Dash Moore examines the years between the two World Wars, a time of settling in and adjustment, through the eyes of Lillian Burstein, an immigrant who arrived in America as a child after the First World War. Jack Wertheimer, in "American Jewry Since 1945," brings the story of America's Jews up to the present, beginning with the aftermath of the Holocaust and then describing the social and political activism, as well as the challenges, that emerged in its wake.

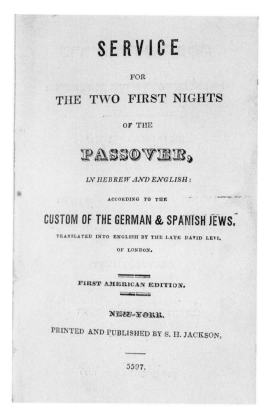

SERVICE

FOR

THE TWO FIRST NIGHTS

OF THE

PASSOVER,

IN HEBREW AND ENGLISH:

ACCORDING TO THE

CUSTOM OF THE GERMAN & SPANISH JEWS,

TRANSLATED INTO ENGLISH BY THE LATE DAVID LEVI,
OF LONDON.

FIRST AMERICAN EDITION.

NEW-YORK.

PRINTED AND PUBLISHED BY S. H. JACKSON,

5597.

The "First American Haggadah" was published in 1837 by Solomon Jackson, a native of England, who was the first Jewish printer in New York. The haggadah's forty-three leaves include the original Hebrew text, as well as an English translation by David Levi of London. Interestingly, the haggadah incorporates both Ashkenazic and Sephardic customs, as well as the prescient and optimistic statement by the publisher that this is the First American Edition—"first," with others sure to follow.

Service for the Two First Nights of the Passover....
(New York, 1837). Gift of Leiner Temerlin, augmented by a grant from the Madison Council. Hebraic Section.

Jonathan D. Sarna's essay on "American Judaism" explores the development of the varieties of American Judaism that have emerged in the uniquely American pluralistic religious and cultural milieu. In her essay on "America's Jewish Women," Pamela S. Nadell weaves a history of Jewish women from colonial times to the present, drawing our attention especially to Abigail Franks, Rebecca Gratz, and Emma Lazarus. Leonard Dinnerstein's overview, "A History of American Anti-Semitism," examines the phenomenon of anti-Semitism in America with special attention focused on the lynching of Leo Frank in 1915 and *The Dearborn Independent*, an anti-Semitic weekly underwritten by Henry Ford in the 1920s. Stephen J. Whitfield analyzes the long-standing and oft-times paradoxical voting patterns of America's Jews over the course of the last century in his essay on "American Jews and Politics." In "American Jewish Popular Culture," Jeffrey Shandler examines the ways in which Yiddish language and culture, social action, and popular culture have helped to shape individual and communal identities. For readers seeking to deepen their understanding of the topics raised in these essays, a bibliography of "Suggested Readings in American Jewish History," compiled by Peggy K. Pearlstein, has been included as a fitting conclusion to this companion volume.

The Library of Congress's exhibition, also titled *From Haven to Home*, includes some hundred and fifty treasures of Judaica Americana from the collections of the Library of Congress, augmented by a selection of singular materials on loan from other cooperating repositories. The exhibition opens in the Northwest Gallery of the Library's Thomas Jefferson Building on September 9, 2004, and will remain on view through December 18, 2004.

From Haven to Home draws on the unparalleled collections of the Library of Congress, featuring books, manuscripts, archival documents, photographs, recorded sound, prints, newspapers, serials, pamphlets, posters, and broadsides. Threaded through the exhibition are early documentary newsreels and film and television footage that help bring to life the American Jewish experience.

The exhibition examines the American Jewish experience in the United States through the prisms of "Haven" and "Home." "Haven" opens with a selection of pivotal documents expressing the ideals of freedom that have come to represent the promise of America. The formative experiences of Jewish immigrants as they struggled to "become American" are also explored in this section. The "Home" section focuses on the challenges and opportunities inherent in a free society and the uniquely American Jewish denominations, institutions, and associations that were created in response. In telling the story of diverse groups of Jewish immigrants, who over the centuries made the United States their home, the exhibition examines the intertwined themes and sometimes conflicting aims of accommodation, assertion, adaption, and assimilation that have characterized the American Jewish experience from its beginnings in 1654 to the present day.

Acknowledgments

I t is a great pleasure to acknowledge the many individuals who have helped make *From Haven to Home: 350 Years of Jewish Life in America* possible. From the outset, this exhibition has received the strong encouragement, steadfast support, and abiding interest of the Librarian of Congress, James H. Billington. It is a special pleasure to note the exceptional generosity and longstanding commitment of Madison Council members Bernard and Audre Rapoport, who, through the Abby and Emily Rapoport Trust Fund that they established at the Library of Congress, have made this exhibit and companion volume possible.

The overall project has encompassed the exhibition and its companion volume, as well as a wide variety of supplementary programs and events. Peggy K. Pearlstein, the Library's Hebraic Area Specialist, has been a close and key advisor on all aspects of this undertaking. A specialist in American Jewish history, she has reviewed all submissions and other project-related documentation, suggested key additions to both the exhibit and this companion volume, and planned multiple outreach programs and special events in connection with this commemoration. This project has also afforded me an opportunity to work closely with Marvin Kranz, an American history specialist in the Manuscript Division. His deep knowledge of the Library's vast holdings of Judaica Americana and his expertise on the history, culture, and lore of American Jewry have contributed mightily to both this book and the exhibition.

I owe a special debt of gratitude to my colleagues in the African and Middle Eastern Division and in the Hebraic Section. I have consulted throughout with Beverly Gray, Chief of the division, and have been the grateful beneficiary of her sound advice and good judgment. My colleagues in the Hebraic Section—Sharon Horowitz, Rachel Becker, and Fentahun Tiruneh—have provided invaluable help in tracking down elusive materials and identifying potential Hebraic exhibit items. I appreciate, as well, the assistance and advice that I have received from division colleagues Levon Avdoyan and Christopher Murphy.

This book has benefited greatly from the strong support and close involvement of the Library's Publishing Office under the direction of Ralph Eubanks, whose wise counsel at the outset of this undertaking set in motion all that has followed. I am deeply indebted to Iris Newsom, an editor in the Publishing Office, whose diligence, care, and extraordinary skill were lavished on this book, and whose patience, persistence, and sense of humor made this publication a pleasure to work on. Aimee Hess of the Publishing Office is to be commended for her key role in coordinating the photography and securing permissions and credits from a multiplicity of sources, both inside and outside the Library. Jim Higgins of the Library's Photoduplication Service photographed virtually all of the images of Library of Congress materials included in this volume with attention to detail, care, and exquisite skill.

Irene Chambers, Director of the Library's Interpretive Programs Office, provided the overall direction of this exhibition and from the project's inception has been an enthusiastic supporter and creative shaper of its form and substance. Exhibit Director Cheryl Regan coordinated every aspect of this exhibition, overseeing the myriad details involved in mounting a large complex exhibition with a traveling component and ensuring that the exhibition's multiple elements fit together and complemented each other. Many of the items in this exhibition were newly "uncovered" through the diligent efforts of Exhibit Specialist Tracey Avant, whose unerring research instincts and technical skills were essential to this undertaking. Tambra Johnson, Registrar, kept track of hundreds of exhibit items (from the Library's collections as well as from the collections of our partners) as they made their way from shelf, to preservation, to exhibit, and back again. Additional Interpretive Programs Office staff who made significant contributions to *From Haven to Home* include Giulia Adelfio; Denise Agee; Seth deMatties, Deborah Durbeck, Carroll Johnson, David Hayward, Martha Hopkins, Antonio La Greca, Kimberli Curry, Betsy Nahum-Miller; Susan Mordan, Chris O'Connor, Pamela Steele, and Rachel Waldron. Sam Serafy conducted media research for the exhibition.

Over the course of this project, I was fortunate to be able to call on the following Library staff members for assistance: Peggy Bulger and Ilana Harlow (American Folklife Center); Stephen Kelley, Shawn Morton, and Geraldine M. Otremba (Congressional Relations Office); Rikki Condon, Annlin Grossman, Yasmeen Khan, and Andrew Robb (Conservation Division); Mark Connor, Sue Siegel, Larry Stafford, and Charles Stanhope (Development Office); Ronald Grim, John Hébert, and Michael Klein (Geography and Map Division); David Kelly (Humanities and Social Sciences Division); Meredith Shedd-Driscol (Law Library); Alice Birney and Mary Wolfskill (Manuscript Division); Sam Brylawski, Alan Gevinson, Michael Mashon, and Josie L. Walters-Johnston (Motion Picture, Broadcasting, and Recorded Sound Division); Ray White and Walter Zvonchenko (Music Division); Joann Walker (Office of Contracts and Logistics); Elizabeth Pugh and Emily Vartanian (Office of General Counsel); Mark Dimunation, Clark Evans, Rosemary Fry Plakas, and Jerry Wager (Rare Book and Special Collections Division); Lesia Bodnaruk and Mark Hauver (Preservation Reformatting Division); Jill Brett, Helen Dalrymple, Audrey Fischer, and John Sayers (Public Affairs Office); Jeremy Adamson, Maricia Battle, Katherine Blood, Beverly Brannan, Verna Curtis, Sara Duke, Mary Ison, Carol Johnson, Harry Katz, Martha Kennedy, and Elena Millie (Prints and

Photographs Division); Georgia Higley (Serial and Government Publications Division); Kim Moden, Elsa Keshishian-Roth, and Bernadette Snead (Special Events Office).

From the inception of this commemorative exhibition, we have been especially fortunate to work with an extraordinary cadre of outside scholars and experts. First and foremost, we owe a debt of gratitude to our partners on the Commission to Commemorate 350 Years of American Jewish History: Greg Bradsher (National Archives and Records Administration); Michael Feldberg (American Jewish Historical Society); and Gary P. Zola (American Jewish Archives). The Commission and the Library have both benefited greatly from the advice and counsel of Pamela S. Nadell (American University) and Jonathan D. Sarna (Brandeis University). Professor Sarna also served as an advisor to the Library of Congress on the exhibition.

It has been a special privilege to be able to call on Grace Cohen Grossman's (Senior Curator of Judaica and Americana at the Skirball Cultural Center) curatorial expertise in helping to shape *From Haven to Home*, which is currently slated to open at the Skirball Cultural Center in the fall of 2005. At the Museum Center (Cincinnati) and at the Center for Jewish History (New York)—both of which are to receive a core group of items on loan from the Library of Congress for inclusion in their own exhibits—we have been fortunate to work with expert curators Karen Benedict (American Jewish Archives) and Karl Katz and Paul Rosenthal (Center for Jewish History).

I have had an opportunity to consult with many individuals across the country on various matters related to this publication and exhibition and would like to give special thanks to Lisa Frankel, Phil Reeker, Dorothy Smith, and Joyce Wise (American Jewish Archives); Pearl Kane and Lyn Slome (American Jewish Historical Society); Irvin Ungar (The Arthur Szyk Society); George Berlin and Rela Mintz Geffen (Baltimore Hebrew University); Jerome Chanes (Barnard College); Robert S. Rifkind and Larry Rubin (Celebrate 350!); Laura Cohen Apelbaum (Jewish Historical Society of Greater Washington); Gail Twersky Reimer and Karla Goldman (Jewish Women's Archive); Bernard D. Cooperman and Shelby Shapiro (University of Maryland); Doris Hamburg, Michael Kurtz, and Richard Marcus (National Archives and Records Administration); Larry Pitterman and Richard A. Siegel (National Foundation for Jewish Culture); Jack Gottlieb (New York City); Isaac Pollak (New York City); Judith Cohen and Sharon Muller (U.S. Holocaust Memorial Museum); Joan Nathan (Washington, D.C.); and Ethan Tucker (Washington, D.C.).

To the President of the United States of America.

Sir

Permit the children of the Stock of Abraham to approach you with the most cordial affection and esteem for your person & merits—And to join with our fellow Citizens in welcoming you to NewPort.

With pleasure we reflect on those days—those days of difficulty, & danger when the God of Israel, who delivered David from the peril of the Sword,—shielded Your head in the day of battle:—And we rejoice to think, that the same Spirit, who rested in the Bosom of the greatly beloved Daniel enabling him to preside over the Provinces of the Babylonish Empire, rests and ever will rest upon you, enabling you to discharge the arduous duties of Chief Magistrate, in these States.

Deprived as we heretofore have been of the invaluable rights of free Citizens, we now (with a deep sense of gratitude to the Almighty Disposer of all events) behold a Government, erected by the Majesty of the People—a Government, which to bigotry gives no Sanction, to persecution no assistance—but generously affording to All liberty of conscience, and immunities of Citizenship:—deeming every one, of whatever Nation, tongue, or language equal parts of the great governmental Machine:—This so ample and extensive Federal Union whose basis is Philanthropy, Mutual confidence and Publick Virtue, we cannot but acknowledge to be the work of the Great God, who ruleth in the Armies of Heaven and among the Inhabitants of the Earth, doing whatsoever seemeth him good.—

For all the Blessings of civil and religious liberty which we enjoy under an equal and benign administration, we desire to Send up our thanks to the Antient of Days, the great preserver of Men—beseeching him, that the Angel who conducted our forefathers through the wilderness into the promised land, may graciously conduct you through all the difficulties and dangers of this mortal life:—And, when like Joshua full of Days and full of honour, you are gathered to your Fathers, may you be admitted into the Heavenly Paradise to partake of the water of life, and the tree of immortality.—

Done and Signed by Order of the Hebrew Congregation in—

NewPort Rhode Island—August 17th 1790.

Moses Seixas, Warden

Prologue to American Jewish History: The Jews of America from 1654 to 1820

Eli Faber

American Jewish history began in the late summer of the year 1654 when, early in the month of September, a small party of twenty-three Jewish men, women, and children disembarked on Manhattan Island at the small town of New Amsterdam, the headquarters of the Dutch colony of New Netherland. In flight from northeastern Brazil in the wake of its recapture by Portugal after twenty-four years of rule by the Dutch West India Company, the twenty-three refugees found two Jewish merchants already present in New Amsterdam; they had arrived just weeks before. It is not unreasonable to suppose that Jewish traders from the Netherlands had visited the colony even before the summer of 1654, but, unlike merchants who occasionally came and went, the newcomers from Brazil soon gave every indication they intended to settle permanently. They did so by stoutly, ultimately successfully, resisting the efforts of New Netherland's hostile director-general, Peter Stuyvesant, who, in consultation with his council and the colony's Calvinist clergy, sought to deport them shortly after their arrival. Two years later, after twice petitioning the director-general and his council, together with a small number of Jewish settlers who had subsequently arrived in the colony, they gave further indication of their tenacity when they acquired land for a cemetery, almost always the first permanent action of a religious nature taken by Jews when they put down roots in new

---

This congratulatory address, written by Moses Seixas, was presented by the Hebrew Congregation in Newport, Rhode Island, on behalf of "the children of the seed of Abraham" to President George Washington on August 17, 1790. Washington's reply—in which he characterizes the government of the United States as one that "to bigotry gives no sanction, to persecution no assistance"—was first used, almost verbatim, in this address by Moses Seixas.

Moses Seixas, "Congratulatory Address to George Washington on Behalf of the Hebrew Congregation of Newport, Rhode Island," August 17, 1790. Papers of George Washington, Manuscript Division.

locations. Furthermore, New Amsterdam's Jewish population continued to oppose Stuyvesant's continuing efforts to constrict their civic and commercial rights. Successively, they won the right to trade throughout New Netherland, to acquire houses, to serve in the militia instead of being forced to pay an assessment, and, at last, to enjoy the same burgher (civic) rights that Jews exercised in Amsterdam. In the end, the only restriction of note that differentiated their condition from that of the Jewish population in Amsterdam was a prohibition upon public worship, a requirement stipulated by the officers of the Dutch West India Company back in Holland. By imposing this condition upon New Amsterdam's Jews, one that applied as well to Protestant dissenters in the colony, the officers of the Company in effect permitted Stuyvesant, their employee, to save some measure of face.[1]

Why the small band from Brazil sought refuge at all in New Amsterdam is puzzling, in light of New Netherland's generally weak economic condition. Significantly, during the thirty years that had elapsed since New Amsterdam's founding around 1625, Jews had not emigrated to it, preferring instead to settle in northeastern Brazil after the Dutch West India Company seized it in 1630. Within fifteen years, Brazil's Jewish population peaked at as many as 1,450 persons, but it declined thereafter, owing to a ferocious guerilla war launched by Portuguese inhabitants bent on retaking their colony. Most of the six-hundred-odd Jews who still resided in Brazil when the Dutch lost it in 1654 returned to their home base: Amsterdam. Simultaneously, a small contingent also made its way to the English colony of Barbados, attracted no doubt by that colony's shift from tobacco to sugar production. Yet another small group chose to emigrate to the French colony of Martinique, likewise a sugar island. During the period they had resided in Brazil, the Jewish population had gained familiarity with the cultivation and marketing of sugar, in a small number of instances as the owners of sugar plantations, in a larger number of cases as middlemen in the sugar trade, and they could use their knowledge of the sugar industry in the two new locations.[2]

New Netherland, of course, did not possess the climate necessary for the production of sugar. Neither did it offer much in the way of promise for merchants engaged in international commerce, the kind of enterprise that most attracted Jews who settled in Europe's New-World colonies. For the first twenty to twenty-five years of its existence, the colony attracted few settlers, limiting possibilities for local commercial activity. Its owner, the Dutch West India Company, was chronically on the verge of bankruptcy. Facing ruin, in 1639 it relinquished its monopoly powers, notably over furs, the colony's one significant natural resource, thereby opening opportunities for enterprising merchants. However, New Netherland's commerce thereafter fell largely under the control of four merchant houses in Amsterdam, none of which was Jewish, a factor that markedly constrained opportunities for Jewish merchants, for this was an era in which familial, ethnic, and religious networks were critical to commercial success. Indeed, thanks to the hold the four Amsterdam houses had on commerce between Holland and New Netherland, merchants who resided in the colony were unable to develop flourishing trading enterprises no matter what their religion or ethnicity.[3]

In sum, New Netherland did not provide fertile economic ground, for either the newcomers from Brazil or the handful of other Jews who appeared in the colony during the course of the decade. Most were gone by the early 1660s. Just two are known to have remained, including Asser Levy, renowned in later centuries among American Jews for challenging Director-General Stuyvesant's refusal to permit him to perform military service.[4] Dutch Jews showed far greater interest in establishing themselves in the Caribbean and South America during the 1650s, while others who settled in North America avoided unpromising New Amsterdam, going instead to Newport, Rhode Island. Approximately fifteen families did so in 1658, emigrating there either from Barbados or from Curaçao or perhaps even from Holland.[5] Historians have explained their choice as arising from Rhode Island's religious toleration; and this may have played a role in their decision. On the other hand, by 1657 the Dutch West India Company had overridden all the impediments Stuyvesant had attempted to impose upon the Jews present in New Amsterdam. His defeat was so complete that, when four of the town's Jews petitioned early that year for full burgher rights, he immediately assented.[6] The decision to head for Newport, therefore, may well have had as much to do with New Amsterdam's economic limitations for locally based merchants as with Rhode Island's willingness to accept Protestant dissenters and Jews.

As the Jewish presence in New Amsterdam faded, Newport's held its ground. In 1677, the town's Jewish inhabitants acquired land for a cemetery. As was usually the case elsewhere, Rhode Island's Jewish settlers turned to commerce, as suggested by two prosecutions in the mid-1680s for alleged violations of England's Navigation Acts by Jewish traders there. In the early 1690s, the Jewish population may have grown with the arrival of approximately ninety individuals from Curaçao because of an epidemic on that island. But thereafter until the 1740s, traces of a Jewish presence in Newport are meager, suggesting that whatever community existed in Rhode Island largely disappeared until the middle of the eighteenth century.[7]

On Manhattan Island, on the other hand, a new—and this time permanent—Jewish community began to arise during the 1680s. Dutch rule had abruptly come to an end in 1664, when, without warning, the British mounted an expedition against New Amsterdam, took possession of it after its burghers demanded that Stuyvesant surrender, and renamed it New York. Jewish colonists did not immediately settle in England's newly acquired colony. Although the British government had permitted Jews to reside in England in 1656 for the first time in more than 360 years, and although Britain proclaimed religious toleration in New York after the conquest of 1664, Jewish settlers were apparently hesitant to migrate there, preferring instead, during the 1660s and early 1670s, to settle in Barbados and Jamaica, major outposts of the British Empire in the Caribbean.[8] But by the early 1680s, a growing number of Jews made their way to New York, perhaps because of trading connections between it and the two Caribbean islands, necessitating the acquisition of land in 1682 for a second cemetery. During the course of the next twenty years, the small Jewish population grew to between one hundred and one hundred fifty individuals. Although largely Sephardic, tracing their ancestry to Spain and Portugal, the town also attracted Ashkenazim, Jews whose origins were in Central and Eastern Europe. In fact, by the 1720s Ashkenazim outnumbered Sephardim, a generalization applicable not only to New York but to the entire Jewish population in America for the next century, despite the fact that the period between 1654 and 1820 is generally known as the Sephardic era in American Jewish history.[9]

Growing slowly but steadily, participating in the town's economic life as merchants engaged in commerce throughout the reaches of the Atlantic trading world, in 1728 New York's Jews were at last able to undertake construction of a synagogue, the first on the North American mainland. The effort brought Sephardim and Ashkenazim together in a cooperative venture, rare at the time because of a lengthy history of animosity and conflict between these two great subdivisions of the Jewish people.[10] Setting aside that heritage, the town's Jews quickly built and dedicated their synagogue, with the undertaking led by Sephardic and Ashkenazic members of the congregation. Thereafter, representatives of the two groups were routinely elected to serve as *parnas* (president) and as assistants, with Ashkenazim actually predominating.[11] On the other hand, the synagogue adhered to the Sephardic rite of worship, despite the fact that the majority of the congregants were Ashkenazim. According to an important principle of Jewish law, the established custom in any given locality is the one that governs, with alternative customs giving way; and it had been largely Sephardic Jews who had arrived in New York in the 1650s and again in the 1680s (as well, probably, as in Newport in 1658), thereby establishing the primacy of the Sephardic ritual in colonial North America. The Sephardic rite was therefore followed not only in New York, but also in the four other Jewish communities that subsequently developed in colonial America, despite the fact that in those localities, too, Ashkenazim were more numerous.

The quarter century between 1725 and 1750 marked a turning point in the development of a Jewish presence in what would eventually become the United States of America. In addition to the communal achievements of the New Yorkers during these years, four additional Jewish communities were established. In Savannah, the first to appear after New York's Jews constructed their synagogue, Sephardim and Ashkenzim were unable to replicate the cooperation that generally characterized relations between the two groups in New York. Georgia, established by the British in 1732 in part to block the Spanish in Florida, was envisioned by its creators as a haven for the impoverished, a humane alternative to debtor's prison. The Sephardic community in London, whose members were descendants and relatives of victims of the Spanish Inquisition (as well as the Portuguese one), were doubtlessly sympathetic to the first of the two reasons for the new colony, but they also welcomed the second. Coping with an influx of refugees from the Portuguese Inquisition during the 1720s, the congregation's resources were stretched thin. Its leaders therefore applied for and received permission to send a small contingent of Jewish settlers to the newly established colony, and in 1733 they dispatched them to Savannah.[12]

The newcomers numbered thirty-four Sephardim and eight Ashkenazim. In 1735, they apparently established a synagogue, but the two groups soon quarreled, split apart with mutual recriminations, and were unable to construct a permanent place of worship.[13] Greater disruption, however, was to come from an external force. Britain found itself once again at war with Spain in 1740, and, apparently fearing the possibility of a Spanish attack at Savannah, most of the Sephardic population left, leaving behind only three Jewish families. Although other Jews settled in Savannah during the 1760s, the number there remained small, perhaps no more than six families by 1771. Despite their resolve in 1774 to meet as a congregation in a private home, successful efforts to create a viable community did not occur until the 1790s, and they did not erect a synagogue until 1820.[14]

Some who left Savannah by 1741 in the wake of war with Spain made their way to New York, but others immigrated to Charleston in the neighboring colony of South Carolina. Like New York and Savannah, Charleston was a seaport offering possibilities for merchants engaged in Atlantic commerce, the economic path favored by Jews who settled in colonial America. All told, during the first half of the eighteenth century, fifteen adult Jewish males are known to have made their way to Charleston, but it was the arrival of several more from London in 1750 that led to the formation of a congregation and the acquisition of a cemetery. Charleston continued to attract Jewish settlers, so much so that in 1775 the town's Jewish inhabitants began to plan for a synagogue, soliciting donations from New York's congregation in order to build it. In the ensuing, unsettled years of the Revolution and the early years of the young republic, the community was forced to abandon its plans until 1792, when at last it was able to undertake construction of its first permanent house of worship, dedicating it for use two years later. By that time, Charleston was on its way to having the largest Jewish population of any city in America, outpacing even New York in the period between 1790 and 1820.[15]

As in Charleston, a Jewish presence developed in Philadelphia by mid-century and, once more, in Newport . In both instances, the possibilities for Atlantic commerce in the two northern towns provided the impetus. In Philadelphia's case, two New York merchant families each sent two sons to the new location in 1737 and 1738 to serve as commercial representatives for their families' firms. More Jewish settlers went to Philadelphia in the ensuing decades before the Revolution, attracted by the fact that the rapidly growing city functioned as a bustling port of entry for large numbers of Scotch-Irish and German immigrants and as the locus of a large export trade in grain, lumber, and wool. The desirability of a career in commerce in Philadelphia is illustrated by a letter written in 1757 by one of London's Jewish merchants to his parents in Eastern Europe, rationalizing the loan he had extended to his brother so that the latter could try his luck for a second time in Pennsylvania: "He was ashamed to return to Philadelphia and be a mere employee, and had no money to be a merchant."[16] Before long, the increase in the number of aspiring Jewish merchants in Philadelphia led to the residence of approximately twenty-five families in 1765 and probably around one hundred individuals in 1770. Formal organization of a community began during the 1760s, culminating in 1771 in the rental of space for worship in quarters larger than the private house previously used. Construction of an actual synagogue building, however, would not occur until 1782, after the hostilities of the Revolution had subsided.[17]

Not so in Newport, where a new Jewish community arose after 1740 and was able in 1759 to undertake construction of what is the oldest synagogue building extant in the United States, dedicating it for use in 1763, although it remained uncompleted as late as 1768. Here too possibilities for commerce abounded, for Newport had evolved since the end of the seventeenth century to encompass trade that stretched along the coasts of North America and then, successively, to the Caribbean, Africa, and England. In conjunction with their transatlantic commerce, Newport businessmen launched whaling expeditions, produced spermaceti candles, and manufactured rum for use in their trade with Africa—for Newport was the largest importer of slaves in the mainland colonies and, after Liverpool, Bristol, and London, the fourth-largest center of the slave trade in the British Empire. The Jewish merchants who immigrated to Newport participated in all these enterprises.[18]

Such merchants are known to have begun to settle in Newport by 1746. By the early 1760s, the town had approximately twelve Jewish families; and by 1774 there were between thirteen and twenty-two families. The merchants included Aaron Lopez, who left Portugal in the early 1750s and reverted to Judaism once he was safely away from the Portuguese Inquisition's oversight. Lopez traded across the length and breadth of the Atlantic world, dealing in virtually all the commodities that were to be had in Atlantic commerce, including slaves, and became one

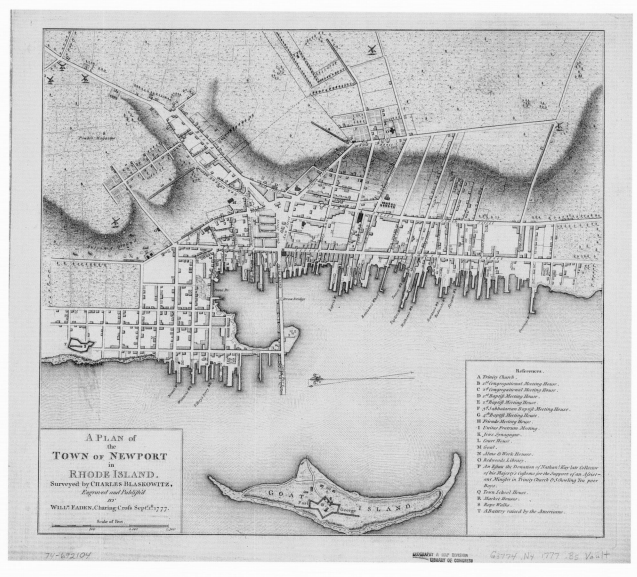

This early map of Newport, Rhode Island, was produced in London in 1777. Referenced on the map are the houses of worship of the various religious groups present in Newport at the time, including Catholics, Congregationalists, Baptists, Quakers, and Jews (see inset).

A Plan of the Town of Newport in Rhode Island, *London, 1777. Geography and Map Division.*

A *Trinity Church.*
B *1st Congregational Meeting House.*
C *2d Congregational Meeting House.*
D *1st Baptist Meeting House.*
E *2d Baptist Meeting House.*
F *3d Sabbatarian Baptist Meeting Hou*
G *4th Baptist Meeting House.*
H *Friends Meeting House.*
I *Unitas Fratrum Meeting.*
K *Jews Synagogue.*
L *Court House.*
M *Goal.*
N *Alms & Work Houses.*
O *Redwoods Library.*

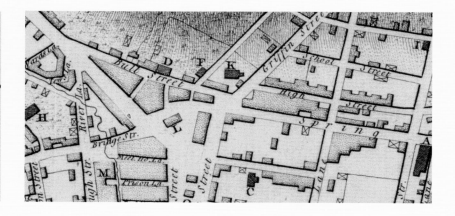

of the wealthiest men in Newport. His is probably the only instance in which a Jewish merchant in colonial America can be said to have achieved a leading position in the economic life of the general community.[19]

Although the Jews of colonial America settled primarily in five of the colonies' Atlantic seaports, a handful were also to be found in what was then the interior, whether in eastern Long Island, New York's Westchester County, New Jersey, or the area around Lancaster, Pennsylvania, among other locations.[20] But in its totality, the Jewish population on the eve of the American Revolution must have amounted to perhaps a thousand souls, comprising a minute fragment of the total colonial population, which in 1776 stood at almost three million people. The largest concentration was in New York, with 242 Jews in 1773.[21] In contrast to the thirteen mainland colonies, the English colony of Jamaica, alone, had an estimated 800 to 900 Jews in 1776, and Kingston, its main port, contained the largest number of Jews outside London in the British Empire. Indeed, Jamaica employed a *haham* (the term for rabbi in the Sephardic tradition) as early as the 1680s, while New York would not have a rabbi, the first anywhere in mainland North America, until 1840.[22]

Minute size continued to characterize the American Jewish population during the first four decades of the early republic. The Jewish population in 1790 amounted to between thirteen hundred and fifteen hundred in a national population of almost four million. In 1820, even following a small measure of immigration from Jamaica, Holland, and France, Jews throughout the United States numbered only 2,650 to 2,750 people, or three one-hundredths of 1 percent of the population reported in that year's national census, and were still concentrated in four of the five towns where they had been during the colonial era. By then, no Jews, save for one in the early 1820s, remained in Newport, whose port and shipping never made a recovery after the Revolution, but new communities had appeared in Richmond, Virginia, and Baltimore, Maryland.[23]

Not only was the Jewish population during the colonial era and the early republic of very limited size, its members cannot be said to have played a significant, much less decisive, part in the life of the larger society. With the exception of Aaron Lopez in Newport, they were not great captains of commerce or finance. The belief by many in later generations that Haym Salomon was the "Financier of the Revolution" must be tempered by the realization that his function was that of a salesman

These circumcision implements belonged to members of the Seixas family, which traced its roots to Portugal and England before arriving in New York in the first half of the eighteenth century. The trunk and its implements were fashioned over time and crafted in different locales, reflecting both the migrations of the Seixas family and its adherence to one of Judaism's main commandments, "that he that is eight days old shall be circumcised among you, every male throughout your generations...." (Genesis 17:12) .

Seixas Family Circumcision Set and Trunk, circa eighteenth century. Courtesy of the American Jewish Historical Society, New York, NY and Newton Centre, MA.

of foreign notes on behalf of the U.S. government, albeit a highly capable one, but only between 1781 and 1784, or after most of the hostilities had ended.[24] In politics, denied the right to vote and to serve in office almost everywhere during the colonial era, Jews had no effect on public life. After the Revolution, they won civic equality in almost all states by 1820, but their numbers were too few to have made a difference in political affairs.[25] Finally, in the cultural realm they were similarly of little if any consequence, for early America's Jews were not intellectuals, writers, philosophers, scientists, or educators.

But despite their seeming inconsequentiality, this small New-World Shearith Israel—this Remnant of Israel, the name the congregation in New York called itself—was of significance in the context of American Jewish history out of all proportion to its size, economic or political impact, or cultural abilities. The Jews who settled in early America were among the first of their faith in the modern world to explore the implications of what it meant for Jews to reside in a benign environment, one that did not subject them to persecution, one that practiced religious toleration. They were the beneficiaries of toleration and of a comparatively negligible amount of anti-Semitism, but such prevailing benevolence raised questions in three distinct realms. First, in the absence of any external pressure to belong to the Jewish community, how could the community achieve cohesion, support itself financially, and recruit officers willing to lead and serve? Second, in a relatively comfortable setting, one devoid of persecution and serious anti-Semitism, would Jews want to maintain their distinctive identity? Could they and their children resist complete assimilation? Finally, would they ever be able to attain civic equality? The high degree of tolerance they enjoyed did not encompass the right to vote and serve in office. Would it, one day?

The issue of the Jewish community's ability to command allegiance, affiliation, and compliance with its dictates was apparent by the middle of the eighteenth century, to judge from the records of the congregation in New York, the only ones dating to the colonial period that have survived. Repeatedly, Shearith Israel asserted that all Jews in the region, whether they resided in the city or in its vicinity, were subject to it. In 1737, it proclaimed that it had the right to tax Jews who resided outside New York City, and that any who refused to pay were to be denied membership in the congregation, honors in the synagogue, and community benefits, the last a meaningful threat because the congregation provided poor relief to the indigent. Ten years later, the congregation adopted new regulations requiring all members to attend meetings on pain of a fine, and imposed an assessment not only on Jews who resided in the city but also on those in the country. Those who complied were to be listed officially as members, receive assigned seats in the synagogue, have all other membership rights, and be empowered to serve in office. Five years later in 1752, the community sharply increased its demands for compliance, when the leadership decreed that anyone who did not attend the synagogue or contribute to it could not be buried in its cemetery unless the officers voted to permit interment, a ban that included wives and children younger than thirteen. This was a powerful threat indeed, and the community's elders invoked it again in 1757, when they dramatically utilized the commencement of the Day of Atonement, the most solemn occasion in the Jewish religious year, to read out an edict against all who violated Judaism's Sabbath and dietary regulations. Any who continued to break religious laws, they warned, would suffer expulsion from the congregation—and would not be buried in the cemetery.[26]

These assertions in New York of hegemony over all Jews in the region and the recurrent demands for subordination to the congregation derived from the model of the Jewish community that still existed in contemporary Europe. There, the officers of the *kehilla*, the official Jewish community, reigned supreme within the borders of the community. Their authority derived from the fact that the secular government designated the *kehilla* as the official voice of the Jewish community. Because Jews in Europe's societies were not recognized as part of the body politic but were classified as a people who stood apart from it, outside of it, the government dealt separately with them through the mechanism of the *kehilla*, which served as the intermediary between the government and the Jewish population, collecting its taxes and transmitting its edicts. Within the Jewish community itself, the *kehilla*'s officials made policy for the community, dispensed its funds, and maintained its communal institutions.

With this model in mind, and through the agency of its officers, the congregation in New York attempted to re-create what was in its essence a compulsory community. But the effort was doomed to fail, for conditions in the English colonies were antithetical to the development of a *kehilla*. First and foremost, the government did not require it. Absent the extremes of anti-Semitism and exclusion that prevailed in Europe, the need for an officially designated body to mediate between the government and the Jewish population did not exist. Concomitantly, there was no external pressure upon the Jews in the colonies to belong to the Jewish community. Then too, geographic mobility in America precluded the enforcement of demands for conformity to religious law or for the payment of communal assessments. If unhappy with attempts by the congregation to impose its will, one could readily settle elsewhere.[27] Finally, mid-eighteenth-century colonial America was a cauldron of antiauthoritarian sentiment. Thanks to the Great Awakening, the religious-revival movement that swept through the colonies and split churches in its wake, challenges to religious traditions and church authorities abounded everywhere and may well have affected attitudes toward authority within the Jewish community, too.

The impossibility of replicating a compulsory community in the American setting contributed to recurring crises in the annual election of officers in New York and to reluctance on the part of the membership to attend meetings. In 1746, the controversy, indeed the uproar, that ensued when a representative of one of the community's leading families refused to serve as president led to threats of ejection from the synagogue and necessitated revision of the community's governing regulations. The issue flared anew in subsequent years, forcing the community in 1748, in 1751, and again in 1771 to adopt new methods for choosing officers.[28]

The search for a viable way to recruit leaders is traceable to a number of causes. Service as president and assistant was time-consuming, for the duties of these community elders included

In colonial times, when synagogues were scarce, traditional Jews conducted prayer services in their homes. This hand-carved wooden lintel was affixed horizontally above the opening of Joseph Simon's personal Torah ark. In the lintel's center is a depiction of the two tablets symbolizing the Decalogue and below it the Hebrew saying, "Know before Whom you are standing," a phrase that often appears in synagogues on the ark lintel or above the reader's lectern.

Torah Ark Lintel, Lancaster, Pennsylvania, mideighteenth century. Courtesy of the American Jewish Historical Society, New York, NY and Newton Centre, MA.

caring for the congregation's buildings and cemetery, maintaining its school, supervising its employees, authorizing expenditures for poor relief, and guaranteeing the *kashrut* (ritual purity) of the meat prepared by the community's official slaughterer. Then too, the officers had to collect dues, as well as impose congregational sanctions upon members who misbehaved inside or in the immediate vicinity of the synagogue: tasks with the potential for difficult or embarrassing confrontations with individual members in what was, after all, a small community.[29] But, perhaps above all, what undermined the attractiveness of service was the fact that the leaders of the Jewish community had no official standing in the larger world. Lacking authority from and recognition by the government, its leaders could not claim the prestige, the status, and the power that officials of the European *kehilla* enjoyed. Disinterest, or worse, hostility, to serving in office was the consequence.

Therefore, rather than being able to assume that theirs was a community based upon compulsory participation, the Jewish population of early America had to devise the creation of a community built on voluntary affiliation. The recurrent search for a foolproof method for recruiting leaders was one important manifestation of the challenge that lay in the disappearance of the compulsory community and the emergence of the voluntary one. The future for Jews who undertook to create viable Jewish institutions in America in fact lay in voluntary organizations; and in this new territory, the Jews of eighteenth-century America blazed the path, unfamiliar though it was to them from their prior experiences in Europe.

They were also among the first Jews in the emerging modern world to confront the possibility of disappearance through a process of acculturation that progressed to outright assimilation. The tension between preserving a distinctive Jewish identity on the one hand and blending into the larger population on the other, a recurring issue in American Jewish life in subsequent eras (and, for that matter, a concern for many other immigrant groups in America), was one already encountered by the small Jewish population of eighteenth-century America, another arena in which they wrestled with the consequences of residence in a tolerant environment.

A great deal of evidence attests to their adherence to traditional Jewish law and practice, which was of course conducive to maintaining their distinctiveness. To begin with, they readily established congregations, prayed together as a community, and eventually constructed synagogues, the core institution in Jewish life. When questions involving religious law arose, they endeavored as laymen, in the absence of a rabbi anywhere in America, to resolve them in accordance with the law, but turned to rabbinic authorities in Europe when they could not.[30] Evidence of their commitment to tradition in their private lives is also abundant. In Lancaster, Pennsylvania, Joseph Simon employed a ritual slaughterer and conducted services in his home. In the interior of Massachusetts, during the Revolution, Jews who fled the British occupation of Newport impressed their new neighbors with their diligent observance of the Sabbath. In Philadelphia shortly after the Revolution, Manuel Josephson successfully undertook to convince the congregation there to erect a ritual bathhouse, an extremely important feature of traditional religious law. And in New York, Uriah Hendricks regarded a man who proposed to marry his aunt with disfavor because the suitor in question did not observe the Sabbath and ate nonkosher food. These are but a few examples that can be cited of the fidelity to Jewish tradition that early American Jews maintained.[31]

Conversely, the suitor whom Uriah Hendricks opposed for his aunt provides evidence of a retreat from the norms that guaranteed the continuity of a distinctive Jewish identity. The edict on the evening of Yom Kippur in 1757 described before, in which the elders of the New York community warned Sabbath and *kashrut* violators they would not be buried in the congregation's cemetery, is a startling illustration of how early American Jews, or at least some among them, had begun to abandon the religious laws. In 1785, two members of the Philadelphia congregation, writing to rabbinic authorities in Amsterdam, bemoaned the "great lack of discipline that prevails in our generation," referring to the decline of traditional law and practice among Jews

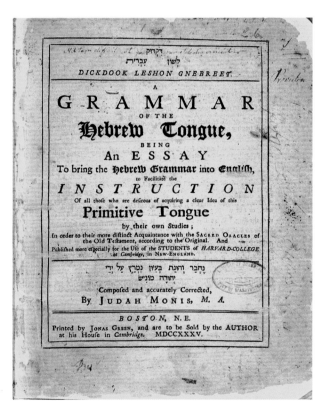

The first Hebrew grammar published in America, its title page shown here, was issued in 1735 specifically for "the ... use of the students at Harvard-College at Cambridge, in New-England," for whom Hebrew was a required subject. One thousand copies were printed, a large edition for an early-eighteenth-century American publication.

Judah Monis. Dikdook Leshon Gneebreet: A Grammar of the Hebrew Tongue, *Boston, 1735. Hebraic Section.*

in America. And non-Jewish observers—who were perhaps more objective than Jews who may have had axes to grind or who were filled with nostalgia for allegedly better days in the past—reported that Jews in America ate pork, especially the young and especially when they traveled, according to one.[32]

Yet another marveled at the fact that the Jews of America did not look like those of Europe: they dressed in the same clothing worn by non-Jews, and the men did not have beards. The many portraits commissioned by eighteenth- and early-nineteenth-century American Jews that have survived amply document his assessment. They also reveal that men did not cover their heads and that women apparently did not crop their hair upon marriage and don wigs.[33] But the most striking development of all, which revealed there was a perceptible drift away from loyalty to the Jewish tradition and community, were the instances of intermarriage that occurred.[34] The New York congregation addressed this issue only once during the colonial era, but between 1790 and 1820 it proved a matter of growing concern, to judge from the references to it in the regulations adopted by the communities in New York, Savannah, Philadelphia, and Charleston. The penalties ranged from forfeiture of membership, to barring the congregation's cantor from officiating at weddings unless both partners were Jewish, to denying burial in the community cemetery to any who married non-Jews.[35]

Through letters to her son Naphtali in England, Abigail Franks (1696–1756) provided historians with an extraordinary portrait of the everyday life of America's colonial Jews. Her correspondence recounts her admonitions to Naphtali to fulfill his religious obligations as well as her shame and despair on learning of her daughter's secret marriage to a non-Jew.

Portrait of Abigail Franks, attributed to Gerardus Duyckinck, New York, circa 1735. Courtesy of the American Jewish Historical Society, New York, NY and Newton Centre, MA.

To resolve the conflict between standing apart from the larger population and its culture and, on the other hand, melding with the majority, the Jews of early America attempted to steer a middle path, one that sought to synthesize the two extremes. The life of Abigail Franks provides an example. An inhabitant of New York during the first half of the eighteenth century and the wife of the Jewish community's leading Ashkenazic member, Franks enjoyed contemporary English literature, followed local politics, maintained personal friendships with non-Jews, and advised her son, who resided in London, to do likewise. To judge from her portrait, she presented herself to the world as a typically well-dressed colonial woman. But while absorbing elements of the larger culture as well as participating in it, she firmly remained Jewish. She admonished the son in London to refrain from making adverse comments about religion, to adhere rigidly to religious requirements like the daily morning prayers and the dietary regulations, and to eat only bread and butter in her own brother's home, voicing doubts about the latter's

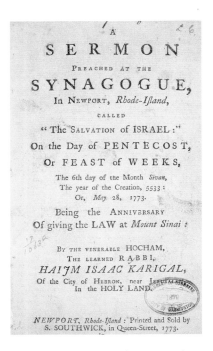

A

SERMON

PREACHED AT THE

SYNAGOGUE,

In NEWPORT, Rhode-Island,

CALLED

" The SALVATION of ISRAEL :"

On the Day of PENTECOST,

Or FEAST of WEEKS,

The 6th day of the Month Sivan,
The year of the Creation, 5533 :
Or, May 28, 1773.

Being the ANNIVERSARY
Of giving the LAW at Mount Sinai :

BY THE VENERABLE HOCHAM,

THE LEARNED RABBI,

HAIJM ISAAC KARIGAL,

Of the City of HEBRON, near JERUSALEM,
In the HOLY LAND.

NEWPORT, Rhode-Island : Printed and Sold by
S. SOUTHWICK, in Queen-Street, 1773.

The first American Jewish sermon to be published was preached by an emissary from the Holy Land, Haim Isaac Carigal. "The venerable hocham, the learned rabbi, of the city of Hebron, near Jerusalem, in the Holy Land," as Carigal was known, preached the sermon, shown here, on the festival of Shavuoth, May 28, 1773, in Newport's synagogue. Delivered in Ladino (Judeo-Spanish), the language of Sephardic Jewry, the sermon was translated into English by Abraham Lopez and published contrary to Carigal's wishes.

Haim Isaac Carigal, A Sermon
Preached at the Synagogue in
Newport, Rhode Island, 1773. *Rare
Book and Special Collections Division.*

compliance with the dietary laws. In one of her letters, she indicated she would probably not have time to keep up her correspondence because of the impending holiday of Sukkoth (Festival of Booths). But above all, when her daughter secretly wed a non-Jew and then six months later divulged the marriage by leaving her parents' home to join her husband, Franks plunged into despair and, deeply ashamed, could not meet or converse with anyone else for some time. Nor would she agree to meet with their daughter when her own husband expressed his willingness to reconcile. Clearly, while relishing participation in the non-Jewish world, Franks insisted upon loyalty to Jewish tradition—in the lives of her children, as well as her own.[36]

On the communal level, the effort to amalgamate the contemporary world and the world of Jewish tradition was vividly apparent in the synagogues that early America's Jews constructed. Architecture generally mirrors prevailing social ideals; and the synagogues in Newport (dedicated 1763) and Charleston (dedicated 1794) were metaphors in wood and stone, plaster and glass, for the ambitious attempt to create a harmonious synthesis of the two cultures.

The exterior of the Newport synagogue was in the Palladian style, then all the rage in England and beginning to come into its own in the colonies. With its derivations from classical architecture, Palladianism had recently been introduced in Newport with the construction of the Redwood Library. By constructing the synagogue in the same style as the Redwood, which was located only a few minutes' walk away, the Jewish population demonstrated not only that it appreciated the very finest in colonial architecture, but, more important, that it was solidly part of the town's civic development, that it was in step with contemporary thinking and trends in Newport.[37]

But a different world awaited worshipers and visitors on the inside. After passing through the Palladian exterior with its classical columns, pediment, and emphasis upon symmetry and balance, one entered an interior that was an exact scale-model replica of the Sephardic synagogue in London.[38] While contemporary in its Palladianism and synchronous with the Redwood Library on the outside, the synagogue was thoroughly Jewish on the inside, dramatizing the harmonious combination of cultures that eighteenth-century American Jewry aspired to achieve.

Thirty years later, the synagogue in Charleston reflected the effort to adapt to and be part of the surrounding environment even more vividly: its exterior was that of a church in the Georgian style, complete with steeple. However, as in Newport, the interior was decidedly in keeping with the Sephardic tradition. Seating for men on the ground floor ranged along the

Designed by noted colonial architect Peter Harrison and opened in 1763, the Touro Synagogue in Newport, Rhode Island, is the oldest standing synagogue in the United States. On the occasion of its designation as a "National Historic Site" in 1946, President Truman wrote: "The setting apart of this historic shrine as a national monument is symbolic of our national tradition of freedom, which has inspired men and women of every creed, race, and ancestry to contribute their highest gifts to the development of our national culture."

"The Old Jewish Synagogue" [Postcard], circa 1910. Hebraic Section.

This pencil sketch of the first Beth Elohim synagogue building in Charleston, South Carolina, which burned to the ground in 1838, was drawn by painter and printmaker John Rubens Smith. American Reform Judaism traces its origins to the Beth Elohim congregation, when a group of synagogue members withdrew from the synagogue in 1824 and established the short-lived Reformed Society of Israelites.

John Rubens Smith, Jews synagogue in Charleston, circa 1812. John Rubens Smith Collection, Prints and Photographs Division.

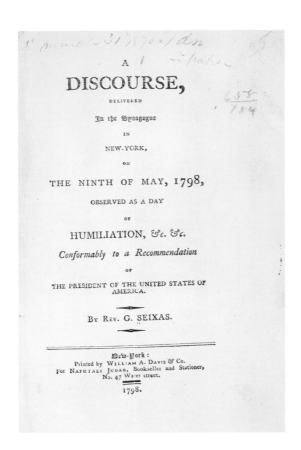

A

DISCOURSE,

DELIVERED

In the Synagogue

IN

NEW-YORK,

ON

THE NINTH OF MAY, 1798,

OBSERVED AS A DAY

OF

HUMILIATION, &c. &c.

Conformably to a Recommendation

OF

THE PRESIDENT OF THE UNITED STATES OF
AMERICA.

By Rev. G. SEIXAS.

New-York:
Printed by WILLIAM A. DAVIS & Co.
For NAPHTALI JUDAH, Bookseller and Stationer,
No. 47 Water street.

1798.

Gershom Mendes Seixas, the "patriot rabbi" of the Shearith Israel Congregation, New York, left the city because of the British occupation during the Revolutionary War and did not return till after its liberation. Through this Discourse *delivered at the synagogue on a national Day of Humiliation, he integrates the synagogue into the new nation's religious landscape. On that day and through this service which was held in response to the "Recommendation of the President of the United States of America."*

Gershom Mendes Seixas, A Discourse Delivered in the Synagogue in New York, on the ninth of May, 1798, New York, 1798. *Rare Book and Special Collections Division.*

northern and southern walls and faced inward to the center of the structure where the reader's desk was located, while seats for the congregation's officers were on the north wall. Women sat upstairs in a gallery, although this was not a feature of the Sephardic synagogue alone, inasmuch as men and women sat separately in Ashkenazic synagogues, too, with the women often seated in a gallery.[39] As in Newport, therefore, the synagogue expressed the ideal of belonging to the surrounding world while at the same time remaining Jewish in identity.

In New York, the effort to create a harmonious blending of American and Jewish culture took form not in the synagogue's architecture (the modest building had been constructed in the late 1720s, perhaps a time when the need to fuse the two cultures was not felt so strongly),[40] but rather inside the synagogue itself, where features of the Protestant ministry were much in evidence in the late-eighteenth and early-nineteenth centuries. They were introduced by the congregation's cantor, Gershom Mendes Seixas, the first Jewish religious functionary born in America, but what is equally noteworthy is that the membership accepted them. Although he was not a rabbi, Seixas introduced the practice of preaching sermons. Rabbis in contemporary Europe did not deliver sermons except on one or two major Sabbaths during the course of the annual religious calendar. Rather than adapting a feature of the synagogue service, Seixas borrowed the institution of the sermon from the Protestant churches, where it was a major component of the weekly church service. But Seixas went even further, utilizing such terms as original sin, salvation, regeneration, and grace in his sermons, all of them theological concepts that came from Christianity.[41]

Staunch traditionalists must have found the exterior of the Charleston synagogue and the sermons with Christian terminology inside the New York synagogue shocking, but these extreme developments occurred because early American Jews were feeling their way in a new and perplexing situation. Like the challenge of replacing the compulsory community of Europe with a new kind of communal organization, the attempt to chart a course between separation from the larger society and assimilation with it required experimentation and innovation. It was as pioneers, therefore, that the small Jewish population during the colonial era and the first four decades of the young republic undertook both to nurture their own religious community and, at the same time, to guarantee the perpetuation of that community in a new world.

But would they be permitted to participate in the public life of the larger community in whose midst they resided? Would religious toleration extend to civic equality in the form of the right to vote and serve in office? This did not occur during the colonial era, when political participation was restricted to propertied white males who were Christian, although some colonies barred Catholics from voting and holding office. As the Reverend Ezra Stiles remarked in 1762, it appeared as if the Jewish people would "never become incorporated with the people of America anymore than in Europe, Asia, and Africa," an assessment occasioned by Rhode Island's denial of naturalization to Aaron Lopez and another member of Newport's Jewish community. Naturalization was a right to which they were in fact entitled under the terms of legislation enacted by Parliament in 1740 but, blithely disregarding that law, Rhode Island asserted in yet another way that Jews were not part of the political order.[42]

The sole exception to the prevailing rule of exclusion was in the colony of New York, where Jews were allowed naturalization as early as 1715 and were permitted to become freemen, which in turn authorized them to vote in municipal elections (they are known to have done so during the 1760s) and serve as constables. Even in New York, however, they could not vote for members of the colony's legislature, a disability that was not eliminated until 1777, when the state adopted a constitution that ended religious qualifications for voting in elections and serving in office. But when the Revolution ended, New York's was the only constitution that accepted Jews as equal citizens by granting them those two key civil rights. It appeared as if the Reverend Stiles's prediction of permanent Jewish disenfranchisement was solidly grounded everywhere else in the new nation, and that not even in an era of a revolution devoted to liberty, the protection of basic rights, and a proclamation that all were created equal could Jews achieve acceptance as full citizens.[43]

If early America's Jews were innovative when it came to formulating a new kind of Jewish community and taking steps to preserve their distinctive identity, it was in making the case for civic equality during and after the Revolution that they were at their boldest. Daringly, they challenged the consignment of Jews to civic inequality, basing their claim to inclusion on their loyalty and service to America during the Revolution. Choosing sides during the Revolution was in and of itself an unprecedented step for the Jewish population, for it was perhaps the first time they had plunged into political life anywhere in the modern world. Although some sided with England, most appear to have backed the American cause by abandoning their homes when their cities were captured by the British, crossing into exile behind American lines, serving in the military, and, in Georgia and South Carolina, serving in civilian institutions established by the rebels.[44] Subsequently, they invoked this record of loyalty to America to argue for civic equality. For example, when the officers of the congregation in Philadelphia protested late in 1783 against the clause in Pennsylvania's constitution that required members of the legislature to swear that the Old *and* the New Testaments were divinely inspired—a requirement that would obviously disbar Jews—they pointed to their adherence to the American cause:

> To the Hebrew Congregation in Newport
> Rhode Island.
>
> Gentlemen.
>
>   While I receive, with much satisfaction,
> your Address replete with expressions of affection
> and esteem; I rejoice in the opportunity of assuring
> you, that I shall always retain a grateful remem
> brance of the cordial welcome I experienced in
> my visit to Newport, from all classes of citizens.
>   The reflection on the days of difficulty and
> danger which are past is rendered the more sweet,
> from a consciousness that they are succeeded by days
> of uncommon prosperity and security. If we have
> wisdom to make the best use of the advantages with
> which we are now favored, we cannot fail, under the
> just administration of a good Government, to become
> a great and a happy people.
>   The Citizens of the United States of America
> have a right to applaud themselves for having given
> to mankind examples of an enlarged and liberal
> policy: a policy worthy of imitation. All possess
> alike liberty of conscience and immunities of
> citizenship. It is now no more that toleration is
> spoken of, as if it was by the indulgence of one
> class of people, that another enjoyed the exercise
> of their inherent natural rights. For happily
>   the

Shown here is Washington's celebrated reply to Newport in which he declared that the government of the United States "to bigotry gives no sanction, to persecution no assistance"—an enduring affirmation of America's fundamental commitment to religious tolerance and pluralism.

George Washington to the Newport Hebrew Congregation, 1790. Courtesy of the B'nai B'rith Klutznick National Jewish Museum, on loan from the Morgenstern Foundation.

the Government of the United States, which gives to bigotry no sanction, to persecution no assistance, requires only that they who live under its protection, should demean themselves as good citizens, in giving it on all occasions their effectual support.

It would be inconsistent with the frankness of my character not to avow that I am pleased with your favorable opinion of my administration, and fervent wishes for my felicity. May the children of the Stock of Abraham, who dwell in this land, continue to merit and enjoy the good will of the other Inhabitants; while every one shall sit in safety under his own vine and figtree, and there shall be none to make him afraid. May the father of all mercies scatter light and not darkness in our paths, and make us all in our several vocations useful here, and in his own due time and way everlastingly happy.

G. Washington

1790. August

Reply of Genl. Washington to Address of the Hebrews of Newport Rhode Island With Autograph Signature of G.° Washington Original & Valuable

The Jews of Charlestown, New-York, New-Port and other posts, occupied by the British troops, have distinguishedly suffered for their attachment to the revolution principles. . . . The Jews of Pennsylvania in proportion to the number of their members, can count with any religious society whatsoever, the whigs [supporters of the Revolution] among either of them; they have served some of them in the continental army; some went out in the militia to fight the common enemy; all of them have chearfully contributed to the support of the militia, and of the government of this state. . . .

Similarly, four years later, one of the congregation's members wrote to the Constitutional Convention, then meeting in Philadelphia, to argue against religious requirements for office, again citing the fact that "the Jews have been true and faithful whigs, & during the late Contest with England they have been foremost in aiding and assisting the states with their lifes & fortunes. . . ."[45]

It was against this background of uncertainty about their status in political America that the small Jewish community of Newport, significantly reduced in size after the Revolution, corresponded with George Washington in August 1790, in what is arguably the most important exchange of letters in American Jewish history. Writing to welcome the president when he visited Newport, they alluded to the fact that, historically, Jews had been denied "the invaluable rights of free citizens," but, in a reference to the new federal government, declared that happily there now existed "a Government. . . deeming every one, of whatever nation, tongue, or language equal parts of the great governmental machine." Washington replied immediately. Repeating the most ringing phrase of all in the congregation's letter, he wrote that the government of the United States "gives to bigotry no sanction, to persecution no assistance." Just as important, however, particularly for the cause of equal political rights, was the statement in his letter that "all possess alike liberty of conscience and immunities of citizenship." In that single sentence (which also borrowed terminology from the congregations's letter but did not repeat it exactly), Washington gathered the Jews of America under the umbrella of equal citizenship. By implication, the hero of the Revolution, the father of the nation, could be said to have supported the case for Jewish enfranchisement.[46]

By this point, many others in the republic agreed to it. Virginia had already joined New York, when it terminated religious tests for voting and serving in office in 1785. South Carolina and Pennsylvania followed suit in 1790, Delaware in 1792, and Georgia in 1798.[47]

And yet, seven of the original states continued to deny Jews the political rights that went with full citizenship. Accordingly, they continued to press the case against religious qualifications for participation in public life, as in 1809 in North Carolina, when Jacob Henry, elected to the legislature, was challenged on the grounds that the state's constitution required an oath affirming the divinity of the New Testament when he sought to take his seat. Henry argued, successfully as it turned out, that he supported the principle that officeholders must subscribe to religious beliefs, but that there could be no legal prescription regarding *which* beliefs. Even more eloquently, Isaac Harby of Charleston argued in 1816 against barring anyone on the basis of reli-

In his letter of May 28, 1818, to America's most prominent Jew, Mordecai M. Noah, Thomas Jefferson sheds light on the nature of democracy, the frailty of the human character, the power of the free human spirit, and Jefferson's faith in humankind. The president cautions, however, that: "More remains to be done, for altho' we are free by the law, we are not so in practice." Jefferson's letter was in response to Noah's published address—a copy of which he had sent to the president—that Noah had delivered at the consecration of New York congregation Shearith Israel's newly rebuilt synagogue building.

Thomas Jefferson to Mordecai M. Noah, May 28, 1818. Papers of Thomas Jefferson, Manuscript Division.

gion from appointment to positions in government, in the process articulating a vision of America as a society in which pluralism and equal inclusion were bedrock principles. Objecting to the removal of Mordecai Manuel Noah as consul to Tunis because, as Secretary of State James Monroe explained, he was Jewish, Harby wrote to Monroe that Jews were "by no means to be considered as a *Religious sect*, tolerated by the government; they constitute a portion of *the People*. They are, in every respect, woven in and compacted with the citizens of the Republic. Quakers and Catholics; Episcopalians and Presbyterians, Baptists and Jews, all constitute one great political family."[48]

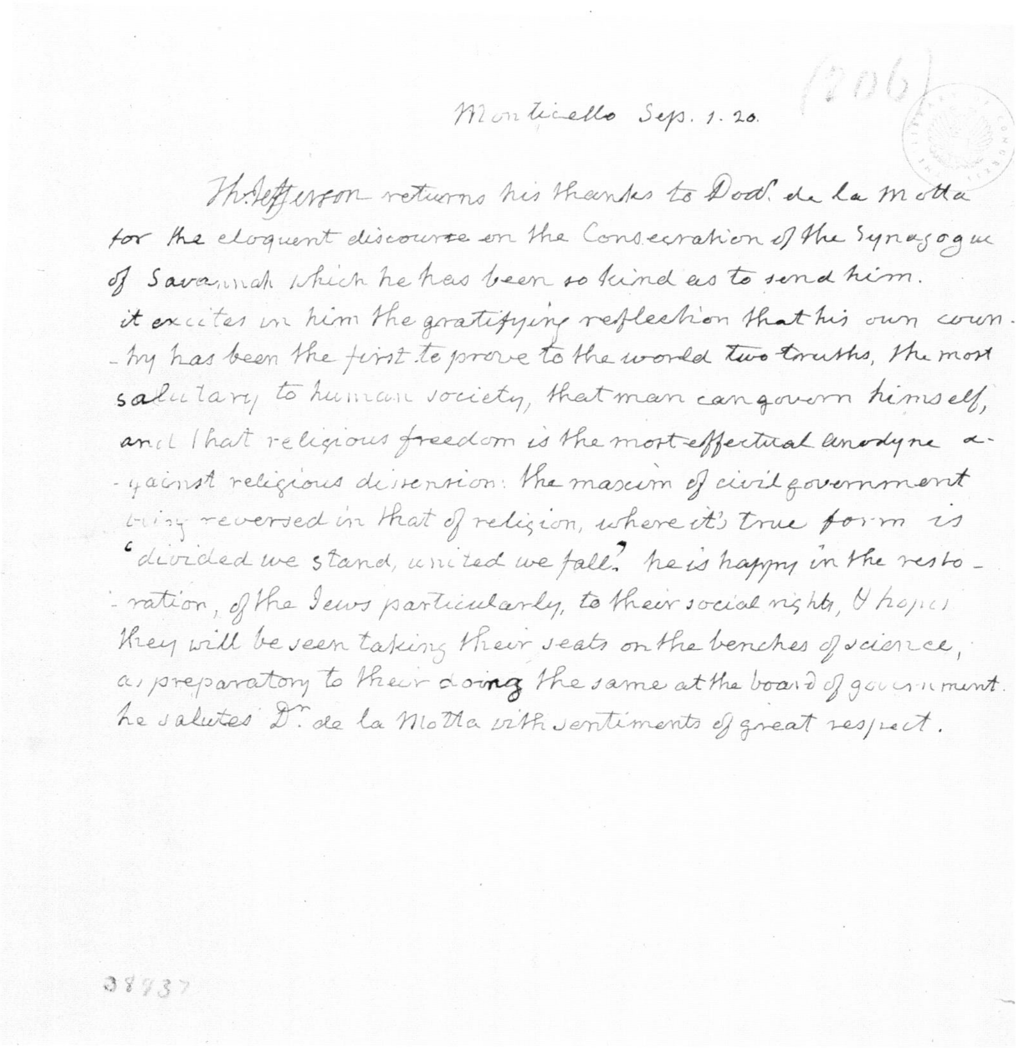

In 1820, Jacob De La Motta sent Thomas Jefferson a copy of the address he delivered at the consecration of Savannah's first synagogue. In Jefferson's response, which is shown here, the sage of Monticello comments upon the true meaning of religious liberty in a pluralistic democracy: "The maxim of civil government being reversed in that of religion, where its true form is, divided we stand, united we fall."

Thomas Jefferson to Jacob De La Motta, September 1, 1820. Papers of Thomas Jefferson, Manuscript Division.

By 1820, another of the original thirteen states, Connecticut, had abandoned religious qualifications for political participation, and Massachusetts was on the verge of doing likewise in 1821.[49] Equally auspicious for the Jews of America at this juncture, Thomas Jefferson, a seminal figure on the political landscape, strongly affirmed that Jews had the right to civic equality. In 1818, Mordecai Manuel Noah sent Jefferson a copy of the speech he delivered during the dedication of a new synagogue building by the congregation in New York, and in his response the former president denounced religious intolerance and suggested that the only protection against it were laws that guaranteed religious and civil equality. As Jefferson wrote, "Our laws have applied the only antidote to this vice, protecting our religious, as they do our civil rights, by putting all on an equal footing." Two years later, Jefferson, responding to yet another speech delivered upon the dedication of a synagogue, this time in Savannah, again offered his unstinting support for equal rights in the political arena. "He is happy," Jefferson wrote describing himself, "in the restoration of the Jews, particularly, to their social rights, and hopes they will be seen taking their seats on the benches of science as preparatory to their doing the same at the board of government."[50]

The Jewish population of the young nation no doubt felt buoyed by and grateful for the support of such figures as Washington and Jefferson. However, they had not passively awaited political emancipation, but repeatedly made the case for it themselves. In this respect too, therefore, the Jews of early America proved innovative and daring, forceful and bold, as they endeavored to create a viable Jewish community, to preserve their identity—and to participate freely in the broader community that was America.

The War Between Jewish Brothers
in America

Eli N. Evans

For Jews in America, the Civil War was a watershed that involved Jewish soldiers from all over the nation. Jews served in both armies and helped in the war effort in many other ways. Serving their countries under fire and fighting side by side with their Gentile comrades in arms accelerated the process of acculturation, not only through their self-perceptions, but also because of the reactions of the community around them. Jewish immigrants who had only recently arrived in America and thought of themselves as Germans came to see themselves not only as Americans, but as Americans who belonged. And the veterans were largely treated that way when they returned home.

By 1860, with a Jewish population of 150,000 (more than 100,000 new immigrants having arrived since 1850, mostly from Germany), there were at least 160 identifiable Jewish communities with synagogues in America, which meant that Jewish families with sons from cities and towns all across the country were involved in the Civil War. There were thirty congregations in New York City, but congregations also existed in cities and towns such as Albany, Utica, Rochester, Syracuse, and Buffalo, New York, as well as Savannah and West Point, Georgia, and Springfield, Illinois.

Judah Benjamin, the first acknowledged Jew to be elected to the U.S. Senate, served as Louisiana's senator from 1853 until that state seceded from the union in early 1861. Benjamin served as a member of Jefferson Davis's cabinet, first as attorney general, then as secretary of war, and finally, as secretary of state. After the collapse of the Confederacy, Benjamin fled to England, where he had a distinguished career as one of England's leading barristers.

Judah Benjamin, attributed to Jesse Whitehurst, photographer, salted paper print, circa 1861. Gift of Janos Novomeszky, Prints and Photographs Division.

For rabbis, ministers, and clergy of all faiths in the Northern cities generally, the sermon was beginning to be used as a patriotic vehicle. Slavery had emerged in the voice of the clergy of all faiths not just as a political matter, but as a spiritual one. The subject of slavery was soon given maximum attention from the pulpit. As the flames ignited in America spread to Jewish pulpits across Europe, rabbis took up the debate, attacking Raphall's interpretation of text and charging him with misreading Jewish history. American antislavery literature based on this event even eluded the Czarist censors and reached Yiddish speaking Jews in the interior of Russia.

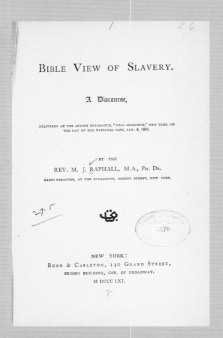

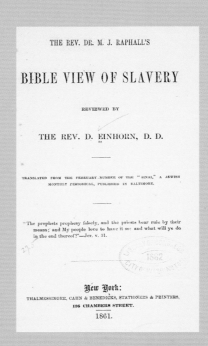

Rabbi Morris J. Raphall of New York Congregation B'nei Jeshrun, whose sermon in 1861, "The Bible View of Slavery," was to become the most controversial statement ever issued by an American rabbi. Raphall claimed that the "very highest authority—the Ten Commandments" sanctioned slavery" because "the Sabbath of the Lord" required one to "rest thy male slave and thy female slave." He asserted "How dare you denounce slavery as a sin? When you remember Abraham, Isaac, Jacob and Job—the men with whom the Almighty conversed, with whose names He emphatically connects to His own most holy name;...that all those men were slaveholders, does it not strike you that you are guilty of something very little short of blasphemy?" The speech brought sensational front page headlines all across the country with special attention in the South.

Morris J. Raphall, Bible View of Slavery: A Discourse ....,
New York, 1861. General Collections.

Rabbi David Einhorn of Baltimore, the leading abolitionist among the American rabbis, and one of the few rabbis who had been opposing slavery from his pulpit since 1856, denounced Raphall's views asking if God had shown any respect for the "historic right" when he emancipated the Hebrew slaves from Egyptian slavery, and arguing that "religious principles of freedom and righteousness must triumph over...ancient prejudices and ... hallowed atrocities." Einhorn's slashing reply eventually received such wide circulation that Southern sympathizers in Baltimore burned his printing press, young men from the congregation guarded him and his house around the clock, and he finally had to flee for his safety to escape the rioting in the city between the proslavery partisans and the abolitionists.

David Einhorn, The Rev. Dr. M. J. Raphall's Bible View of Slavery. *New York, 1861. General Collections.*

Slavery evolved into the lightning rod and the sword that made a civil war on this divided continent inevitable. The divisive political, economic, social, and moral upheavals brought about by the struggle over slavery gripped the nation for decades. There was no one Jewish position on slavery, but German Jews, who in 1848 had begun the great journey to America in search of religious liberty, gravitated to the newly formed Republican Party in the North. There were many Jews who stood up for what they believed in on all sides of the issues, but on the whole Jews in both sections of the country, especially the struggling new immigrants, preferred political neutrality to outspoken participation in the bitter arguments over abolition. In the end, as Naomi Cohen pointed out in *Encounter with Emancipation,* "geographical location determined which army they fought in; for whom the women rolled bandages, and for which side the rabbis invoked divine aid." Finally, as the war clouds gathered, Jewish neutrality was tested from an unexpected quarter—an improbable clash of rabbis impassioned by Old Testament interpretation.

The War Years

Anti-Semitism, or what one historian refers to as "Judaeophobia," during and in the aftermath of the Civil War was as great as anytime in American history. That Jews didn't fight, but just made money off the war, is a canard that gained great currency in the press during and in the years after the war. The charges took on the coloration of the fierce regional divisions that were at the core of the conflict. When the presence of Jews in the South during the Civil War was even acknowledged, the image in the Northern press was often of the cunning merchant-cheat and the speculator. The Southern press depicted Jews as "scavengers" who were unpatriotic and therefore "un-Southern," outsiders safely behind the lines, feeding off the troubles of the South in its most desolate time. In the North as well, the Jews were accused of undermining the war effort and Jewish financiers of making money off the war. The truth for both sides is a more dramatic story of participation and sacrifice.

Shocked by the charges that Jews avoided the dangers of the war and that no Jews even fought in the war, in 1895 Simon Wolf, a lawyer who had supported Abraham Lincoln and was the major lobbyist for Jewish causes in Washington, assembled a list of as many Jewish soldiers as he could find and published it in his book, *The American Jew as Patriot, Soldier and Citizen* (which contains 300 pages of lists and biographical data taken from his interviews with families, citing their recollections, Jewish names, testimony, and other inexact sources). Wolf estimated that approximately twelve hundred Jews served in the Confederacy, including twenty-four army officers and eleven navy officers. But his contacts were not as good in the South as they were in the North. Confederate Secretary of War James A. Seddon placed the number in the South as high as 10,000. However, most scholars have concluded that the figure is closer to between 2,000 and 3,000, but no accurate number has ever been established.

In the North, 6,000 Jews served, according to Wolf's account, but only sixteen were officers. (Eight hundred more names were listed but not classified.) There were six Jews awarded the Congressional Medal of Honor for bravery in battle. In the South, Jews even organized two Jewish companies—at West Point, Georgia, in the first month of the war, and at Macon, Georgia, in 1862, for the stated purpose of the defense of Savannah. Jewish companies were also organized in the North—in Chicago and Syracuse. However, most Jews, Northern and Southern, were reluctant to separate themselves as Jews and chose to enlist in the regular army units.

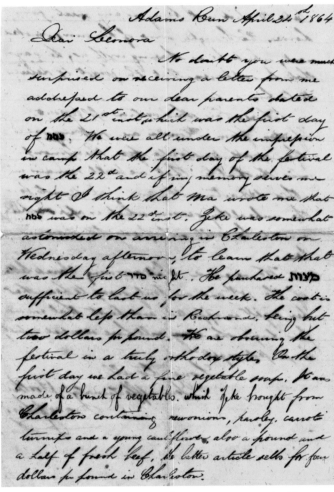

In a letter to his sister Leonora from an encampment in Adams Run, South Carolina, Isaac Levy described his preparations for celebrating Passover in the field. He reported that their brother Zeke had traveled to Charleston for provisions, including matzot (written in Hebrew letters in the middle of the page), and they both were "observing the festival in a truly orthodox style."

Isaac J. Levy to Leonora Levy, April 24, 1864. Courtesy of the Jacob Rader Marcus Center of the American Jewish Archives.

The South

All over the South, Jews rallied to the Confederacy as ardent Southerners. Now that fate had cast the gauntlet, they would fight for the glory of the Southern flag, as steeped in the honor and insult as the other white men they fought with.

In Charleston, 180 Jews joined the Confederate Army; M. C. Mordecai's steamer *Isabel* was outfitted into a blockade runner; Benjamin Mordecai organized the "Free Market of Charleston," which was supporting more than six hundred families at a cost of $8,000 a month by late 1862; and David Lopez, a talented builder and architect, constructed one of the torpedo boats, *David*, which in 1863, in Charleston harbor, seriously damaged the federal warship *New Ironsides* in the first successful torpedo attack in naval history.

In Montgomery, Alabama, Mayer Lehman was cut off from his brother Emanuel in New York City, but because the Lehman family was so trusted by the Governor of Alabama, Emanuel was sent to England to raise funds for the Confederacy. (Little wonder then that Mayer named his eighth child after his friend Hillary Herbert, Confederate colonel and congressman from Alabama. Herbert Lehman would become Governor and U.S. Senator from the State of New York.)

In Chattanooga, Tennessee, the war split the Ochs family. Julius Ochs (the father of Adolph Ochs, who would ultimately buy and build the *New York Times*) joined the Union Army, but his wife Bertha remained loyal to the Confederacy and was once arrested for trying to smuggle quinine in a baby carriage to wounded Confederate soldiers. Bertha was a charter member of the Chattanooga Chapter of the United Daughters of the Confederacy and when she died she requested that a Confederate flag be placed on her coffin. Julius was buried next to her in a coffin draped with the Stars and Stripes.

Down in the ranks, the stories of bravery would be passed from generation to generation as Southern Jewish families swelled proudly at the portraits of Confederate infantrymen over their mantels.

Max Frauenthal, from Port Gibson and Summit, Mississippi, served as a member of the 16th Mississippi Infantry and distinguished himself at Bloody Acute Angle during the Battle of Spottsylvania Court House in Virginia. A veteran from his company remembered Frauenthal as "a little Jew, who, though insignificant, had the heart of a lion in a battle. For several hours, he stood at the immediate point of contact amid the most terrific hail of lead, and coolly and deliberately loaded and fired without cringing. . . . I now understand how it was that a handful of Jews could drive before them a hundred kings–they were all Fronthals." It would not be the last time that a Jewish name was mispronounced; for years in Mississippi, Confederate veterans referred to any brave man as "a regular Fronthal."

Private Isaac Gleitzman of Arkansas fought under the daring command of Nathan Bedford Forrest. While the Confederacy awarded him its Cross of Honor for "conspicuous gallantry in the field," he was proudest that he had never eaten any *trefa* or nonkosher food during his entire four years of military service. His family retains to this day the two mess kits he carried with him during the war, one for meat and one for dairy.

Robert Rosen reports in *The Jewish Confederates* that there were "Jewish Johnny Rebs," who were the enlisted men in the trenches who did the fighting as well as the unglamorous work of the army. They were "cooks, sharp shooters, orderlies, teamsters, foragers... who dug trenches, cut trees, guarded prisoners, and served on picket duty." And they were the infantry, casualties at every major battle of the war. The book records the story of family after family with losses of sons and fathers and quotes from the unintended poetry of diaries. There is the story of Simon Baruch, the father of Bernard Baruch, a Prussian immigrant from Camden, South Carolina, who served as a surgeon (with the equivalent rank of major), treating the wounded of the 3rd South Carolina Battalion, known as Kershaw's Brigade, and others wounded at Gettysburg for weeks after the battle. Baruch later wrote that Union doctors shared their supplies. And there is the very poignant story of Lieutenant Joshua Lazarus Moses, a Citadel graduate and one of five brothers to serve in the Confederacy. He was killed in action at

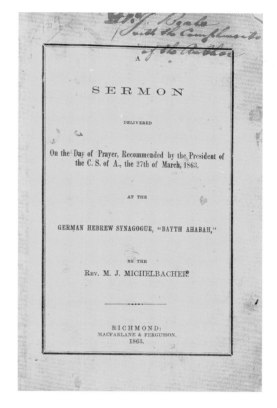

On March 27, 1863, on the "Day of Prayer" recommended by Jefferson Davis, President of the C.S.A., Reverend M. J. Michelbacher preached this sermon, to which he added a prayer for the Confederate States of America "to crown our independence with prosperity," and for its president to "grant speedy success to his endeavors to free our country from the presence of its foes."

M. J. Michelbacher, A Sermon Delivered . . . at . . . "Bayth Ahabah" (House of Love), Richmond, 1863. Rare Book and Special Collections Division.

Fort Blakely, outside of Mobile, Alabama, on April 9, 1865, the same day that Lee surrendered at Appomattox.

The Levy Sisters of Charleston

Eugenia and Phoebe Levy were Jewish Southern belles who became legends in the South from their unusual adventures during the Civil War. We know a great deal about them because of Eugenia's wartime diary in the Library of Congress collection and Phoebe's book written after the war, *A Southern Woman's Diary* (1875). Eugenia's 1902 obituaries noted the two Confederate Jewish sisters as "toasts of the day" and that "two more brilliant women...could not be found."

T. C. Deleon, writing in his *Belles, Beaux, and Brains of the Sixties* (New York, 1909), a paean to Southern women during the war, wrote that "Eugenia...was one of the most picturesque personages in Confederate history... most potent and popular..."; and that Phoebe "was a belle and early a widow, she made herself loved in the army camps by that good work of her Chimborazo Hospital."

They were raised in a prominent family of considerable wealth in Charleston, with all the privileges of young women of their class, and especially the self-confidence and high-spirited élan for which Southern women have been celebrated in Southern literature.

Both married well, as one would expect, but Eugenia, after being pursued by many, at the age of sixteen married Philip Phillips, a twenty-nine-year-old brilliant young Jewish lawyer in Charleston who moved her to Mobile where he represented the major commercial interests and eventually was elected to Congress from Alabama.

A fiery and outspoken Confederate sympathizer, Eugenia Levy Phillips often found herself at odds with Union officials. The opening page of her journal, reproduced here, describes her arrest in Washington, along with two daughters and her sister Martha, on August 23, 1861 by federal officers. Released after a three-week imprisonment, Phillips relocated to New Orleans, where she ran afoul of the notorious General Benjamin "Beast" Butler, who issued a special order imprisoning her at Ship Island, where conditions were harsh and primitive.

Eugenia Levy Philips, Journal, 1861. Papers of the Philip Phillips Family, Manuscript Division.

When the war broke out, they remained in Washington for a time because Phillips was opposed to slavery and secession while Eugenia was an outspoken Confederate patriot. Korn called her "a fire-eating secessionist in skirts." She even enlisted in a form of female espionage using her charms on gullible Union officers and politicians to get information that she managed to deliver clandestinely to the young Confederate government. She and others were arrested by Union authorities, and Mary Chesnut referred to her and fellow spy Rose Greenhow as "saints and martyrs and patriots."

Moving with their nine children to New Orleans, which they thought would be a relatively safe haven far from the battlegrounds of Virginia, she became embroiled in the episode which sealed her story in the annals of Confederate history. When New Orleans fell to the Union Navy in early 1862, Major General Benjamin Butler of Massachusetts took over the occupation and eventually became known as "Beast" Butler for the harshness of his administration. Accusing Eugenia of teaching her children to spit from the balcony of their home on Union officers and "laughing at and mocking" the passing remains of a Union officer during a solemn funeral procession, Butler decided to make an example of her. He reported that when he confronted her as to why she had done those things, she replied "I was in good spirits that day." T. C. Deleon reported, "it was Mrs. Phillips' contempt of the general and her cool sarcasm that caused her imprisonment." Butler ordered her to be isolated till further orders on Ship Island, sixty-five miles from New Orleans, an isolated prison site infested with mosquitoes and the threat of disease, certainly no place for a "lady" among so many male soldiers acting as guards. She would later complain that "their conversation, evidently to insult me, was of the basest and foulest character." When notified of her sentence, she replied, "It has one advantage over the city, sir; you will not be there." And when informed it was a yellow fever station, she stated, "It is fortunate that neither the fever nor General Butler is contagious."

News of her imprisonment spread all over the South—for Butler had challenged the code of Southern chivalry. After all, he had warned in his notorious "The Woman Order" that if the Confederate women of New Orleans insulted the occupying forces in any way, they would "be treated as a woman of the town plying her avocation." Diaries of the time indicate that such language and attitude inflamed women across the South and Eugenia became a symbol of injustice for standing up to the Union occupation. Moreover her fervently patriotic letters from the island were widely circulated and she became an overnight heroine for her unflinching loyalty to the cause and her acid tongue. When she was released three and a half months later (some said by intervention of friends in Washington) she and her husband were greeted with standing ovations and cheers everywhere they went. Crowds made pilgrimages to their home, and a relative wrote to her, "future historians will vie with each other for the honor of writing your biography." Robert N. Rosen summarized her life as follows, "raised nine children, incarcerated twice for her pro-Southern sympathies, and lived to the age of eighty-three."

Her younger sister, Phoebe Yates Pember, widowed shortly after her marriage, was drawn to serve the cause after the war began and worked herself up from simple nursing tasks to become the first female administrator of the sprawling Chimborazo Hospital. It was a remarkable achievement for a Southern woman, especially one from the aristocracy, for this was the largest hospital in the world at that time, at its height with 150 wards and over the course of the war serving 76,000 patients. In truth, all of Richmond became a vast hospital, with thousands of bloodied and bandaged men hobbling back to the city, some blinded and missing limbs, helped by comrades or in carts, wagons, and litters. Inside the wards, it was a scene of unspeakable carnage and suffering, as the wounded and dying were brought to the hospital from surrounding battlegrounds to be treated, or into the amputation room to be hacked or sawed and then cauterized with a hot poker, or just left to die if they were too far gone.

Union soldier David Urbansky was awarded a Medal of Honor for gallantry at Shiloh and Vicksburg. Displayed here is Urbansky's second medal, which was issued in 1879, after he petitioned the government for a medal to replace the first one that had been lost or stolen in 1865.

Medal of Honor of David Urbansky. Courtesy of the Jacob Rader Marcus Center of the American Jewish Archives.

It was inconceivable for most Southerners to imagine a woman of such fine upbringing as Phoebe Pember in such circumstances, and she later wrote that many thought "such a life would be injurious to the delicacy and refinement of a lady." But she had a strong character that enabled her to be around death and misery all day and still summon the strength to read to the suffering wounded from the Bible, give a sip of water or soup, hold a hand, or bind a wound, or write a farewell letter home for the illiterate soldiers. In her book, she wrote that she was not prepared or trained to be a Florence Nightingale. Instead she was able to call on a forceful nature fueled by an unlikely combination of moral outrage and warm humanity in the face of the agony all around her, possessed of an extraordinary determination and resilience, not unlike her sister. One of the most famous scenes portraying the role of women in the war described her standing guard over the whiskey barrel, with a pistol on her hip, protecting it from thievery so that it would be available for the wounded and those facing the surgeons. "Hers was a will of steel," Deleon wrote.

The North

There were also legendary Jewish immigrants who fought for the Union, whose stories are better documented, both in the better-staffed Northern newspapers and by Simon Wolf's interviews. Wolf tracked down the stories of six Jewish soldiers of the Union Army who received the first Congressional Medal of Honor, created by President Lincoln "to reward non-commissioned officers and privates as shall most distinguish themselves by their gallantry in action." Sergeant Leopold Karpeles was born in Prague and in 1850, when he was twelve years old, came to the United States to live with his brother in Texas. He joined the Union Army at Springfield, Massachusetts, and received the Congressional Medal for "rallying the men of the 57th Massachusetts Volunteers around his flag" in a major battle, "turning retreat into victory."

Private Abraham Cohen, of the 68th New York Regiment, rose in the ranks to be a sergeant major and won the Congressional Medal "for conspicuous gallantry displayed at the Battle of the Wilderness, in rallying and forming, under heavy fire, disorganized troops"; also "for bravery and coolness in carrying orders to advanced lines under murderous fire." After rising to the rank of captain of his regiment, sickness and wounds caused surgeons to declare him "unfit for service" and he was given an honorable discharge. But after an extended recovery, he reenlisted as a private in the 6th New Hampshire Volunteers and served with such distinction at the Battle of

Petersburg, once again risking life and limb by "carrying orders from and to advanced outposts under a barrage of fire," that he received new promotions in a second career.

Wolf counted fourteen families in both armies who gave the ultimate sacrifice of no less than fifty-one lives: families who lost three, four and five brothers; a father and three sons; a father and four sons, all of whom were "volunteers in a deadly strife."

Many others with roots in one region fought for the other side. On September 2, 1891, former Captain Joseph B. Greenhut, a Jewish Union officer recalling the unforgettable panorama of death and courage seared into his memory of his service as a twenty-year-old in the Illinois 82nd Infantry, walked the fields of Gettysburg to Cemetery Hill to deliver the dedication at the unveiling of the monument to the soldiers of the Illinois 82nd who fought there. Appointed by the governor of Illinois as one of three veterans to erect the monument, it must have been difficult for Greenhut to imagine that the boy born in Austria in 1843, who immigrated with his parents to Chicago at the age of nine, worked for several years in Mobile, Alabama, but returned North after secession to join the Union Army as an eighteen-year-old recruit, twenty-eight years later would be standing in the middle of the battlefield where he saw unbelievable carnage and tragedy that he never thought he would survive.

In his capacity as Secretary of the Board of Ministers of the Hebrew Congregations of Philadelphia, Isaac Leeser wrote to President Lincoln on August 21, 1862, asking that a Jewish chaplain be appointed to minister to the spiritual needs of sick or wounded soldiers in military hospitals in Philadelphia and its vicinity. The letter was referred by the president to the surgeon general, who advised that, it is "both legal and proper, that Chaplains of the Hebrew faith should be appointed in the Army."

Isaac Leeser to Abraham Lincoln, August 21, 1862. Papers of Abraham Lincoln, Manuscript Division.

The two highest-ranking Jews in the Union Army were Brigadier Generals Edward Solomon and Frederick Knefler. Solomon left Germany at the age of eighteen, settled in Chicago in 1854, and at the outbreak of the war joined the 14th Illinois as a second lieutenant. By the summer of 1862, as a major, he was instrumental in organizing the all-Jewish company for the new 82nd Illinois with a full complement of ninety-six men, supported by funds raised by the local community. Praising the patriotism of "our Israelite citizens," the *Chicago Tribune* trumpeted that "the rapidity with which the company was enlisted has not its equal in the history of recruiting...Can any town, city or state in the nation show an equally good two days work?" Solomon became a lieutenant colonel and led his company through the battles at Chancellorsville and the three-day battle at Gettysburg (possibly firing at Proskauer in the 12th Alabama). Looking back thirty years later, Major General Carl Schurz told Simon Wolf: "He was the only soldier at Gettysburg who did not dodge when Lee's guns thundered; he stood up, smoked his cigar and faced the cannon balls." At the end of the war, in June of 1865, Secretary of War Edwin Stanton, with the ratification of the U.S. Senate, awarded him the rank of brigadier general.

At the age of twenty-six, Frederick Knefler of Hungary immigrated to the United States and arrived in 1859 on the eve of the outbreak of the Civil War. He enlisted as a private in the Army in response to Lincoln's first call for volunteers in the 79th Regiment of the Indiana Volunteers. He took part in many battles over the course of the war with the Army of the Cumberland and served for a time under General Grant. For heroic conduct in the bloody Battle of Chickamaugua, he attained the rank of major general and subsequently joined General William Tecumseh Sherman in the "total war" March to the Sea that broke the back and the spirit of the South.

With regard to Jews in the government, the South would reward with its highest honors the generation of Sephardic Jews, by 1860 almost totally assimilated, made up of men who had married outside their faith and drifted away from Judaism until they blended smoothly into the slave-holding plantation life of the aristocracy—men like Judah P. Benjamin, who served as U.S. Senator from Louisiana before becoming Attorney General, Secretary of War, and Secretary of State to the Confederacy; Henry Hyams, the Lieutenant Governor of Louisiana; and Dr. Edwin Moise, the Speaker of the Louisiana legislature. Even though they were indistinguishable from other Southerners in style and language, they could retain a cultural curiosity about their Jewishness, both an awareness and a respect, that would astound a visitor who had assumed they had long since abandoned any consciousness of their roots.

Just before the war, Salomon de Rothschild of the Parisian branch of the noted banking family traveled to New Orleans, where he met with Benjamin, Hyams, and Moise. "What is astonishing here," he wrote home, "or rather what is not astonishing, is the high position occupied by our coreligionists, or rather by those who were born into the faith and who, having married Christian women, and without converting, have forgotten the practices of their fathers . . . and what is odd, all these men have a Jewish heart and take an interest in me, because I represent the greatest Jewish house in the world."

Judah P. Benjamin

There is much that is intriguing about how deeply Jews and Southerners are alike–stepchildren of an anguished history–and yet different. Whereas the Jewish search for a homeland contrasted with the Southerners' commitment to place, Southern defenders of the Confederacy often used Old Testament analogies in referring to themselves as "the chosen people," destined to survive and triumph against overwhelming odds.

Judah P. Benjamin was called "the dark prince of the Confederacy" by Stephen Vincent Benet in *John Brown's Body*. He was an extraordinary figure in the Civil War who achieved greater political power than perhaps any other Jewish American in history. Benjamin was the first acknowledged Jew in the U.S. Senate, and after Secession he became Jefferson Davis's

Bearing Judah Benjamin's likeness, this twenty–year bond was issued by the Congress of the Confederate States of America on August 19, 1861, and offered an interest rate of 8 percent, reflecting the investment's high degree of risk. The last coupon redeemed was dated January 1865.

Five Hundred Dollar Bond, Confederate States of America, Authorized by an Act of Congress, C.S.A., August 19, 1861. *Confederate States of America Collection, Manuscript Division.*

right-hand man, serving initially as Attorney General, a job that expanded because the president needed a prodigious administrator to help organize the government. Subsequently, Davis appointed him Secretary of War, to which he was named because Davis wanted to have a dependable and trusted friend who would not question the president's decisions and yet would accept the blame for military defeats. Even after the harsh denunciations of Benjamin for failures on the battlefield, Davis once again appointed him to a third cabinet post, Secretary of State, which put him in charge of all efforts to bring England and other nations into the war and fatefully, as it would turn out, involve him in the spy efforts in Canada and elsewhere. Yet this brilliant, cultured man, who came to be called "the brains of the Confederacy," has been largely overlooked by history because he chose obscurity by burning his papers in the closing days of the war. Still, he left letters to others, thousands of official documents, and many impressions.

Judah P. Benjamin was fascinating because of the extraordinary role he played in Southern history and the ways in which Jews and non-Jews reacted to him. He was the prototype of the contradictions in the Jewish Southerner and the stranger in the Confederate story, the Jew at the eye of the storm that was the Civil War. Objectively, with so few Jews in the South at the time, it is astonishing that one should appear at the very center of Southern history. Benjamin himself avoided his Jewishness throughout his public career, though his enemies in the Southern press and in the halls of the Confederate Congress never let the South forget it. The virulence of the times, which saw an outpouring of anti-Semitism such as had existed in no previous period in American history, required a symbolic figure as a catalyst for an ancient hostility and perhaps contributed to his intentional elusiveness.

Judah Benjamin would abandon formal Judaism, but neither the South nor the North would allow Judaism to abandon him. Cruelly, anti-Semitism stalked him throughout his career, as if to mock his success with ancient hatreds. When the South began to sink in despair, Benjamin, as Secretary of War, emerged as a convenient target of attack for the military failures, the lack of supplies, and the gathering disillusionment with the cause. Thomas R. R. Cobb, a brigadier general and member of the Provisional Congress of the Confederacy, said, "a grander rascal than this Jew Benjamin does not exist in the Confederacy, and I am not particular in concealing my opinion of him." In the Confederate House of Representatives, Congressman Henry S. Foote of Tennessee affirmed that he "would never consent to the establishment of a supreme court of the Confederate States as long as Judah P. Benjamin shall continue to pollute the ears of majesty Davis with his insidious counsels." A writer to the *Richmond Enquirer* believed it "blasphemous" for a Jew to hold such high office and suggested that the prayers of the Confederacy would have more effect if Benjamin were dismissed from the cabinet.

Blamed by the South for its miseries, Benjamin also was bitterly denounced in the North and rarely mentioned in the Northern press without some reference to his being a Jew. Other senators bitterly attacked both him and another Jew, Florida Senator David (Levy) Yulee, known as the "Florida fire-eater" because of the passion of his proslavery views. Andrew Johnson, as a senator, later to succeed Lincoln as the seventeenth president, told Charles Francis Adams of

Boston, "There's that Yulee; miserable little cuss! I remember him in the House—the contemptible little Jew—standing there and begging us to let Florida in as a state. Well, we let her in, and took care of her and fought her Indians, and now that despicable little beggar stands up in the Senate and talks about her rights." The future president also had choice words for Judah Benjamin: "There's another Jew—that miserable Benjamin."

Isachar Zacharie

In a private meeting in 1863 in Richmond, Judah P. Benjamin met with Isachar Zacharie, who was the closest Jewish friend to President Abraham Lincoln. Lincoln had personally issued Zacharie a pass to cross Confederate lines to make an unofficial visit to explore peace talks after the fall of Gettysburg and Vicksburg and had sent one of his closest confidantes on the mission. The two Jews closest to their respective presidents met for the discussion, and subsequently with other members of the Confederate Cabinet as well.

It was an improbable choice of emissary on Lincoln's part. Zacharie was an English immigrant and a chiropodist or foot doctor who had periodically visited the president to remove bunions and treat other presidential foot ailments. But Zacharie was also a man of great intelligence and enormous charm, who used language with flair and knew America well since he had family in Savannah and had traveled widely in his profession. As the president was being treated, Zacharie sensed Lincoln's loneliness and need for companionship and began to converse with Lincoln about all manner of subjects including affairs of state and the condition of the Jewish community. Zacharie also must have had much Washington gossip to report because his medical specialty had enabled him to treat the most influential feet in the capital—other members of the cabinet such as Secretary of State Seward and Secretary of War Stanton, and Union generals McClellan, Banks, and Burnside, as well as members of Congress such as Henry Clay and William Cullen Bryant. Zacharie clearly intrigued the president. In 1864, the *New York World* reported that Zacharie "enjoyed Mr. Lincoln's confidence, perhaps more than any other private individual...(and was) perhaps the most favored family visitor to the White House."

He did not pass through Washington unnoticed. The *New York Herald* described him as "a man distinguished by a splendid Roman nose, fashionable whiskers, an eloquent tongue... great skill in his profession, an ingratiating address...and a plentiful supply of social moral courage." On the other hand, the *World* disparaged Zacharie as a "toe-nail trimmer" and reported, "the President has often left his business-apartment to spend an evening in the parlor with his favored bunionist."

A year before Zacharie's trip to Richmond, after the fall of New Orleans to the Union, realizing that a foot doctor could move with ease between social classes as well as among the influential in the Confederacy, Lincoln had sent Zacharie to New Orleans on a sensitive mission to interview local people, including Jewish friends, to assess public opinion in the aftermath of General Nathaniel P. Banks's assumption of command as a successor to the hated General

English-born Isachar Zacharie was President Lincoln's chiropodist, political confidante, and special emissary. At Lincoln's behest, Zacharie crossed over to the Confederacy during the war and presented a secret peace proposal to Confederate officials in Richmond.

Portrait of Isachar Zacharie. Courtesy of the American Jewish Historical Society, New York, NY and Newton Centre, MA.

Benjamin "Beast" Butler. Zacharie treated the feet of General Banks and numerous other leading citizens of New Orleans to seek information and frequently wrote letters back to Lincoln describing what he discovered. (He also sent the President baskets of bananas, oranges, and pineapples, addressing him as "My Dear Friend.") The letters, which are preserved in the Library of Congress, tell an extraordinary tale of spying and observation, even observing Confederate troop movements to uncover future military plans. With $5,000 in Confederate currency issued by the military quartermaster, Zacharie employed and outfitted as peddlers Jewish businessmen who had lost their livelihoods, who could, thus disguised, move around the countryside as familiar figures on the rural landscape.

Zacharie also was able to befriend and help Jewish visitors from the North who had been unable to return home from New Orleans after the Union capture of the city as well as numerous concerned Southern Jewish families who had relatives there now living under Union rule. Among them had been the sister of Judah P. Benjamin, for whom Banks had arranged safe passage out of the city. One of Zacharie's missions to Richmond was to obtain the South's approval to allow General Banks to discuss possible peace negotiations, and Zacharie wrote back to General Banks, "Benjamin ...spoke of you *in the kindest manner* and said...he was under obligation to you for your kindness *toward his sister.*"

Zacharie claimed that he was the originator of the so-called peace plan that he brought to Richmond, but the politically ambitious General Banks also claimed authorship and wanted to represent the Union in any subsequent peace talks. (Banks was one of Lincoln's notorious "political generals" with no military training who was given military command because he had served before the war as Governor of Massachusetts, a two-term congressman from the state, and Speaker of the U.S. House of Representatives.) The plan became known and ultimately was ridiculed by the Northern press as the product of an overactive imagination. The idea, discussed over two days in Richmond, and later reported in the *New York Herald*, was that Jefferson Davis, with Union support and supplies, would assemble 150,000 soldiers of the Confederate Army to attack Napoleon III's French troops in Mexico, conquer that country, and oust Emperor Maximilian. Davis would then proclaim himself president of the Mexican republic, after which the seceding states would be readmitted to the Union, thereby ending the Civil War.

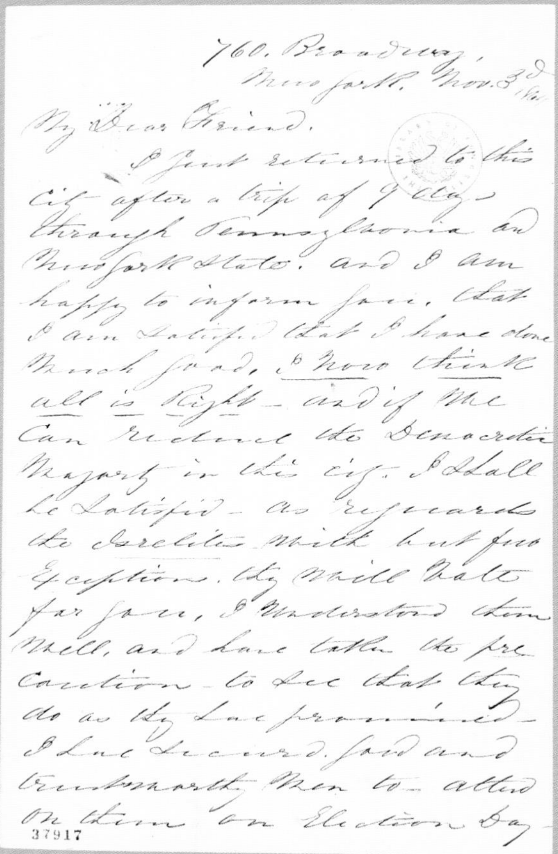

760. Broadway,
New York, Nov. 3d
1864

My Dear Friend.

I just returned to this city after a trip of 9 days through Pennsylvania and New York State. and I am happy to inform you, that I am satisfied that I have done much good, I now think all is Right — and if We Can reduce the Democratic Majority in this city, I Shall be Satisfied — as regards the Isrelites with but few Exception, they will Vote for you, I Understand them Well, and have taken the precaution — to See that they do as they have promised — I have Secured good and trustworth Men to attend on them on Election Day —

37917

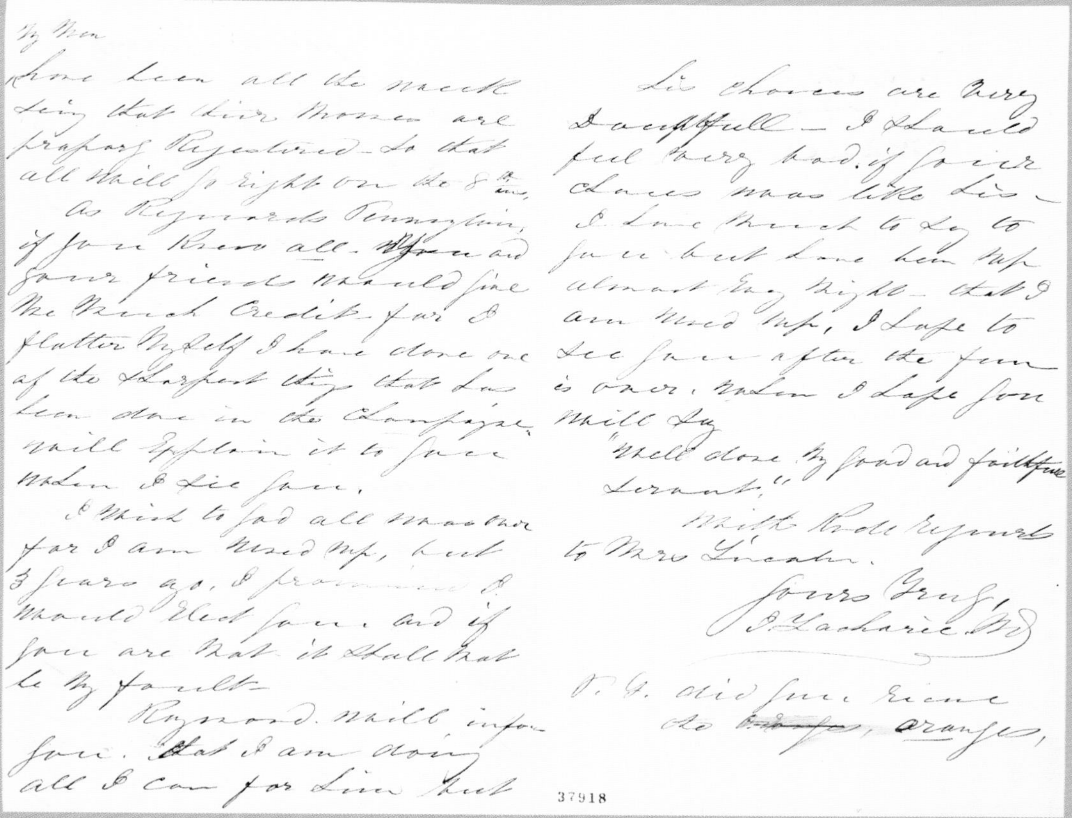

My Men have been all the Week Seing that their Women are properly Registered—So that all Will go right on the 8th ins.

As Regards Pennsylvia, if you Knew all. You and your friend Would give Me Much Credit. for I flatter Myself I have done one of the Sharpest thing that has been done in the Champaign will Explain it to you When I See you.

I Wish to god all was Over for I am Used Up, but 3 years ago. I promised I Would Elect you. and if you are Not it Shall not be My fault.

Raymond. will inform you. that I am doing all I can for him but

Sir chances are very doubtfull — I Should feel very bad, if your chances was like his — I have much to Say to you but have been Up almost Every Night — that I am Used Up, I hope to See you after the fun is over. When I hope you Will Say "Well done thy good and faithful Servant,"

With Kind Regards to Mrs Lincoln.

Yours Truly,
B Zacharie MD

P.S. did you receive the oranges,

37918

Isachar Zacharie involved himself in helping Abraham Lincoln secure the Jewish vote. In a letter to Lincoln on November 3, 1864, Zacharie wrote:
"*I just returned to this city after a trip of 9 days through Pennsylvania and New York state, and I am happy to inform you, that I am satisfied that I have done much good, I now think all is Right . . . . As regards the Isrelites—with but few Exceptions, they will vote for you, I understand them well, and have taken the precaution—to see that they do as they have promised—I have secured good and trustworthy men to—attend on them on Election Day—My Men have been all the week seeing that their masses are properly Registered—so that all will go right on the 8th ins.*"

Isachar Zacharie to Abraham Lincoln, New York, November 3, 1864. Papers of Abraham Lincoln, Manuscript Division.

It was a grand scheme that had a certain breathless naiveté to it. Though Zacharie wrote that he discussed the matter for two hours with President Lincoln behind closed doors, ultimately it was also opposed by Stanton and other hard liners in the Cabinet.

In 1864, after campaigning for Lincoln's reelection among Jews across the North, and hinting in almost every letter to Lincoln of his merit and hope of future recognition, Zacharie was honored by Jewish leaders at a testimonial evening in New York. He responded to the praise in remarks stating that "in this republican and enlightened country, where we know not how soon it may fall to the lot of any man to be elevated to a high position in the government, why may it not fall to the lot of an Israelite as well as any other?" Bertram W. Korn asked in *American Jewry and the Civil War:* "Did he conceive of himself as another Jewish premier, like Judah P. Benjamin, wielding the power of statecraft for an affectionate President? It is not altogether unlikely."

In an interesting footnote to the story, Henry Wentworth Monk, described by Korn as a "strange...Canadian born Judeophile" and "early Zionist...visionary" once went to Washington to discuss still another peace plan with Lincoln and mentioned "his pet project" of the Jewish return to their ancient biblical homeland in Palestine. It was reported that Lincoln agreed that it "was worthy of consideration" and that "I myself have regard for the Jews. My chiropodist is a Jew and he has so many times 'put me on my feet' that I would have no objection to giving his countrymen 'a leg up.' "

Korn sums up Zacharie's role in history as a man Lincoln listened to, trusted enough to send on missions, read reports from, and accepted on merit as a Jewish foreigner who had no "mass following or well-placed backers" and was "unknown and unimportant." Korn concludes that "whatever his role—sycophant, court jester, politician, spy or sincere friend—his relationship with Lincoln was one of the strange corners of the personal and public life of the Civil War President."

As the war dragged on and the structure of the South began to unravel, the romantic dreams of easy victory turned to blood, death, starvation, and destruction; and the nation, at its most desperate moment, erupted with the most virulent explosion of anti-Semitism that America had yet experienced. The press and officials in the North and the South, including Union officers, attacked the Jews. In the North the Jews were the secessionists, the "rebel spies," the "speculators," the "counterfeiters driving Anglo-Saxon firms out of business," the "cause of the inflation," the dark and shadowy presence behind all the troubles. An Associated Press writer in New Orleans wrote an article stating that "the Jews of New Orleans and all the South ought to be exterminated. They run the blockade and are always to be found at the bottom of every new villainy."

Of course, the anti-Semitic charges against Jews ignored the nature of the crisis in the Southern economy after the outbreak of hostilities. As an agricultural economy, the South imported most of what was needed from the North and from Europe. Once the Northern blockade became the "anaconda" that was designed to strangle the South, all imports were cut off. With instantaneous shortages of every kind of goods imaginable and rapid inflation, blockade runners and smugglers were able to earn fantastic fortunes for their cargoes; and everyone who bought and sold commodities benefited from the scarcity–farmers, merchants, tradesmen, shop owners, farm supply storekeepers–whether they were Jews or Gentiles, native born or foreigners, patriots or traitors. The South needed scapegoats, and who better than the Jews, who had served such a role for centuries and whose dishonesty and vilification were part of the church preaching on Sundays and holidays.

General Order No.11
"the most sweeping anti-Jewish regulation in all American history"

The South lay in ruins, decimated by fire and plunder, its ports isolated for years by blockade, its factories turned to charred rubble by a deliberate scorched-earth policy, its money worthless, and its economy in turmoil. Without foodstuffs or farmers to raise food in the midst of battle, the scarcity sent prices soaring beyond imagination to make a broken people more miserable. In Memphis, on the Mississippi River, at the line of battle, thousands of bales of cotton sat in the warehouses, half hostage and half gold, the target for speculators and adventurers and Yankee soldiers, who saw unprotected cotton as a way to steal whatever the South had left of any worth. But cotton could be turned into a huge profit by selling it in the North to the reopening textile factories so long deprived of Southern cotton. President Lincoln told a friend, "The army itself is diverted from fighting the rebels to speculating in cotton." Charles A. Dana wrote to the Secretary of War, "Every colonel, captain, or quartermaster is in secret partnership with some operator in cotton; every soldier dreams of adding a bale of cotton to his monthly pay."

Generals Ulysses S. Grant and William Sherman considered all the speculators as leeches on the system, bringing in gold for cotton that would be convertible into arms. Sherman had earlier complained of "swarms of Jews and speculators" who were flocking into Memphis. For Sherman, the terms were synonymous.

On December 17, 1862, Grant issued what Bertram Korn called in his volume, *American Jewry and the Civil War*, "the most sweeping anti-Jewish regulation in all American history," General Order No. 11, providing that "the Jews, as a class violating every regulation of trade established by the Treasury Department and also department orders, are hereby expelled from the department [of Tennessee] within twenty-four hours from the receipt of this order."

Southern Jews who had lived in Tennessee for decades, even former Union soldiers, were forced to pack up their families hurriedly and leave. When one man and his wife questioned a soldier, they were told, "It's because you are Jews and neither a benefit to the Union nor the Confederacy." But the political struggle to rescind the order would not be argued on behalf of the Jews in the South; instead it would be based on the more blatant injustices to Jewish loyalists to the Union cause.

Cesar Kaskel of Paducah, Kentucky, had seen thirty men, some with Union military service, and their families deported, without trial or hearing, and he hastened to Washington to see President Lincoln. He stopped in Cincinnati to ask the assistance of Rabbi Isaac Wise and

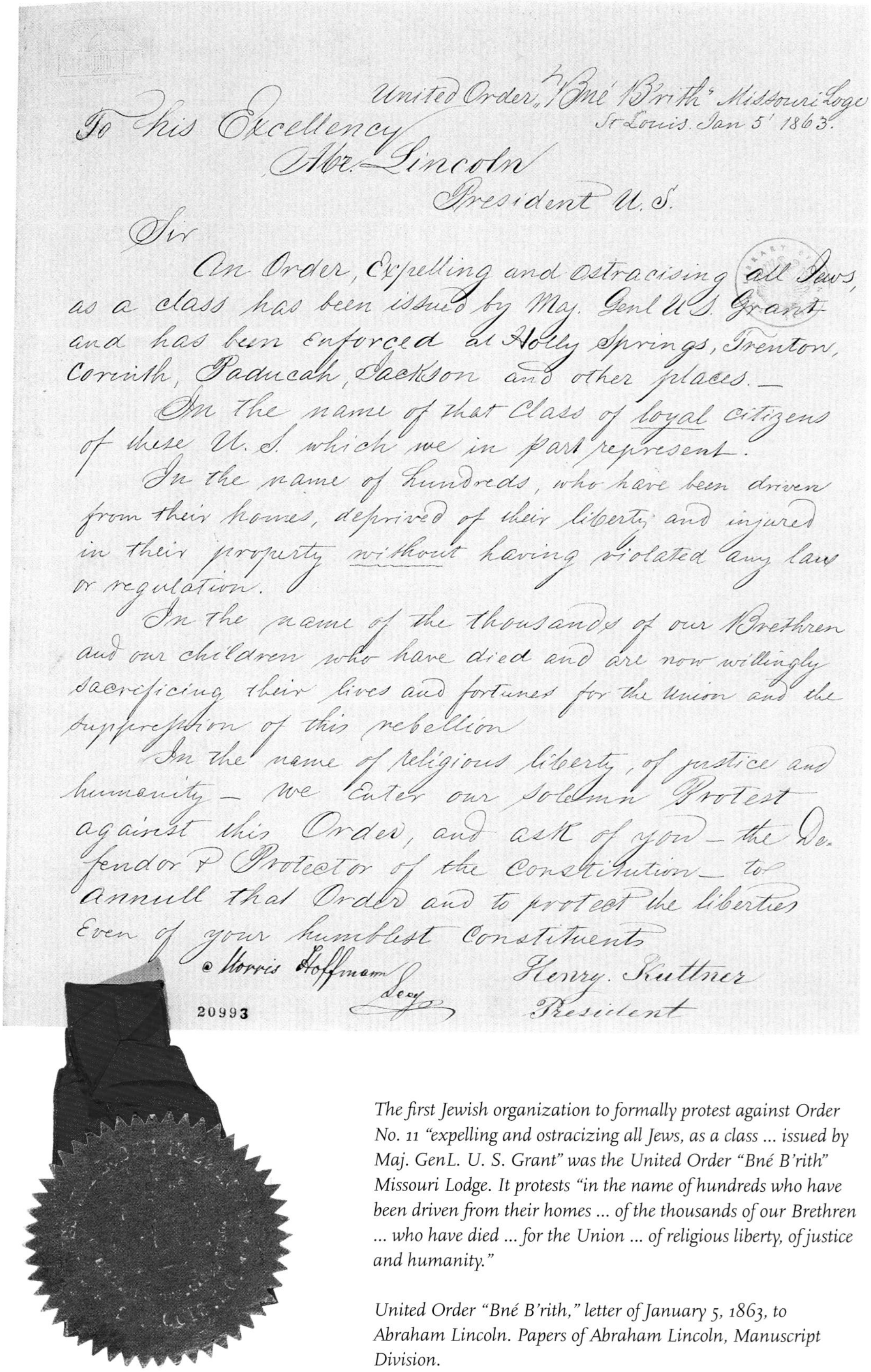

United Order, "Bné Brith" Missouri Loge
St Louis. Jan 5ᵗ 1863.

To His Excellency
    Abr. Lincoln
        President U. S.

Sir

An Order, Expelling and ostracising all Jews, as a class has been issued by Maj. Genl U S Grant and has been enforced at Holly Springs, Trenton, Corinth, Paducah, Jackson and other places.—

In the name of that Class of loyal citizens of these U. S. which we in part represent.

In the name of hundreds, who have been driven from their homes, deprived of their liberty, and injured in their property without having violated any law or regulation.

In the name of the thousands of our Brethren and our children who have died and are now willingly sacrificing their lives and fortunes for the Union and the Suppression of this rebellion

In the name of religious liberty, of justice and humanity — we Enter our Solemn Protest against this Order, and ask of you — the Defendor & Protector of the Constitution — to annull that Order and to protect the liberties Even of your humblest Constituents

Morris Hoffmann
    Secy

Henry. Kuttner
    President

20993

The first Jewish organization to formally protest against Order No. 11 "expelling and ostracizing all Jews, as a class ... issued by Maj. GenL. U. S. Grant" was the United Order "Bné B'rith" Missouri Lodge. It protests "in the name of hundreds who have been driven from their homes ... of the thousands of our Brethren ... who have died ... for the Union ... of religious liberty, of justice and humanity."

United Order "Bné B'rith," letter of January 5, 1863, to Abraham Lincoln. Papers of Abraham Lincoln, Manuscript Division.

together they began to stimulate petitions, letters of protest from Jewish leaders to Washington, and resolutions demanding revocation of the order. Congressman Gurley of Ohio, a friend of Rabbi Wise, arranged an appointment with the president, and Kaskel brought affidavits from leading Republican Party members and military authorities. Korn's book reported the following quiet conversation with the president—almost charming in view of the intensity of his visitor.

Lincoln: "And so the Children of Israel were driven from the happy land of Canaan?"

Kaskel: "Yes, and that is why we have come unto Father Abraham's bosom, asking protection."

Lincoln: "And this protection they shall have at once."

Lincoln walked over to a big table and wrote a note to the General-in-Chief of the Army, Henry W. Halleck, directing him to telegraph instructions canceling the order. He wished Kaskel well and told him that he was free to return home. When a delegation of rabbis and other Jewish leaders called on the president to thank him, Lincoln told them that he could not understand what compelled the general to issue it. "To condemn a class is, to say the least, to wrong the good with the bad. I do not like to hear a class or nationality condemned on account of a few sinners." In Allan Nevins's words, "All honor to Lincoln!"

The *New York Times* referred to the order as "one of the deepest sensations of the war" and criticized Grant, saying, "men cannot be condemned and punished as a class without gross violence to our free institutions." Most newspapers gave the popular general every shadow of a doubt; some, like the *Washington Chronicle,* called the Jews "the scavengers. . .of commerce," while others criticized the general as "thoughtless," while praising his military record. The order followed Grant into politics and became one of the major issues in his election as president in 1868. He never apologized or explained, though he wrote a congressman during the campaign, "I have no prejudice against sect or race, but want each individual to be judged by his own merit. Order No. 11 does not sustain this statement, I admit, but I do not sustain the order. It would never have been issued if it had not been telegraphed the moment it was penned and without reflection."

The *Cincinnati Enquirer* suggested that Grant and Sherman had been influenced by powerful cotton buyers and their officer cohorts in the army to make way for larger profits. The price of cotton was lowered from forty cents a pound to twenty-five cents a pound the day after the order was issued; thus the speculators who remained profited from the order. Isaac Wise charged in his journal a few months after the order, "The Jews bought cotton from planters at forty cents a pound; the military authorities with their business partners, agents, clerks, porters, etc., intended to buy that staple at twenty-five cents a pound. . . they could sell it in Eastern cities just as high as the next man—and the Jews must leave, because they interfere with a branch of military business."

Lincoln's cancellation of the order diminished greatly the rising fear of Jews in the South that the Union victory would thrust them again into the kind of anti-Semitism they had fled from in Europe. The Northern Jewish community had stood beside the Jews in the South, demonstrating a sense of community that transcended sectional bitterness. Northern Jews had

Board of Delegates of American Israelites

At a Special Meeting of the Executive Committee of the Board of Delegates of American Israelites held at the City of New York Thursday evening January 8th 1863, Henry I. Hart Esq. President in the Chair.

The President laid before the Committee a copy of General order No. 11 issued by General U. S. Grant commanding Department of the Tennessee December 17, 1862, and also communications received by him from Washington with reference to the revocation of the same.

Whereupon the following Preamble and Resolutions were proposed, seconded and unanimously adopted.

Whereas the attention of this Committee has been called by the Chairman to the following general order No. 11.

" Headquarters thirteenth Army Corps Department of the Tennessee Oxford Miss. Dec 17
" 1862
" The Jews, as a class violating every
" regulation of trade established by the Treasury
" Department, also department orders, are hereby
" expelled from the department within twenty
" four hours from the receipt of this order by
" post commanders. They will see that all
" this class of people are furnished with passes

" and required to leave, and any one returning
" after such notification will be arrested and
" held in confinement until an opportunity
" occurs of sending them out as prisoners
" unless furnished with permits from these
" headquarters. No passes will be given these
" people to visit headquarters for the purpose
" of making personal application for trade
" permits. By order of
" Major General Grant
" John A. Rawlins A A G"

Be it therefore Resolved, that we have read with surprise and indignation intelligence that in this present Century and in this land of freedom and equality an Officer of the United States should have promulgated an order worthy of heathen Europe in the dark ages of the World's history. ―

Resolved that in behalf of the Israelites of the United States, we enter our firm and determined protest against this illegal unjust and tyrannical mandate depriving American Citizens of the Jewish faith of their precious rights, driving them, because of their religious profession, from their business and homes by the military authority and in pursuance of an inequitable proscription.

Resolved that the Israelites of the United States expect no more and will be

---

content with no less than equal privileges with their fellow Citizens, in the enjoyment of "life, liberty and the pursuit of happiness" as guaranteed by the Constitution of this Republic.

Resolved that it is peculiarly painful to the Israelites of the United States, who have freely tendered their blood and treasure in defence of the Union they love to observe this uncalled for and inequitable discrimination against them. Claiming to be second to no class of Citizens in support of the Constitutional government, they regard with sadness and indignation this contumely upon the Jewish name this insult to them as a community, in the obvious ground that individuals if proved to be Jews have violated "regulations of trade established by the Treasury Department and department orders." ―

Resolved that it is in the highest degree obnoxious to them, as it must be to all fair minded American Citizens, for the general body to be made accountable for acts of particular persons supposed to belong to their denomination, but as has been frequently demonstrated, in many cases really professing other creeds. That if an individual be guilty of an infraction of discipline or offence against military law or treasury regulations punishment should be visited upon him alone, and the religious community to which he is presumed to be attached should not be subjected to insult, obloquy or disregard of

---

its constitutional rights as a penalty for individual offences. ―

Resolved that the thanks of this Committee and of the Israelites of the United States be and they are hereby tendered to Major General H. W. Halleck General in Chief U.S.A. for the promptitude with which he counted General Grant's unjust and inequitable order, so soon as it was brought to his attention.

Resolved that a copy of these resolutions duly attested be transmitted to the President of the United States, the Secretary of War, Major General Halleck and Major General Grant and that the same be communicated to the Press for publication.

From the Minutes

Myer S. Isaacs
Secretary

publicly petitioned their government to revoke an order by its most popular general in the midst of a war, and the head of the nation had agreed. For Northern and Southern Jews who had escaped from countries where such unfairness would have been shrugged off, the decision by Lincoln made them know that they had found a home in the new land, and that its paper promises as the protector of minorities were real and concrete. The war itself had given Jews on both sides the opportunity to stand and fight with their neighbors, and when it was over, for most of them, they were much more "American" than when it began. The Civil War had been a totally American battle without foreign troops or clash of foreign ideology—only brothers could fight. Bitter as that experience was for the nation, it enabled Jews in the North and the South to taste the fire of American dissension and be welcomed by other Americans into the bosom of the nation.

The Aftermath of the War

After years of struggle and turmoil, the devastated and wrecked Southern economy began to show signs of life. A recovering South suggested opportunity to the new Jews streaming from Russia and Poland to the "Promised Land"—2.8 million from 1881 to 1924—crowding into the pushcart pandemonium of the Lower East Side of New York City, packing the tenement houses, and scrambling for wages in the sweatshops of the streets.

Only fifteen years after the end of the Great War almost four million black slaves were newly freed, Atlanta was just beginning to rebuild from the devastation of Sherman's march, and the South was still smoldering in the lawlessness and racial violence of Reconstruction. Only the most foolhardy or the most desperate immigrants would take the chance. But why not try? First, stock a peddler's pack at the Baltimore Bargain House—little risk in that—then look for a place to settle and send for the family. Surely then his relatives would come.

Another generation of Jews was poised to play out the drama again.

Opposite: The outrage of American Jewry against General U.S. Grant's Order No. 11, which expels the "Jews as a class" from territories under the Thirteenth Army Corps, is conveyed to President Lincoln by this set of calligraphically inscribed resolutions, adopted January 8, 1863.

Board of Delegates of American Israelites, "Resolutions to Abraham Lincoln," January 8, 1863. Papers of Abraham Lincoln, Manuscript Division.

A Century of Migration, 1820-1924

Hasia Diner

The century spanning the years 1820 through 1924 witnessed a massive Jewish population movement that surged westward. It accompanied great upheavals of European Jewish life ushered in with emancipation, industrialization, population growth, and urbanization. The Jewish migration went along with a wrenching internal Jewish debate accompanying the *haskalah*—the Jewish enlightenment—and the breakdown of the coherent, self-governing Jewish communities. Jews embarked on their physical journeys as their political and legal status underwent dramatic changes, and Jews not only went out of Europe but they did so as they also moved out of their ghettos, both literally and figuratively.

Of the massive Jewish population movements of that century, none loomed as large as that which crossed the Atlantic and brought Jews in the millions to America. The westward emigration of Jews from Europe had a dramatic impact on Jewish life. About one-quarter of Europe's Jewish population went to the Americas, most of them opting for the United States. About one-third of all East European Jews left in the latter decades of the nineteenth century and the early decades of the twentieth. About 80 percent of them chose the United States. By 1924, when free and open immigration to the United States ended, it housed one of the largest and most significant Jewish communities in the world.

Lady Liberty, her cap labeled "America" in Yiddish, opens America's gates to allow Jewish immigrants to enter. The inscription on the left reads: "Open the gates and let a righteous nation enter" (Isaiah 25:2), while the one on the right continues in the same vein: "Open the gates of righteousness for me" (Psalms 118:19).

Lady Liberty Opens America's Gate, 1909. From the HUC Skirball Cultural Center, Los Angeles, California. Photography by Lelo Carter.

The European context of the immigration changed dramatically in this century. At the beginning of the era Jews came to America from small, relatively isolated villages of, for example, Bavaria or Bohemia. They came with little exposure to warring political ideologies or to any profound debates over the nature of Jewish identity. Young people from small towns in the main, most of the immigrants of the 1820s through the 1860s, came from poor and traditional Jewish communities.

By the time the Congress of the United States brought the migration to an end, Jews came as urbanites, dwellers of cities in the Soviet Union and Poland, places that had not existed earlier. Those immigrants who made their way to the United States after the 1890s had witnessed and sometimes participated in new social and political movements. Socialists, members of various Jewish worker groups, Zionists, those who stressed secular education, all struggled against each other and against the established religious authority structure to win over the Jewish masses of Eastern Europe.

Published by the Hebrew Immigrant Aid Society and intended for new immigrants, this map of the United States cited the states, their capitals, important mountain ranges, and major rivers and lakes in Yiddish and English.

Yiddish map of America, in The Jewish Immigrant, *vol. 2, no. 1 (New York, January, 1909). Hebraic Section.*

The massive westward movement of Jews to the United States did not even begin until the fledgling American republic emerged as an attractive destination for large-scale European immigration. Until the 1820s America could not have been the goal of a substantial number of voluntary immigrants from anywhere because the avenues of transportation both within the continent and across the Atlantic proved highly unreliable. Similarly, the American economy proved to be as unreliable as its transportation links to Europe. Only with the first stirrings of its industrial development in

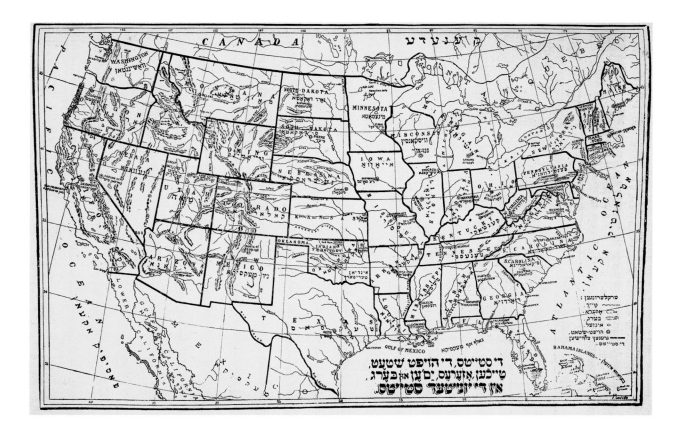

the cotton mills of New England in the 1820s—as well as the revolution in the young nation's transportation system, connecting the Atlantic Coast with the hinterlands through the development of canals—did the mass migration take place from Europe to America. If any event can be cited as pivotal to facilitating immigration and making America the Europeans' most coveted overseas destination it was the 1825 completion of the Erie canal, linking New York with the Middle West.

Likewise, wholesale emigration from Europe commenced only when the Napoleonic Wars ended in 1815. Europe then entered into a century of quasi-continental peace, with skyrocketing birth rates and profound industrial developments that upset local economies. New forms of transportation shook up long-standing relationships between peasants and markets. About thirty million Europeans made their way to America in the century of migration.

About three million Jews joined the European exodus. Like all other immigrants, Jews responded to both the pushes that compelled them to leave their homes and the pulls that attracted them to another. Most made strategic decisions about their economic prospects and those of their families. They sought out places where they could work. Over time they gravitated to those destinations where they had relatives and townspeople who had paved the way for them by sending money, leads on jobs, and information about America. Once there they began a process of adaptation. Yet they retained ties to hometowns, to parents and other relatives who would not join them in their new homes.

Popular ideas about the history of Jewish immigration assume that the first immigrants, those who arrived between 1820 and 1880, came from Germany while in the decades after 1880 they hailed from Eastern Europe. The former, it has been assumed, came as middle class Jews, steeped in German culture, and experienced little discomfort in their adaptation to America, where they quickly assimilated American standards of behavior. The latter immigrants have been seen as quite different, emerging in history and memory as more urban, more "ethnic," more "Jewish" and more resistant to change. The Germans, historians and others have said, came for essentially positive economic reasons, while the later Russian-Jewish immigrants fled pogroms—bloody and vicious attacks on Jews.

Rather than being absolutely wrong, these popular categorizations are just overly simplistic. The 250,000 Jews who came to America between 1820 and 1880 tended to come heavily from those areas that either had been incorporated into a unified Germany in 1871 or which—like Austria, Hungary, Bohemia, and Moravia—housed an urban elite deeply influenced by German culture. Similarly, the vast majority of the two-and-a-half million Jews who arrived in

This miniature daily prayer book was printed in Germany in 1842 "especially for travelers by sea to the nation of America." It is the first of three editions of this tiny prayer book published between 1840 and 1860—a period that saw Jews from the German lands immigrate to the U.S. in the tens of thousands (between 1840 and 1850 the Jewish population of this country tripled from 15,000 to 45,000). Political unrest and economic hardship were the primary reasons for this migration.

Minhah Ketanah (Minor Offering), Fuerth, 1842. Hebraic Section.

On this journal cover, published by the Hebrew Immigrant Aid Society, Lady Liberty, wearing a cap bearing the legend "America" in Yiddish, holds a key in one hand and opens a gate to waiting immigrants with the other. Two verses from the Hebrew Scriptures flank the open gate. On the right, the verse reads: "Open the gates of righteousness for me " (Psalms 118:19) and on the left, "Open the gates and let a righteous nation enter" (Isaiah 26:2).

The Jewish Immigrant, New York, January, 1909. Hebraic Section.

the United States after 1880 did leave lands east of the Elbe River, with those hailing from Czarist Russia making up the largest chunk of the migrating Jewish population.

The complications emerge, however, when we ask who migrated and why. For one, in the pre-1880 contingent many of the "German" Jews who left for America came from Polish provinces like Silesia and Posen, which had been annexed by Prussia and were later incorporated into Germany. On paper these Jews appear as German, and many described themselves in later years as German. But in their poverty, their high level of religious traditionalism, and the kinds of Jewish communities they left, "German" explains little about them. Even matters of language link the earlier and later Jewish immigrants to each other. The Bavarian Jews, at the time of their migration to the United States, spoke western Yiddish, and Bavarian authorities passed numerous pieces of legislation intended to transform them into German speakers. The Jews of Posen spoke Yiddish as well, a dialect no different from that spoken in other parts of Poland. Jews from Posen, at the time of their emigration, differed little from the Jews who by dint of circumstance lived in those areas of Poland that had been incorporated by Russia or by Austria-Hungary.

Indeed in the 1820–1880 migration, Jews already began to flow to America from Lithuania, Western Russia, and Galicia. These emigrants resembled in most ways those Jews of Eastern Europe who would begin their large-scale exodus to America in later years. In terms of their Yiddish language, their dense settlement patterns in large Jewish enclaves, their economic profile as small-scale artisans, and their adherence to traditional religious practice little differentiated those who came early and those who came in subsequent decades from other parts of Eastern Europe. Local circumstances, including epidemics, famines, and wars, as well as the general migratory trends in their towns and regions, sent them westward to America somewhat before the great exodus of the latter part of the nineteenth century.

By 1880 when the massive flood out of Eastern Europe began to crest, one-sixth of America's Jews had been born someplace east of Germany. Well before 1880 many synagogues in America worshipped according to *minhag Polin*, the Polish rite. Enough Russian Jews lived in New York City by the early 1850s that they founded a congregation of their own in 1852, Beth Hamedrash Hagadol, and in that same decade contingents of Jews from the Lithuanian provinces of Kovno and Suwalk settled in Buffalo, Chicago, Philadelphia, San Francisco, and other American cities. Los Angeles Jews in the late 1850s—the pioneer Jews who went to southern California—all listed their birthplace as "Russian Poland." A Jewish newspaper in Odessa, *Hamelitz*, reported in 1869 on the large number of Polish-Jewish families going to America. It noted at that seemingly early date, "There is virtually no family in Poland which has no relatives in America." [1] The first Rumanian Jews came to America in the late 1860s and early 1870s.

Many of these East European Jews made the journey to America in steps, spending some time in German states and the British Isles. The latter immigrants came to the United States in the 1860s and 1870s with a smattering of the English language acquired by peddling in Scotland, Wales, or England, but in all important ways they still resembled the later Jewish immigrants from Lithuania, Poland, and Russia.

THE PEDDLER'S WAGON.—DRAWN BY C. G. BUSH.—[SEE PAGE 394.]

Many early nineteenth-century Jewish immigrants from the German lands took up peddling to earn a living. Here, a country family examines the wares of an itinerant peddler, his wagon laden with household goods for sale.

Charles Green Bush, "The Peddler's Wagon," in Harper's Weekly, June 20, 1868. Prints and Photographs Division.

The rigid division of American-Jewish immigrants into "German" and "East European" also erases from history the 30,000 Jews from the Balkans, Turkey, and Greece who came to America during the first quarter of the twentieth century. The largest group among this Sephardic contingent spoke Ladino, or Judeo-Spanish. Along with arrivals from elsewhere in the Levant, they settled in New York, occupying a distinctive space on the Lower East Side along Allen Street. Contingents of Levantine Jews headed for San Francisco, Seattle, Los Angeles, and Portland. Like their coreligionists from Europe's heartland, they formed themselves into ethnic synagogues, created charitable societies, and sought ways to educate their children. In 1910 Moise Gadol, a Bulgarian-born Jew launched *La America*, a Ladino weekly publication which survived until 1925. These Jews united in their practice of the Sephardic rite, but manifested deep divisions among themselves based on place of origin and the constant political turmoil in their home communities. Their arrival in the United States, like that of Lithuanian and Polish Jews in the period before 1880, demonstrates why the conventional bipolar categories of a German and then an East-European period do not conform to historical reality.

But most Jews who came to America in the decades flanking the Civil War did indeed come from those states which in 1871 would make up a unified Germany. The first to make the migratory journey left small towns in Bavaria, Baden, Westphalia, and the Rhineland. From the

1820s through the 1840s tens of thousands of young Jewish men in particular left these places for America. After the 1840s as this migration continued, it came to include recruits from Posen, Silesia, Bohemia, Moravia, Hungary, and other communities to the East, as well as Alsace in France. Both the earlier and the later immigrants appear to have been the least Germanized of their cohort, the poorest, the most traditional, and the least able to take advantage of the fruits of emancipation being offered to the Jews by the states where they lived. Given state policies, the devastating impact of industrialization on the Jewish economy, and the high Jewish birth rate, they could not stay home, where they would have no chance to work or to marry.

The sons and daughters of Jewish peddlers, horse traders, and semiskilled artisans and some women, who had labored as domestic servants, turned to America, seeing no alternative at home. They migrated along well-articulated family chains and they developed a distinctive migration pattern. Typically one son left for America, serving as the family pioneer. He worked there, almost invariably in the occupation of his forebears, peddling and petty business. After saving money he sent passage for one or more of his brothers to join him in America, share in his enterprise, and lay away enough money to bring over more siblings, all the while sending money back home to help aging parents and siblings not participating in the American migration.

Over time the brothers now reunited in the United States would have squirreled away enough money to be able to fulfill the ultimate goal of the migration. One of them returned home, where he could see his parents for the last time, and he could also find a young woman who, like him, had no real marriage prospects. The two would wed. She might have sisters, cousins, and other female friends. The newlyweds often convinced these unmarried women to join them on the return journey to America. They would all travel to America, where a cohort of Jewish bachelors awaited them.

These Jewish men and the women whom they married became the proprietors of countless dry goods stores and other kinds of retail establishments in small towns, moderate sized cities, and large urban centers. Retail functioned as their economic métier and by the latter part of the nineteenth century no region or state lacked one of their stores. These kinds of stores which sold the basic needs of life to American customers made Jews, whatever the size of the town, highly visible. Their stores, which usually clustered in the main business districts, boldly displayed on awning and signs Jewish—and as such foreign sounding—names, such as "Levy," "Cohen," "Friedman," or "Zeckendorfer," and the like, drawing public attention to the merchant's ethnicity and religion.

These shops tended to remain small, certainly in the immigrant generation. In many cases men continued to peddle during the week while women and children ran the stores. But an impressive number of these immigrants experienced in their lifetimes a rapid rise from being humble peddlers, to solid shopkeepers, to "merchant princes." Some of the sons of this migration came to play prominent roles in the world of American merchandizing, having started with little capital but tremendous determination. Edward Filene, who came from Poznan started his American business life as a peddler, tailor, and glazier. Lazarus Straus peddled first and then

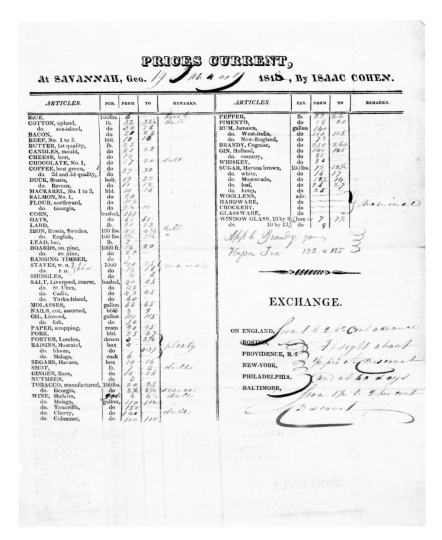

PRICES CURRENT,

at SAVANNAH, Geo. _____ 1818, By ISAAC COHEN.

The goods enumerated on Isaac Cohen's January 19, 1818 "Prices Current" list reflect a diverse and well-stocked inventory, featuring foodstuffs, spices, cotton, tobacco (including Havana "Segars") building supplies, wines and liquors, and, at a "nominal" cost: "woollens, hardware, crockery, and glassware."

Isaac Cohen, "Prices Current," Savannah, Georgia, 1818. Courtesy of the Jacob Rader Marcus Center of the American Jewish Archives.

ran a small country store in Talbotton, Georgia. Jakob Kaufmann, son of a horse and cattle dealer in Bavaria also began in the United States as a peddler. His first actual store on the outskirts of Pittsburgh measured no more than 17 by 28 feet. Adam Gimbel abandoned a village in the Rheinland-Pfaltz region as an eighteen-year old with no money and took up a peddling route in the area around Vincennes, Indiana. Each one of these men ended up the owners of massive department stores which bore their names and testified to the close fit between their skills and the developing needs of the American marketplace.

Jewish immigrant men were not the only ones to seize the opportunities of the American marketplace. Jewish women in this immigrant era combined their migration to America with the chance of making a success for themselves. Sarah Nathan Goldwater's husband came to America first and she and her children joined him in California after a three-year hiatus. "Big Mike" Goldwater moved, usually unsuccessfully, from one business venture to another. Sarah, frustrated with her husband's failure not only declared herself in 1858 not responsible for her husband's debts, but she ventured out into her own enterprises. She ran her own, highly successful dressmaking shops, first in Los Angeles and then San Francisco. Likewise Mary Ann Moejian and her husband Isaac arrived in San Francisco from the Netherlands in the 1850s. Her husband labored as a picture frame maker and gilder while she hand sewed garments—children's wear and women's undergarments—that her husband sold from a pack on his back. By the time the couple changed their last name to Magnin, Mary Ann had built up a substantial clientele and the store they opened, I. Magnin, became a watchword for elegant wear for women and children.

An even smaller number from this immigrant generation made an even more substantial ascent and entered into the realm of America's financial elite. The Seligmans, Guggenheims, Lehmans, Goldmans, and Wertheims also arrived with modest means. They saved their money and spent little on themselves, set up networks of family distribution, and took advantage of being in the right place at the right time.

The story of Joseph Seligman, while atypical in that he ended up one of America's wealthiest individuals, still offers a window into the world of the Jewish immigrant of this era and the opportunities which could have been had. Born in 1819 in Bavaria, the oldest son of a weaver and itinerant woolen merchant, Joseph emigrated to the United States in 1837. Here he peddled in and around western Pennsylvania, selling to the miners and farmers. Within a brief period of time, like so many of the other Jewish immigrants of his era, he sent for his brothers who together pooled their resources and carved out a peddling territory for themselves. They indeed moved their operation to Missouri and Alabama, although they had acquired enough capital to also have a New York wholesale headquarters. At the same time they opened a store in Watertown, New York, where along with selling cloth, they also acquired a new friend, one Ulysses S. Grant. In 1849, when news of the discovery of gold in California electrified the world, the

Uncle Sam is the "Modern Moses," waving the wand of "liberty" and parting the ocean so that a long line of Israelites can escape the "oppression and intolerance" of the old country and find refuge in America. This cartoon aroused controversy and criticism because of the depictions of the Jewish immigrants with hook noses, beards, and kinky hair.

Frederick Burr Opper and Joseph Keppler, "The Modern Moses," in Puck, 1881. General Collections.

Under the Imperial Russian coat of arms, traditionally dressed Russian Jews, packs in hand, are lined up on Europe's shore gazing across the ocean. Waiting for them under an American eagle holding a banner with the legend "Shelter me in the shadow of your wings" (Psalms 17:8), are their Americanized relatives, whose outstretched arms simultaneously beckon and welcome them to their new home.

"A Happy New Year," New Year's Postcard, ca. 1900. Alfred and Elizabeth Bendiner Collection, Prints and Photographs Division.

Seligman brothers decided to capitalize on the excitement and the prospects for business. They relocated their operation to San Francisco and occupied the city's only brick building as their offices. The Seligmans managed to obtain a virtual monopoly on the clothing business of the city. By the time the Civil War broke out, much Seligman wealth was concentrated in the family's New York bank. During the Civil War Joseph Seligman had placed over 200 million dollars worth of United States Government bonds in European banks and as of 1864 J & W Seligman & Company had branches in London, Paris, Frankfort, New Orleans, and San Francisco. The fortunes of the Seligman family only increased in the post-Civil War period and by the late nineteenth century the firm played a key role in such diverse enterprises as steel making, railroad construction, and public utilities around the world.

Such a massive financial empire hardly typified the business experience of the Jewish immigrants of the middle of the nineteenth century. The vast majority came poor and ended up moderately comfortable. But the fact that the son of a relatively poor Bavarian Jew could end up as one of America's—and the world's—wealthiest and most powerful individuals demonstrated the confluence of Jewish experience and American opportunity. The details of the Seligmans' meteoric rise to extravagant success however contained certain elements that also appeared in the more common life histories of the immigrants of this era.

The details of this migration, the chain migration by which brothers pulled brothers, and sisters pulled sisters to America, led to a class- and age-specific transfer of Central European Jewish population to America. These immigrants affirmatively chose never to return to Germany, other than perhaps for a nostalgic trip to visit elderly relatives or to find a suitable Jewish bride. Although the Jews as a whole understood their political prospects to be improving throughout Central Europe, in Germany, Alsace-Lorraine, and Austria-Hungary, those who went to America had no interest in returning with their earnings to take part in the new realities. While some of them developed a fondness for certain elements of German culture, among them, its music, beer gardens, theater, literature and libraries, as well as athletic clubs and shooting societies, they did so on the American side of the Atlantic. The fact that hardly any of them returned to Europe demonstrated the immigrants' understanding that back home offered them little, while America offered much.

For these Jews migration to America after the 1820s represented a chance to fulfill such basic goals as marriage and raising a family. Even after the various states lifted the most discriminatory laws against Jews in the late 1840s the out migration from, for example, Bohemia continued. "It is conspicuous," observed a Jewish newspaper account in 1849, "that despite the emancipation, the desire for emigration, especially to North America, increases here from day to day. Hundreds of Bohemians emigrated even this year. The second-class cabins of the boat that is leaving Bremen on April 15 are completely taken by Jews from Prague. The captain is prepared to supply *kosher* food if desired....One can see that there is little faith in the future of Austria. From Hungary, too, a large number is emigrating to America." [2]

The Jewish immigration of the midnineteenth century took place in a specifically Jewish context, for Central European Jews experienced periodic outbursts of violence and hatred. In 1819, on the eve of the exodus,

First- and second-class passengers above, steerage passengers below, in Alfred Stieglitz's famed photograph taken in 1907.

Alfred Stieglitz, "The Steerage," New York, 1907. Alfred Stieglitz Collection, Prints and Photographs Division.

Central Europe experienced an explosion of mob attacks on Jews. It began in the city of Wurzberg, in the province of Baden. It quickly engulfed much of southern and western Germany, then spread northward. This upsurge of violence came to be known as the "Hep! Hep!" riots (a phrase of unknown origin shouted by the marauding mobs). Communities saw Jewish property destroyed and Jews attacked on the streets. It engulfed Jews in Frankfurt, Danzig, and Hamburg. Over the course of the next decades, as the migration hit its stride, sporadic outbursts of anti-Jewish violence left their mark on the Jews of Central Europe as some among them pondered the benefits and liabilities of staying put versus emigrating to the United States.

More importantly, Jews left for specifically Jewish reasons. The Jewish economic niche as peddlers and middlemen had been deeply eroded, and only some Jews could make it in the new economic order. Laws limiting Jewish marriage made life hopeless for the young. Jews also migrated in different ways and from different places within this vast region. The enormous exodus of Christians out of Central Europe, an emigration of approximately a million better-off peasants and small landowners from Bavaria, Wurttemberg, and Baden, took place in the years between 1820 and 1860. They tended to migrate as full families and among them a sizable number returned to their German homes. Jews who migrated from these places, migrated primarily as single men, first. They and the women who joined them in America did so for good. They also emigrated in a mass out of proportion to their numbers in the population. Jews, for example, made up about 1.5 percent of the population of Bavaria, but accounted for 5 percent of the emigrants to the United States. From Posen, whose Christians left later than its Jews, Jews predominated among those who decided to leave for America. Between 1824 and 1871, 46,640 Jews left, compared to 18,790 Christians. Jews also made up a disproportionate number of those who preferred to find new homes in America rather than remain in Alsace, Bohemia, Moravia, Western Russia, and such Lithuanian provinces as Suwalk and Kovno.

All in all, from 1820 through 1840 about 50,000 Jews left Europe for America, and from 1840 through 1880 that number quadrupled as 200,000 Jews made the move. The emigration encompassed much of the middle of the continent and covered an area from Alsace in the west through Western Russia in the east. Although the migration took place in a segmented fashion, women and men migrated in roughly equal numbers. Few children and older people joined the outward flow. Able-bodied, working-age Jewish women and men went, while those less able to contribute their labor stayed home. They settled in America's cities, New York in particular. They created Jewish enclaves in Philadelphia, Baltimore, and other older cities. They gravitated as well to newly formed urban hubs in the Middle West and West, with Jewish communities springing up in Pittsburgh, Cincinnati, St. Louis, Chicago, Portland, Oregon, and San Francisco. A good number of them spent some amount of time in small towns, operating retail establishments, usually opened after peddling in the hinterlands.

Starting in the 1870s, the Jewish emigration from Europe grew in number and included substantially larger contingents from the massive population centers of Eastern Europe. In the years after 1880, considered conventionally as the beginning date of the East-European Jewish emigration, the number of Jews coming to America grew wildly. Between 1881 and 1924 over 2.5 million moved to America, a tenfold increase over the exodus of the previous six decades. Looking at a shorter period of time, the numbers become even more dramatic. In the years between 1899 and 1910, 750,000 Jews left Russia, particularly Lithuania, amounting to one-seventh of that country's Jewish population.

In the decades after 1880 about one-third of East-European Jews changed residence. Most did so by moving within their home countries into cities like Odessa, Lodz, Bialystok, or Kishinev, where factory jobs began to absorb tens of thousands of Jewish laborers. In general they shifted from the overcrowded poor, northwest, particularly Lithuania, to the less dense and developing southeast, Ukraine in particular. Indeed most migratory Jews stayed in Eastern Europe. They may have listened to the stern advice of many rabbis who counseled against America, warning that in the United States, a godless place, Jews would lose their Jewishness.

Of those who went across national boundaries, between 80 to 90 percent chose America. The basic demographic facts of the migration demonstrate the inner workings of the Jewish strategies. Of those who went to America, able-bodied workers, young adults at the peak of their physical ability to labor, far outnumbered children or older people. This was a labor migration, and it drew in those who could work and earn a living.

It was notable that approximately one-quarter of the East European Jewish immigrants to the United States did not fall into this group, and a sizable number of children and older people, less able to contribute economically, also joined the immigration.

So too, gender patterns tell much about the immigrants. After the 1880s, Jewish women were just as likely as Jewish men to leave their home communities, either on their own or with friends or siblings. When fathers emigrated to the United States in order to earn money and then send for the rest of the family, they took their older children with them. They brought along daughters just as often as sons. Birth order and age rather than gender determined which family members from Jewish Eastern Europe spearheaded the family relocation.

In the great East-European Jewish migration, class mattered. The economically disadvantaged chose to migrate to America, while the better-off stayed put. And as in nearly all migrations, the very poorest also did not participate in the exodus. In the East-European, post-1880 emigration, young people with experience in certain occupations chose to emigrate more often than those with other work backgrounds. Skilled workers, those previously employed in manufacturing, made up 64 percent of the Jewish emigrants, but constituted only 40 percent of the Russian-Jewish population as a whole. Those who made a living in commerce in Russia found themselves underrepresented among the immigrants to America, and Jewish women who in

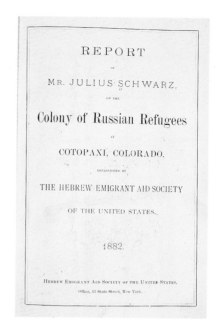

In his report to the board of the Hebrew Emigrant Aid Society, which sponsored the colonization activities of a small group of Russian Jewish settlers in Cotopaxi, Colorado, Julius Schwarz wrote: "It is with much satisfaction and justifiable pride that I pronounce the agricultural colony of the Rocky Mountains a full and complete success and the question whether Jews are fit to be farmers, solved and answered in the affirmative."

Julius Schwarz, Report ... on the Colony of Russian Refugees at Cotopaxi, Colorado ..., New York, [1882]. General Collections.

A view of the bustling street market scene on New York's Lower East Side at the turn of the twentieth century, bursting with activity and commerce.

"Mulberry Street, New York City," [ca. 1900]. Detroit Publishing Company Photograph Collection, Prints and Photographs Division.

Russia spent their young adulthood in domestic service far outnumbered the percentage in the Jewish population at home and swelled the ranks of those who left.

Finally, southern and southwestern Russia sent out proportionately fewer Russian-Jewish immigrants than did northern and northwestern Russia, including Lithuania, which contributed the most and the earliest immigrants. Additionally, the immigration included Jews from regions of Eastern Europe that were not part of the Russian Empire. Galician Jewry participated in substantial numbers in the flood to America. Rather than coming from the Czarist land, they had lived under the more benign rule of the Habsburg monarchy. Its Jews had actually experienced some forms of emancipation in 1867, as did those of Hungary. But migration to America proved attractive to these Jews because of the poverty they endured. Galician Jews were indeed among the poorest in Europe and by the 1880s some 60 percent of them ate and lived on Jewish communal charity. Making up approximately 10 percent of the province's population, Galicia's Jews lived under conditions "even worse than in Russia....Emigration alone offered them an escape from misery."[3]

The origins of this massive migration of two and a half million Jews lay in the confluence of a number of factors. First, the Jewish population had grown exponentially. Despite the continuous outward flow, the Jewish birth rate soared, causing unprecedented competition for a dwindling number of jobs in the traditional Jewish trades, tailoring in particular. The stirrings of industrialization in Eastern Europe and the importation of goods by railroad undermined the Jewish economy precisely at the point in time when more Jewish laborers struggled to find a livelihood.

The number of industrial jobs opening up in the large cities in Russia and elsewhere in Eastern Europe could not sustain the increasing number of Jews who clamored for them. Young people had little prospect of establishing families amidst the growing impoverishment. Those with tailoring skills saw that they could successfully transfer their work experience to the United States, a place that had in the middle of the nineteenth century assumed premier place as the world's manufacturer of ready-made garments. New York in particular functioned as the heartland of that industry.

To emphasize the selective nature of the East-European Jewish emigration and the economic forces which fuelled it does not diminish the specific Jewish context from which it took its shape. Jews emigrated from Eastern Europe in much greater number and intensity than did non-Jews. Jews constituted about 5 percent of the population of the vast Russian Empire, but made up nearly half of its emigrants. The numbers and proportions for Galicia and Rumania appear even more dramatic when set against the general figures. Of all the emigrants from Galicia, Jews who made up about 10 percent of the population and accounted for 60 percent of the emigrants; and from Rumania, they were 90 percent of those who left.

Russia had long been an inhospitable place for the Jews. Its Jewish "problem" had long roots. At the end of the eighteenth century Catherine the Great realized that her acquisition of vast chunks of Poland had brought to Russia vast reservoirs of Jews. She and her successors crafted various policies to deal with them, most importantly creating a zone of Jewish residence, the Pale of Settlement where they were to live and be useful to the Empire. Until 1917 and the end of the Czarist regime, Jews had no inherent rights, including that of residence. What benefits they might enjoy at one moment could easily be rescinded at another. The emigration that had commenced in the 1870s needed only a predictable means of transportation, a dramatic economic downturn, and a destination where Jews could believe that they had the chance of earning a living and living their lives as they chose.

The Jewish context of the immigration raises the issue of the pogroms, the bloody riots against the Jews that surfaced periodically beginning in 1881, the first one flaring up in Elizabetgrad in the Kherson province. That month three score more Russian cities experienced pogroms. By the end of the year, 300 more had been visited upon Jews in communities throughout southern and southwestern Russia. Pogroms continued to spurt up sporadically in this region for the next few years, coming to an end in 1884. In 1903 a second cycle of violence broke out and lasted until 1906, while in the years during and after World War I and coinciding with the Russian Revolution and the subsequent Civil War, from 1917 through 1921, a third, more devastating wave of attacks descended upon the Jews of Russia. The pogroms themselves took place in a particular economic setting in which issues of livelihood and religion blurred. After the first set of pogroms, the government promulgated the "Temporary" May laws of 1882, which prohibited Jewish settlement in large numbers of rural villages within the Pale of Settlement. The new laws removed Jews from the rural liquor trade and forbade carrying on business on Sunday. Even within the Pale, Jews could no longer buy land or build houses.

Ironically, this set in motion a dynamic that created more tension between Jews and non-Jews. As a result, nearly half a million Jews found themselves expelled from their homes. Most of them went to the cities where they joined the Jews already there. The new Jewish city dwellers had to compete even more fiercely with their coreligionists for the limited number of jobs available to Jews. But more crucially, upon their arrival in the cities they also had to compete directly with newly arrived, unskilled, poor Christian peasants who had also been spat up by the emerging forces of economic modernization.

The general condition of the Jews, their poverty, their deviance from the national, religious Christian norm became, after the 1880s, a matter of debate at the state level. Administrative authorities harassed Jews repeatedly, restricting their already limited entry into educational institutions and vigorously enforcing the residence of Jews in restricted cities. One government official expressed his wishes and probably those of the state when in 1891 he predicted that, "one-third of the Jews will convert, one-third will die, and one-third will flee the country."[4]

The pogroms haunted the Jews of Russia. They shaped the Jews' political consciousness, leading many of them to embrace Marxist socialism and others to subscribe to Zionism. The imagery of the pogroms suffused the Jewish literary impulse around the world. After the first batch in 1881, the American Emma Lazarus, best known for her poem, "The New Colossus," engraved on the base of the Statue of Liberty, penned *Songs of a Semite* (1882) in which she decried the pogroms, the fate of Russian Jewry, and held Christianity responsible for the tragedies visited upon the Jewish people. In "The Crowing of the Red Cock," she asked with passion: "Where is the Hebrew's Fatherland?" Lazarus continued her rhetorical questioning:

When the long roll of Christian guilt
 Against his sires and kin is known,
The flood of tears, the life-blood spilt,
The agony of ages shown,
What oceans can the stain remove,
From Christian law and Christian love? [5]

Protest meetings against each wave of violence took place as Jewish communities around the world organized mass meetings. In the United States eighty rallies in 1903, from Boston to San Francisco, drew attention to the pogroms and the suffering of Russia's Jews. The meetings raised money to help the victims and they generated sympathy for the Russian-Jewish immigrants landing in America at that moment. The meetings drew the attention of the American press. Editorials in newspapers across the country held up the pogroms as evidence of Russia's barbarism and backwardness. The meetings brought together upon stages and platforms Christian clergy and local elected officials with rabbis and leaders of American Jewish organizations. Declarations of sympathy with the Jews and disgust with the pogromists passed the U.S. Congress. In June 1906, for example, Congress passed a resolution which stated that "the people of the United States are horrified by the report of the massacre of the Hebrews in Russia." [6]

Indeed from the 1880s onward, each surge of pogroms in Russia played a key role in galvanizing American Jews politically. They provided a powerful rallying cry for Jewish organizations—the B'nai B'rith founded in 1843, the Board of Delegates of American Israelites of 1859, the American Jewish Committee organized in 1906, and the American Jewish Congress of 1918—and they all responded, each in its own way, to the outbreaks of anti-Jewish violence in Europe. Each one of these American Jewish communal organizations depicted the horrors of the pogroms in order to lobby for U.S. government involvement and to advocate for the Jews then emigrating to the United States.

Probably, though, the emigration would have happened in the way it did even if the pogroms had not taken place. The Jews of Eastern Europe had learned that America, its cities in particular, held out the prospects of work in either the garment industry or in small business. In those places they could establish families and communities unhampered by the fact of their Jewishness.

The communities that they founded in the United States stood out for the elaborateness of their institutions and for the blend of the traditional with the new, for their Jewish flavor and their embrace of American idioms. The East European Jewish women and men who settled in American cities—and they emphatically opted for urban life and for life in New York City in particular—settled in densely packed neighborhoods. In these neighborhoods, like New York's

Pictured here is a crowded garment sweatshop in the first decades of the twentieth century. The scene was photographed by Lewis Hines in connection with his work investigating the garment industry's use of child labor for the National Child Labor Committee.

Lewis Wickes Hine, "People in a Tenement Working for the Garment Industry," in Tenement Homework Album, ca. 1912. National Child Labor Committee Collection, Prints and Photographs Division.

Lower East Side, by far the largest and most significant, but also Chicago's Maxwell Street Market, Boston's West End, Baltimore's Lloyd Street section, as well as in nodes in Cleveland, Philadelphia, St. Louis, and elsewhere in America's largest cities, Jewish immigrants literally took over the streets.

In their work, their leisure, and their political behaviors, they created institutions which suited their needs as immigrants, Jews, and new Americans.

In the realm of work, nearly half went into small business and they opened retail shops of all kinds. They sold clothing and dry goods, watches, religious objects, shoes, dishes, paper, books, cigarettes. They purveyed food, raw and prepared, in stores and from pushcarts. Indeed the selling and buying of produce, fish, bread, meat, dairy products, and pickles abounded in Jewish immigrant enclaves. Neighborhood residents used these food markets as dense social spaces. Kosher butcher shops and bakeries in particular satisfied the Jews' religious needs and made possible the practice of Judaism in the home, the tradition's sacred center. Signs with Hebrew letters touting the ritual purity of the foods—as well as their freshness and tastiness— became a visible marker of the Jewish presence in these American urban spaces. An official 1899 survey of New York City's Eighth Assembly District which included much of the Jewish immigrant enclave enumerated 631 foodshops which:

American flags top two columns labeled "Zion" (in Hebrew) on this illustrated cover of the Register of the Home for the Aged, established in 1914 by "Cincinnati's Orthodox women." Between the columns, we see an elderly couple walking, he with a cane, she leaning on him for support. Above their heads is a banner with the legend: "Do not cast us out in old age, when our strength fails us, do not abandon us," a common variant of Psalm 71, verse 9.

Joseph Magrill (artist), Pinkas Moshav Zekaynim (Register of the Home for the Aged), Cincinnati, Ohio, 1914. Courtesy of the Jacob Rader Marcus Center of the American Jewish Archives.

catered to the needs of the inhabitants of this area. Most numerous were the 140 groceries which often sold fruits, vegetables, bread and rolls as well as the usual provisions. Second in number were the 131 butcher shops which proclaimed their wares in Hebrew characters. The other food vendors included: 36 bakeries, 9 bread stands, 14 butter and egg stores, 3 cigarette shops, 7 combination two-cent coffee shops, 10 delicatessens, 9 fish stores, 7 fruit stores, 21 fruit stands, 3 grocery stands, 7 herring stands, 2 meat markets, 16 milk stores, 2 matzo...stores, 10 sausage stores, 13 wine shops, 15 grape wine shops, and 10 confectioners.[7]

Additionally cafes, restaurants, "coffee and cake parlors," and cafeterias made the retailing of food the commercial spine of Jewish immigrant space in America. In 1905 the *Forverts*—the Jewish Daily Forward—a Yiddish newspaper which sold over 100,000 copies a day coined the word "oysessen," or, eating out, something that the immigrants had never done at home, but in America enjoyed and indulged in.

Other parts of their communal repertoire had long histories and connected the immigrant Jews to the world they had left. In their neighborhoods the Jews organized small congregations, usually made up of men who came from the same small towns, cities, or regions in eastern Europe. Known as *hevrot* (informal fellowship groups) or *anshes* ("men of" then followed by the place name), these groups organized religious worship along the lines familiar from back home. They also made fellowship and familiarity integral parts of religious services.

Often these groups met in rented storefronts. They as likely as not provided mutual aid to members in the forms of loans and some of them evolved into *landsmanshaftn*, or home town societies which operated according to bylaws and offered as perquisites of membership unemployment insurance, medical care, burial, and survivor benefits.

At times *anshes* took over synagogue buildings which had been built by earlier Jewish immigrants who with greater affluence left the "old neighborhood" of first settlement and moved out to newer, nicer areas. On New York's Lower East Side the building put up in the late 1840s by Anshe Chesed, a predominantly German congregation with a lofty name—the people of righteousness, ended up by the second decade of the twentieth century as the home of Anshe Slonim, the house of worship of a group of men from the town of that name.

Some of the best off of the East European immigrants formed new, elaborate traditional congregations. The first Russian synagogue in New York, Congregation Beth Hamedrash Hagadol, had been founded in 1852. In 1872 it changed its name to Kahal Adat Jeshurun Anshe Lutz, "the congregation of the community of Jeshurun, the people of the town of Lubtz." In

1887, as newcomers from Eastern Europe poured into the Lower East Side in a flood, the synagogue dedicated an ornate building on Eldridge Street. The Eldridge Street Synagogue, with its elaborate windows, soaring roof, and magnificent painted ceiling, represented the effort of the newest Jewish immigrants to claim their place on the city's skyline.

The tempo of the East European Jewish neighborhoods came not just from the commercial and the religious spheres, but cultural, social, and political needs fueled the process of making Jewish space. Some of the East European Jews came with an orientation towards socialism and other forms of political radicalism. Some became radicalized in the garment factories of the United States where so many of them worked.

Their socialism became a force in the creation of labor unions with massive Jewish membership and leadership. The Amalgamated Clothing Workers' Union founded in 1900 by Jewish workers, immigrants from Russia and Poland, brought together those who made a living sewing men's clothing, while the International Ladies' Garment Workers Union, created in 1914, served those who made women's clothing. Regardless of whether they made men's clothing or women's clothing, Jewish workers in the garment unions fused in their activities Jewish and socialist rhetoric and challenged the idea that employers had the right to determine the terms of labor. So too Jewish workers, printers, furriers, bakers, cigar makers, and hat and cap makers organized themselves and made their presence felt in the cities where they labored and in the nation as at large.

The immigrants who settled in the large cities of the United States also became consumers of the Yiddish press. They read newspapers published in New York—the *Forverts* (founded 1897), being the most popular, but also *the Morgen Zhurnal* and *Der Tog*—as well as local Yiddish papers published in Chicago, Philadelphia, Milwaukee, and many other cities. These newspapers provided a range of services to their readers. They gave the general American and world news, they reported on key events in the Jewish world, and they explained America—baseball, politics, youth culture, fashions and homemaking, to name a few—to the new immigrants. The newspapers served as a kind of guide to the newcomers, bridging their desire for news from back home and the news of their new home in a language they knew.

The Yiddish press as an authentic voice of the immigrant generation existed in a culture of publishing. Yiddish books and pamphlets, ranging from fiction to nonfiction, poetry, short stories, political tracts, translations from the repertoire of world classics, original works penned in the United States and reprints of works that circulated in Eastern Europe, all found their way to the immigrant Jewish enclaves. The books covered every imaginable topic, spanning religion, politics, economics, manners, science, and history. The books demonstrated the continuing resonance of Jewish issues and the embrace of American ideas. One example will have to suffice. In 1901 Hinde Amchanitzki published America's first Yiddish language cookbook. In this book she directly addressed the "Jewish daughters" who hoped to improve her culinary skills in order to "excite her husband and family with the best, tastiest foods, which will excite the soul and strengthen the body." She provided guidance on cooking both traditional East European dishes

לעהר-בוך
וויא אזוי
צו קאכען און באקען.
אריגינאל פערפאסט פון א אידישע פרוי, וועלכע האט
45 יאהר ערפאהרונג אין אייראפעאישער און אמעריקאני-
שער קיך.

הינדע אמהאניצקי.

פרייז 15 סענט.

צו בעקומען אין ספרים סטאר פון ר. קאנטראראוויץ 4 רוטגער סט. ניו יאָרק.

Written in the language understood by the majority of newly arriving Jewish immigrants, this cookbook served as an introduction to American as well as traditional Jewish cuisine. The recipes, which are based on Amchanitzki's forty-five years of experience in European and American kitchens, include traditional Jewish dishes as well as American fare. In her introduction, the author promises that using her recipes will prevent stomach aches and other food related maladies in children. The first American Yiddish cookbook pictures the author on the cover.

Hinde Amchanitzki. Lehr-bukh vi Azoy Tsu Kokhen un Baken (Textbook on How to Cook and Bake), New York, 1901. Hebraic Section.

Opposite: Yiddish theatrical productions were especially popular among the over 2.5 million Jewish immigrants who arrived in America between 1880 and 1925. This elaborate poster from 1897 heralds a series of "star-studded" productions on biblical themes at the Thalia Theatre, located in New York City's Bowery district on the Lower East Side.

"King Solomon at the Thaila Theatre," New York, 1897. Prints and Photographs Division.

—gefilte fish, chicken soup, blintzes, kugel—as well as "French soup," "French balls," "Lemon Pie," and "Lemon Short pie." The recipes reveal an immigrant world that stood between the known and the new and a cultural outlook that embraced both.[8]

Similarly the Yiddish theater, a product of the last decades of the nineteenth century, enjoyed a golden age in the 1910s and 1920s. Like the press, New York's Lower East Side functioned as the epicenter of the Yiddish theatrical culture, but smaller though similar houses opened up in other big cities. Traveling troupes from New York likewise made the circuit and entertained Yiddish-speaking immigrants around the country. Audiences enjoyed musical works and tragedies, plays drawn from biblical themes and others that translated Shakespeare into Yiddish. Some of the most popular plays explored the immigrant experience and in comedies and in dramas highlighted the conflicts between "old world" parents and American children and delved into the many crises brought to the surface by the migration.

Concern in the Jewish community over these issues, as reflected on the stage, also became the focus of hundreds of social service projects. Jewish charities and social welfare agencies in New York and around the country tried to create programs and provide services which would help the immigrants negotiate the problems they confronted in their homes. Some of these projects flowed from the top down. Well-off American Jews, many of them the descendants of the earlier immigration, wanted to ease the sting of poverty and aid in the process of adjustment to the United States. In 1893 some of New York's most active Jewish philanthropists created the Educational Alliance in the immigrant quarter. The Educational Alliance offered something for nearly everyone. For children, it had classes in religious education, summer camps, and sports. For adults, classes in practical skills such as stenography, typewriting and bookkeeping, as well as cooking and sewing, offered immigrant workers the chance to improve their job situation or elevate the tenor of domestic life. Students could take classes in how to pass the citizenship exam, and for those who were already citizens, how to pass the U.S. Civil Service examination so that they could qualify for government jobs.

Likewise the National Council of Jewish Women, which had been founded in 1893 by affluent American Jewish women, took as its particular focus the needs of the newly arriving immigrant Jewish women. National Council hired agents who waited at Ellis Island and gave assistance to young Jewish women traveling on their own. It provided these young women with places to live—Council Homes—and job training so that they could support

themselves. One chapter of National Council, the one in Milwaukee, which had opened the Milwaukee Jewish Mission house, decided to offer cooking classes. In this it followed a common pattern. Jewish settlement houses around the country provided classes for married Jewish women on how to cook better and how to prepare American-style food. The Milwaukee project proved to be particularly notable because in 1901 Lizzie Black Kander, a member of National Council, decided that the women in the Milwaukee Mission would band together and collect their favorite recipes as a fundraiser for the settlement house. Out of this came *The Settlement Cookbook* in 1901. Originally a Yiddish pamphlet, *The Settlement Cookbook* remains in print, now in English, at the beginning of the twenty-first century.

East European Jewish immigrants in the United States did not, however, wait for their American coreligionists to help them. They also provided for themselves. Certainly they availed themselves of the services rendered by those Jews who already lived in the United States and had achieved a modicum of comfort and status. But the new immigrants also built their own institutions as they saw fit. The *landsmanshaftn* represented a truly grassroots organization, directed by no one other than the members themselves. These organizations provided some of the basic needs for the immigrants, making it possible for immigrants to get interest-free loans, insurance, and medical care.

Often the services rendered by the *landsmanshaftn* proved too meager for the gravity of the problem and the immigrants needed to create larger institutions to address their concerns. In the 1910s a group of neighborhood women in Boston, all immigrant mothers, complained that they had no regular medical facility in to which to take their children. They decided to raise money, rent an apartment and hire a doctor to come in for a few hours a week. They organized themselves to collect money and recruited members of the local *bikur holim* societies—religious associations dedicated to visiting the sick—to help them solicit donations. Over time the efforts of these women not only succeeded—the apartment got rented and the doctor hired—in a limited sense, but out of their efforts grew Boston's Beth Israel hospital, now the teaching hospital of Harvard University's medical school.

Examples of immigrant self-help, mutual aid, and institution building could be drawn from every city where the East European Jewish immigrants settled. They saw themselves as women and men who had

Featured on the title page of this piece of sheet music are the three favored icons of the American Jewish immigrant sensibility: George Washington, Abraham Lincoln, and the Statue of Liberty.

Leo Rosenberg and M. Rubinstein, Leben Zol Amerika (Long Live America), *New York, n.d. Hebraic Section.*

affirmatively chosen America and in so choosing went about the business of creating communities for themselves. They had no intention of going back and consequently they considered themselves empowered and entitled to take advantage of the openness of America to make Jewish life possible.

Like the earlier immigrants from Central Europe, the newcomers from Eastern Europe had left a place where they believed life had become impossible. There, they understood, they could not make a living and support their families, in large measure because they were Jews. They decided to cast their lot with the twenty-five million other Europeans who saw in America the chance for economic security. They understood, whether in 1820 or 1920, that their home communities had little to offer them as Jews and as people in search of a decent standard of living. The three million Jews who made the move to the United States voted with their feet for a place that offered them precisely what Europe did not.

Shown here is the Inspection Room on Ellis Island, where new immigrants were interviewed by inspectors after passing a medical examination.

Detroit Publishing Company [Inspection room, Ellis Island, New York, New York], New York, circa 1912. Prints and Photographs Division.

The Crucial Decades

Deborah Dash Moore

In December 1920, "our ship had to wait its turn to get to Ellis Island." It took ten days, Lillian Gorenstein recalled. "During this time visitors came in small boats and pulled up alongside the ship to greet their relatives." Lillian, her mother, and two brothers spent over a year on their journey to the United States to join their father. While they waited in the harbor, a friend "from Providence came many times." But her mother asked only one question: "Is he alive?" "Yes, yes, he is alive," was the reply. Lillian "had another question," but she didn't ask it aloud. "If he is alive, why didn't he come?" Lillian never received an answer. When they finally arrived at the Boston train station, they saw "lines of people waving and running" to greet the newcomers. But no one waved to them, so they made their way in a horse and buggy to a tall building in Chelsea, Massachusetts.

"A lady looked out of the window from a high floor." She came down "to see who these people were with their bundles." After "she read the name on Ma's tag," she "motioned to us to follow her upstairs. On the third floor she opened the door." Then she asked a daughter, "Bessie, go call Harry. Tell him his family is here." Lillian heard her father "walking up the stairs in great haste." After all those years of wartime separation, "Ma and Pa met, embraced, and then Ma started to cry. Father held her close, but she continued to cry for some time. The three of us

---

In 1989, at eighty-three years of age, Lillian (Burstein) Gorenstein composed a memoir recounting her early years of privation and hardship in Kamen (Ukraine) during World War I, her family's postwar journey to America, and her experiences in her new home in Chelsea, Massachusetts. Pictured from left to right are Lillian, her brother, Morris, and her mother, Rose.

Burstein Family Portrait, Kamen (Ukraine), circa 1914. Courtesy of Arthur Goren (Jerusalem and New York) and Judith Ronat (Kfar Saba, Israel).

stood aside and watched." Finally Lillian's father turned first to the son he had never seen, kissing him, and then to his older son, and finally to Lillian. "You are so grown up?" he said. "As lightning struck me I was about to say, 'Where were you all the time we got so grown up?'" But Lillian didn't say what she felt and she promised herself "never, never to say anything about Kamen [Ukraine] or about what happened to us since Father left until we came to America. Never, never would I say a word." She turned to her brother. "Now we have a father," she explained. "Now we have a lot to learn in America, and now we have a lot to forget."[1]

What Lillian vowed to forget at age fourteen were the incredible years of starvation during World War I that marred her childhood and prematurely ended it. What she could not understand was why her father, co-owner of a grocery store, failed to come to welcome them to America. The gap between his wartime life, earning a living while enjoying the security of the United States, and her own desperate struggle to survive between warring armies would never be closed. Fate, international politics, and her father's insecure prosperity dealt her family radically different war experiences. Lillian would become an American, and her story as an adult during the Second World War, whose horrors would far exceed those of the First World War, would recapitulate her father's experience. Immigration to the United States created an almost insurmountable chasm separating the New World from the Old. No matter how bad anti-Semitism got in the United States, it never came close to the murderous fury and hatred of Jews that poisoned European politics and culture.

Like so many Jewish immigrants before her, Lillian turned her back on the Old World and focused her considerable energies on mastering America: getting new clothes and a new hairdo (though she refused to wear a corset), learning English, going to school, becoming a Zionist. All were part of crafting an American Jewish identity. Lillian did not know that she was among the lucky ones admitted to an increasingly xenophobic United States. In 1921 strict quotas regulating immigration were put into effect; in 1924 they were reduced further. The number of Jewish immigrants plummeted; only 73,000 settled in the United States between 1924 and 1931.[2] The era of immigration had ended and the age of the immigrants' children, the second generation, was beginning. Lillian worked hard to position herself within that generation, to catch up to the two million Jewish immigrants from Eastern Europe who had preceded her to the United States.

The drama of Lillian's late arrival obscured less dramatic but no less important journeys started by earlier cohorts of second-generation Jews from urban slums throughout the Northeast and Midwest to freshly built homes in suburban sections of expanding cities. Many of those apartment buildings and multifamily houses were built by American Jews eager to enter the construction industry and ready to develop an ethnically distinct market catering to second-generation Jews. When Lillian's father lost his grocery store, he returned to his trade as a carpenter and soon made a modest living in the construction business. As Lillian settled down to her new life in a two-parent family in Chelsea, a working class area of Boston, thousands of Jews were moving to the more middle-class neighborhoods of Roxbury, Dorchester, and Brookline. The same saga repeated itself in Chicago and Philadelphia, Cleveland and St. Louis.

In this World War I poster, a monumental female figure holds a tray of food, poor women and children at her feet, and the skyline of New York City and the Statue of Liberty in the background.

"Share: Jewish Relief Campaign," lithographed by Sackett & Wilhelms Corporation, Brooklyn, New York, circa 1917. Prints and Photographs Division.

But nowhere did the migrations of American Jews register more profoundly than in New York City, the acknowledged Jewish capital city of the United States. With well over a million Jewish residents, New York easily outranked Warsaw, its nearest competitor, as the world's largest Jewish city. Even before 1921, the year of Lillian's arrival, observers had already noted the thinning of the dense immigrant population on Manhattan's Lower East Side and the burgeoning of new Jewish neighborhoods on the Upper West Side as well as in Brooklyn and the Bronx. Things were changing, but what the changes meant would be hard to decipher.

Louis Wirth, a young Jewish immigrant from Germany studying at the University of Chicago in the 1920s, thought he saw a pattern. Part of the emerging school of sociologists fascinated with urbanism as an American way of life, Wirth posited a series of progressive departures and settlements radiating outward from immigrant slum to second-generation neighborhood to third-generation suburb. Each area was more prosperous and more American; each encouraged a different social psychology among Jews; each pointed toward what Wirth hoped would be the culmination of assimilation into American society and the eradication of differences between Jews and their neighbors. "If you would know what kind of a Jew a man is," Wirth wrote, "ask him where he lives; for no single factor indicates as much about the character of the Jew as the area in which he lives." It was, Wirth thought, "an index not only to his economic status, his occupation, his religion, but to his politics and his outlook on life and the stage in the assimilative process that he has reached."[3] Jews accepted Wirth's insight as just so much common sense.

Moving up the social scale in America meant moving out of one's old home and into a new one. It meant trading a nominal traditionalism in religion for a modernized Judaism expressed in spacious and elegant synagogue centers that catered to the entire family, young and old, men and women. Mobility, both physical and social, lay at the heart of the American dream, a dream Jews were eager to embrace. But mobility did not mean leaving behind Jewish identification and a concern for other Jews. Rather, Jews accepted mobility as a collective endeavor; they would all move together to new urban neighborhoods and there create diverse American Jewish worlds. American Jews would remain city dwellers.

There were many paths to follow to fulfill the dream. Lillian Gorenstein chose a popular one: she learned bookkeeping. Although she could not afford tuition, she talked the business school into a loan, promising to pay once she had a job. In a short time Lillian repaid the money. Then she met a man who had actually graduated from college, a dream beyond her reach as an immigrant Jewish woman. Jewish families would scrimp and save to put sons through school because it promised a middle-class, white-collar job. Daughters usually had to settle for less. Saul and Lillian married and by 1926, five years after she had arrived in America, she gave birth to a son.

Other Jewish women, especially in New York City, chose teaching. "My daughter, the teacher," rivaled "my son, the doctor" as gendered aspirations of immigrant parents for their children. Becoming a teacher fulfilled not only the practical requisites any young woman had to

consider of acquiring a skill that would support her, but it also expressed an impractical idealism and love of learning that fired Jewish imaginations. And in New York City, teachers could marry, have children, and keep their jobs. Thus second-generation women prepared for both work and marriage, leaving behind the sweatshops of their parents for white-collar employments. But although they married Jews, as their parents expected, most Jewish women eagerly practiced birth control. They limited the number of their children. Lillian's mother had four children, including one son born in Chelsea. Lillian would have only two.

Most Jewish women did not continue to work once they had children but followed American middle-class patterns of staying at home to raise their children. Lillian proved the exception to the rule. When Saul moved to Washington, D.C., where he worked for the Internal Revenue Service, Lillian continued to work as a bookkeeper. Her husband's choice of a career as a civil servant rather than a life in business reflected both the severe economic

The WPA Adult Education Program and New York City's Board of Education sponsored free English classes to help parents "learn to speak, read, and write the language of your children." In addition, naturalization classes and "special classes for educated foreign born" are advertised on this Yiddish and English poster.

"Free Classes in English!" New York, between 1936 and 1941, Works Progress Administration Poster Collection, Prints and Photographs Division.

pressures of the Great Depression and opportunities for Jews in an expanding civil service bureaucracy. Franklin Delano Roosevelt's New Deal proffered Jews not only a social safety net of unemployment insurance and social security, but also increasingly equal employment.

Jewish men often preferred the path of small business and self-employment as professionals rather than trying to scale the significant hurdles erected to prevent Jews from gaining jobs in large corporations. Barred by discrimination from positions in heavy industry, insurance, telephone companies, prestigious law firms, and banking, Jews turned to light industries as well as wholesale and retail trade. Ironically, their choices, dictated as much by anti-Semitism as cultural bias, served them relatively well during the Depression. Although many Jews lost ground and moved back into cheap apartments, or doubled up with other family members to save on rent, they often managed to avoid turning to welfare to survive. Still, financial worries during the Depression led Lillian to postpone a second pregnancy, waiting nine years after the birth of her son to have another child, a daughter.

Like many married Jewish women, Lillian poured significant energies into Jewish volunteer organizations. She soon became a stalwart of Pioneer Women, the women's organization of the Labor Zionist movement that championed cooperative pioneering settlements in the Jewish national home. Although committed to women's equality, both Zionists and Socialists allowed women to organize separately to pursue their own agendas. Pioneer Women cooperated with the Labor Zionists and helped support an indigenous American youth movement, Habonim (the Builders), but it failed to recruit middle-class women as fully as Hadassah, the independent Zionist women's organization. In response to the crisis of Nazism, Hadassah developed its program of Youth Aliyah, sending teenagers from Hitler's Germany to the Jewish homeland in Palestine. Thousands of Jewish women joined its ranks eager to do something constructive to help Jews suffering persecution.

Had Lillian not been a Zionist, she could have joined the socialist Workmen's Circle, founded in 1901, which blended commitments to Yiddish culture, union organizing, and labor activism. Further on the left was the recently established communist International Workers Order that had separate Jewish fraternal societies, with their own schools and camps for children and adults. Had she not been politically involved, she could have joined a synagogue sisterhood and developed new forms of American Judaism. Sisterhoods rallied to sustain congregations struggling to survive sharply reduced incomes during the Depression. Had her husband prospered, she might have aspired to become a member of the National Council of Jewish Women, which recruited affluent women from American homes. Their agenda included Americanization projects for immigrant Jewish women as well as participation in the international women's movement.

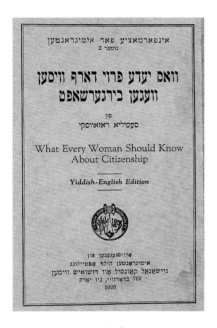

This citizenship guide for women was issued in both English and Yiddish by the Immigration Assistance section of the National Council of Jewish Women. Founded in 1893, the Council focused on helping unmarried women immigrants learn English, secure citizenship, and find employment.

Cecilia Razovsky, Vos yede froy darf visen vegen birgershaft ... What every woman should know about citizenship. Yiddish-English. New York, 1926. Hebraic Section.

But Lillian's understanding of solidarity radiated outward from Jews. She believed that Jews were a nation, that they needed to return to their ancient homeland in Palestine, that the anti-Semitism which she had suffered in Europe could only be overcome if Jews had a state, and that the most just way to structure Jewish life was to build a democratic socialist society. As a democrat, Lillian did not find the dreams of a worker's paradise in the Soviet Union particularly appealing. She rejected the ideal of a dictatorship of the proletariat, though she often debated the merits of Zionism, Socialism, and Communism with her friends and neighbors.

Lillian's choice of Pioneer Women expressed the viewpoint of a small minority of approximately four million American Jews. Many eschewed ideologically driven organizations. They preferred to join *landsmanshaftn*, hometown mutual aid societies created by the immigrant generation. Others formed their own family societies, linking extended cousins through regular meetings and mutual assistance. In the years after World War I, American Jews established several new organizations and expanded existing ones. In 1924 the B'nai B'rith, a fraternal society started in the nineteenth century, responded to pleas for help for increasing numbers of Jewish college youth. In creating Hillel, named after a famous rabbi, B'nai B'rith developed a nondenominational model for Jewish campus life that would become influential after World War II.

Perhaps the most important new organization on the American scene appeared in 1921, the year Lillian arrived. Then Stephen Wise, outspoken rabbi of the Free Synagogue in New York City, established the American Jewish Congress. Wise wanted to unite American Jews in an organization dedicated to fighting for social justice for Jews and other minorities in the United States and abroad. His list of concerns included the revived Ku Klux Klan that targeted Jews, Catholics, and African Americans; quotas that limited Jews attending colleges and medical schools; and restrictive covenants that prevented Jews from renting apartments or hotel rooms. Had some Jews told him that the prestigious American Jewish Committee led by the widely respected lawyer, Louis Marshall, possessed a similar mandate to fight for civil rights, Wise would have pointed to his organization's mass membership base and support of Zionism as being different from the Committee. Wise saw Zionism as an expression of social justice; Marshall saw Zionism as a potentially dangerous form of Jewish nationalism. Jews needed minority rights in Europe and they needed a place of refuge in Palestine, especially after the United States restricted immigration, but whether they also needed a state was a matter of debate. As a Reform Jew, Marshall preferred to see all Jews as members of a religious group, not a Jewish nation. Despite similar goals, ideology mattered, as did religion.

Although the lines between Orthodox, Conservative, and Reform Judaism were not sharply drawn, increasingly distinctions of religious

Rabbi Stephen S. Wise, American Jewry's leading spokesman in the first half of the twentieth century, was a founder of the American Jewish Congress, which played a leading role in the anti-Nazi boycott and in combating anti-Semitism.

Underwood & Underwood, Photographic Portrait of Rabbi Stephen S. Wise, circa 1930. Prints and Photographs Division.

The "ou" symbol on the top right corner of the Krispy Crackers box signifies that the product was prepared under rabbinic supervision and conforms to the laws of kashrut (i.e., Jewish dietary laws). The purpose of the symbol was to serve as a guide for "the observant Jewish woman desiring to uphold the traditional dietary laws."

"Sunshine Crispy Crackers Guaranteed Kosher," in Kosher Food Guide, *New York, 1950. General Collections. Courtesy of Kellogg North American Company.*

This cookbook was one of a series published by the Manischewitz Company based on recipes solicited from its customers. In Yiddish and in English, the recipes "cover every range of cookery, from a half-dozen ways to prepare the ever useful Matzo Knoedel to a delightful method of making Strawberry Shortcake."

Ba'Tampte Idishe Ma'cholim: Tempting Kosher Dishes, *Third Edition. Cincinnati, 1930. General Collections.*

belief and practice mattered. Differences over accommodation to contemporary society divided the Orthodox into two camps. Modern Orthodox Jews advocated a blend of scientific knowledge with Torah learning. The establishment of Yeshiva College (later University) on the bluffs of Washington Heights overlooking the Harlem River proclaimed the synthesis. So did the creation of a new symbol certifying that prepared foods were kosher. The Union of Orthodox Jewish Congregation's OU modernized *kashrut* supervision, making many canned goods available to observant Jews. Traditionalist Orthodox Jews rejected such accommodations. Nor did they look with favor upon Mizrachi, the modern Orthodox Zionist movement.

On the other hand, Conservative Jews surpassed the modern Orthodox in their acceptance of American life and support of spiritual Zionism. Not only did Conservative Jews value college education, an ideal for many American Jews, but they also encouraged the education of Jewish girls. A growing sense of equality for men and women in synagogue life took hold. Although neither the Jewish calendar nor life-cycle events changed, shifts in emphasis occurred. Bar mitzvahs became more important; the High Holy Days of the Jewish New Year assumed major significance, especially for Jews who rarely went to synagogue at other times during the year; Chanukah increasingly became a holiday for children; late Friday evening services acquired popularity.

Reform Judaism, once largely uncontested, became a denomination, one among three. Its rejection of many rituals and observances, including the use of Hebrew in prayer, and its willingness to adopt such congregational practices as organs and mixed choirs that seemed Protestant in the eyes of Jewish immigrants marked it as more American than Jewish for many.

But if religion and ideology divided American Jews, culture and politics united them. Lillian Gorenstein would have been a young mother when she saw *The Jazz Singer*, the first talking movie that revolutionized film production even as it portrayed the saga of a cantor's son who falls in love with American popular culture. Based upon the life of vaudeville singer Al Jolson, *The Jazz Singer* epitomized a move from sacred to profane art, from the music of the synagogue to the songs of the Broadway stage, from the primacy of home and tradition to the glorification of individual achievement. This classic tale of assimilation proclaimed Jews' unadulterated love for America. *The Jazz Singer* imagined a world where talent, pluck, luck, and the essence of Jewish experience—the special sorrows they suffered— translated into success and universal adulation. "You ain't heard nothing yet," Jack Robin assured his adoring mother.

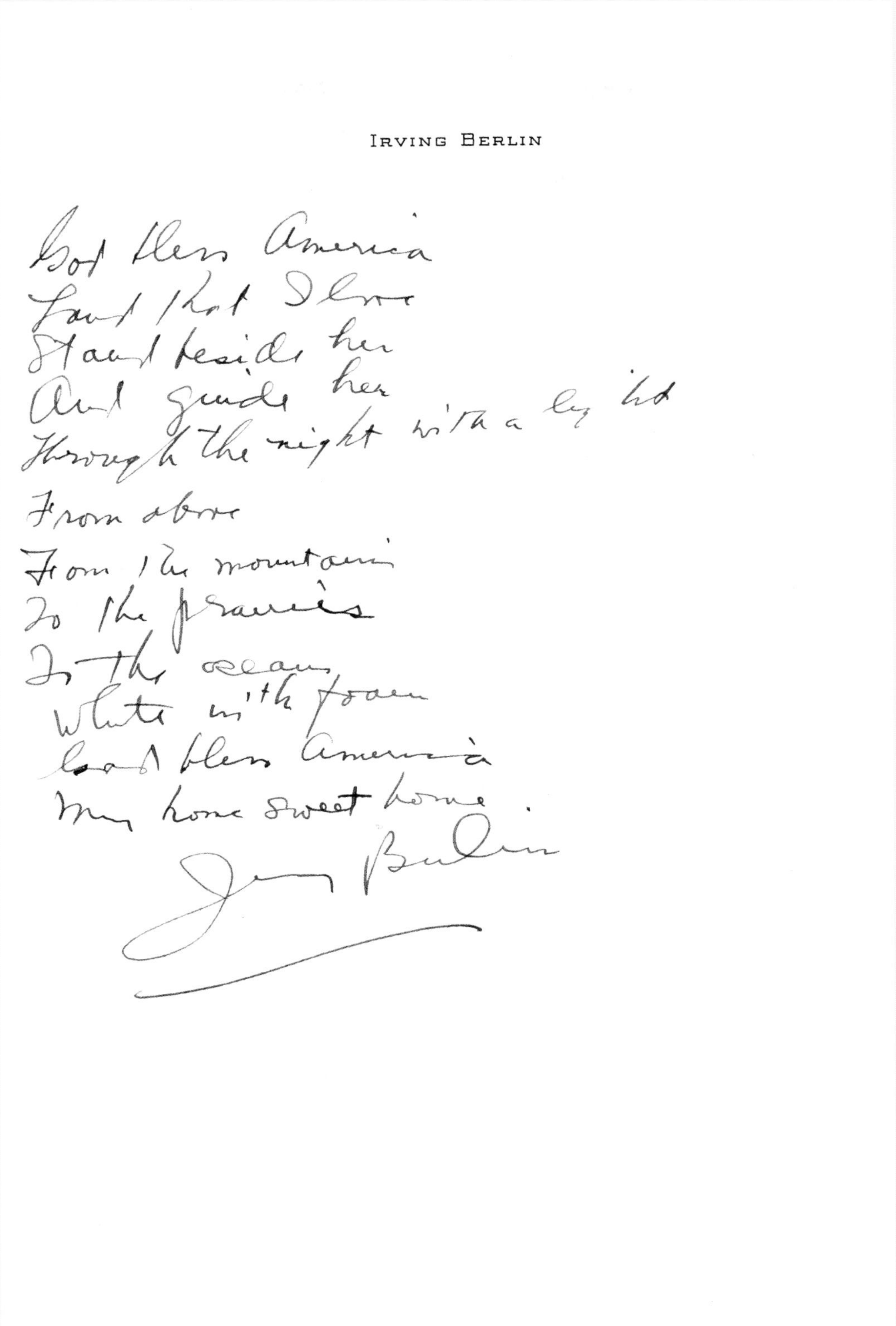

God Bless America
Land that I love
Stand beside her
And guide her
Through the night with a light
From above
From the mountains
To the prairies
To the oceans
White with foam
God bless America
My home sweet home.

Irving Berlin

In 1955, President Eisenhower conferred a special gold medal on Irving Berlin, "in recognition and appreciation of his ... composing many patriotic songs." Berlin told reporters that he wrote "God Bless America" to express his gratitude to America for the opportunities it had given him. Displayed above is a signed holograph copy of the song that has become a second national anthem.

Irving Berlin, "God Bless America," December 28, 1940. Music Division.

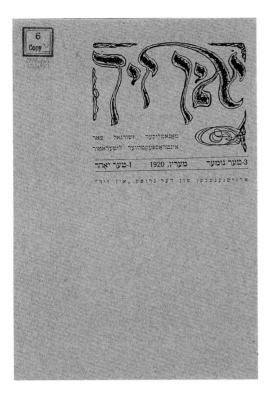

The American Yiddish introspectivist movement's journal In Zikh (In Oneself) posited the radical notion that Jewish poetry need not deal with Jewish themes to be considered "Jewish"; as long as the poetry reflected the poet's own experience it qualified as "Jewish" poetry.

In Zikh (In Oneself), New York, March 1920. Hebraic Section.

Opposite: Born in 1896, Benjamin Leiner changed his name to Benny Leonard so that his observant parents would not know that he had taken up professional boxing. He became the world lightweight champion in 1917 and held the title for some eight years. This 1945 issue of The Ring magazine recognizes Leonard's World War II service as a lieutenant commander in the U.S. Merchant Marine. After the war, Leonard became a boxing referee, collapsing and dying in the ring in 1947.

"Former Lightweight King, Lieut. Com. Benny Leonard of the U.S. Merchant Marine," in The Ring, January 1945. General Collections. Courtesy of London Publishing Company.

His prophetic statement would be fulfilled as Jews enthusiastically entered American culture industries. Movies, popular song, musical theater, and radio broadcasting enticed Jewish performers and entrepreneurs. Structured around disguise and fantasy, dreams and desires, American popular culture rubbed the rough edges off ethnic and religious differences. Who could object to Irving Berlin's "God Bless America," which he wrote during World War I, but only unveiled on the eve of World War II? Possibilities existed for all kinds of crossovers, as the history of "Bei mir bist du sheyn" reveals. Sholom Secunda's song made its way from Second Avenue's Yiddish theater up to Harlem, where it acquired a lively beat and then, in English, rose to the top of the charts as a hit for the Andrews Sisters.

Yet Yiddish theater, music, film, and radio also flourished in these years, coexisting in comfortable tension with the mainstream. After World War I, the center of Yiddish culture shifted from Europe to the United States. New movements in poetry, vigorous literary magazines, and experimental and expressionist theater marked a period of intense creativity alongside the mass circulation Yiddish newspapers, musical comedies of the Yiddish stage, klezmer bands, and radio broadcasts that brought news, skits, and commercials into Jewish living rooms. The two worlds of Yiddish often clashed, yet both spoke to the diversity of American Jewish culture.

That varied world could be seen, as well, in American Jews' leisure practices. Although Saul and Lillian could not afford a car, they often sent their son with his grandparents to enjoy a day at Boston's Revere Beach. Parents who could manage the fees shipped their city children to summer camps in the country. Jewish philanthropic organizations sponsored camps, as did ideological fraternal societies. New York Jews tried to vacation for at least a few weeks each year, taking the train up to the Catskills in the summertime to savor the fresh air and abundant food. Even the garment unions provided members with vacation places. There were leisure opportunities for every pocketbook and ideological conviction. It mattered less whether one stayed in a big hotel like Grossinger's or a small bungalow colony than that one participated in an American rite of summer.

Sports also promised Jews a common bond with other Americans. Baseball, basketball, and boxing generated the most enthusiasm. The last represented a poor boy's ticket out of ghetto poverty. Jews followed the Irish into the sport, on occasion adopting Irish nicknames. But American Jews rooted for them even if they didn't wear a Jewish star on their shorts, like Benny Leonard. Less rough than boxing, basketball became the urban Jewish sport of choice. It required little space, could be played in groups of

THE LEONARD-WHITE THRILLER

25 Cents
P.D.C.
In Canada 30 Cents

The RING

JANUARY
1945

BUY
UNITED STATES
WAR
BONDS
AND
STAMPS

Former Lightweight king,
Lieut. Com. Benny Leonard
of the U. S. Merchant Marine

BOXING OUTLOOK IS BRIGHTER

varying sizes, and demanded a mixture of teamwork and individuality. As new laws made high school education mandatory, Jewish teenagers discovered the game's joys in citywide competitions. Jewish Community Centers, which had always championed sports as a healthy form of recreation and a path to Americanization, fielded teams. But baseball remained the American sport. All American Jews were thrilled when Hank Greenberg hit home runs, whether or not they rooted for the Detroit Tigers. An American hero, he transcended Jewish differences.

As FDR's New Deal gathered steam, American Jews increasingly flocked to the Democratic Party. Roosevelt's willingness to appoint Jewish advisors—the welcome extended to Sidney Hillman, the head of the Amalgamated Clothing Union—and his criticism of Hitler's Nazi Party indicated an openness to Jews and Jewish concerns. Both labor unions and the more radical Popular Front suggested that FDR's blend of domestic social welfare programs combined with an antifascist internationalist posture deserved the support of American Jews. In 1936 overwhelming numbers of American Jews voted for his second term. The creation of the American Labor Party in New York City by the Jewish garment workers' unions allowed dedicated Socialists to pull the lever for FDR without voting for the hated Democratic Party bosses of Tammany Hall.

Yet even as Jews lined up behind Roosevelt, Hitler's success in consolidating his power in Germany and then in Austria and Czechoslovakia brought ever more brutal attacks upon European Jews. An Anti-Nazi Boycott, initiated in 1933, expressed American Jews' anger at Nazi persecution but did not weaken the Third Reich. Jews also failed in their efforts to get Americans to boycott the 1936 Olympics held in Berlin. It was not easy to sway American opinion, especially when Hitler had his admirers in the United States, including such a popular figure as the aviator Charles Lindbergh. But *Kristallnacht* shocked all Americans. The Night of Broken Glass on November 9, 1938, when Nazis and German police destroyed hundreds of synagogues, smashed thousands of shop windows, and then interned tens of thousands of Jewish men, represented the prewar culmination of anti-Semitic violence and pointed to an even darker future.

Jewish refugees, desperate to leave Germany, looked to the great democracies, the United States and Great Britain. But Congress refused to increase immigration quotas, even to admit refugee children, and the State Department erected endless paper barriers to prevent the meager quotas from being filled. Then in May 1939, as Europe teetered on the edge of war, Great Britain drastically curtailed Jewish immigration to Palestine. American Jews, trapped in the ordinary demands of making a living, struggled to influence American and British policy through protests, rallies, and persuasion. Urged to give money to help European Jews, they combined their fund-raising into a United Jewish Appeal, hoping to leverage their cooperation into more effective aid.

Jewish refugee children, en route to Philadelphia, aboard the liner President Harding, *waving at the Statue of Liberty.*

"Jewish Refugee Children," New York, 1939. © AP/Wide World Photos. New York World-Telegram and Sun Newspaper Photograph Collection, Prints and Photographs Division.

American Jews urged Roosevelt to help European Jews caught in the Nazi dragnet, but they also created their own organizations devoted to rescue. Orthodox Jews, Jewish Socialists, and Jewish academics tried to identify and assist fellow rabbis, labor leaders, scholars, and intellectuals. Few were saved in comparison with those who were murdered, but the efforts did produce an impressive intellectual, artistic, and religious migration that transferred important and diverse segments of European Jewish culture to the United States from the Frankfurt school of Marxist philosophers to the Lubavitcher rebbe and his pious hasidim.

World War II started on September 1, 1939, when Germany invaded Poland. American Jews were divided over the best response. The Hitler-Stalin pact that preceded the invasion fractured the Popular Front, as Communists defended the Soviet Union's deal with Nazi Germany. Socialists claimed to see little difference between the imperialist Allies and the fascist Axis. Zionists, furious at Great Britain, debated the virtues of neutrality versus support of England. But many American Jews quickly lined up on the side of England and FDR. They voted by large majorities for his reelection in 1940, demonstrating confidence in his policies and leadership. The issues in the war seemed clear to them: Hitler, Nazism, and fascism needed to be opposed. But what actions should the United States government take? After France fell to the Germans in June 1940, Nazi persecution reached even more Jews.

When the Germans invaded the Soviet Union in June 1941, they initiated the mass murder of Jewish civilians. Specially trained forces assisted the regular German army in the killings. News of these atrocities on the eastern front slowly leaked out. American Jews already knew that the Nazis had forced Jews into ghettos created in Polish cities. There miserable conditions produced unprecedented death rates. Through the American Jewish Joint Distribution Committee, American Jews tried to alleviate starvation and treat disease. But the mass murder of civilians was unheard of. Even as Jews debated the meaning of the awful news, many decided that U.S. participation in the war was inevitable. England and the Soviet Union could not defeat Nazi Germany. And Nazi Germany had to be defeated.

December 7, 1941, shocked all Americans. No matter how aware of the war they were, the Japanese attack on Pearl Harbor stunned them. Now there was no choice. American Jews threw themselves into the war effort along with all other Americans. Lillian worried that her son, who had become bar mitzvah in 1939, might soon be old enough to be drafted. But he didn't think about such things. Like most teenagers, he focused on his high school studies. Lillian and Saul did what they could to help the war effort. Swept up in patriotic enthusiasm, younger, unmarried American Jewish men rushed to enlist, like so many other Americans. Others waited until the draft caught them. In the initial optimism of 1942, patriotism produced rosy expectations of a short war. American Jews had no idea of the genocide Hitler planned for all Jews.

News of the Final Solution and the death camps built to murder thousands of Jews each day reached Rabbi Stephen Wise in the summer of 1942. Although Wise waited for State Department permission to announce to the press the horror of two million dead, he shared what he had learned with other American Jewish leaders. It was difficult, almost impossible to

WESTERN UNION CABLEGRAM

THE COMPANY WILL APPRECIATE SUGGESTIONS FROM ITS PATRONS CONCERNING ITS SERVICE   1280

CLASS OF SERVICE — This is a full-rate Cablegram unless its deferred character is indicated by a suitable symbol preceding the address.

R. B. WHITE PRESIDENT   NEWCOMB CARLTON CHAIRMAN OF THE BOARD   J. C. WILLEVER FIRST VICE-PRESIDENT

SYMBOLS — LC Deferred Cablegram / NLT Cable Night Letter / Ship Radiogram

(27)   1942 AUG

8/29/42

NV15 CABLE=LIVERPOOL 122 1/63 NFD

NLT STEPHEN WIS (CARE MRS SCHNEEBERGER
 250 WEST 94 ST) WORLD JEWISH CONGRESS NYK
(330 WEST 42 ST SEE SPL INSTNS ON FILE (RELAY VIA SI)=

HAVE RECEIVED THROUGH FOREIGN OFFICE FOLLOWING MESSAGE FROM
RIEGNER GENEVA STOP (RECEIVED ALARMING REPORT THAT IN FUHRERS
HEADQUARTERS PLAN DISCUSSED AND UNDER CONSIDERATION ALL JEWS
IN COUNTRIES OCCUPIED OR CONTROLLED GERMANY NUMBER 3-1/2 TO
4 MILLION SHOULD AFTER DEPORTATION AND CONCENTRATION IN EAST
AT ONE BLOW EXTERMINATED TO RESOLVE ONCE FOR ALL JEWISH
QUESTION IN EUROPE=

CFM 3-1/2 4. QUICKEST, SUREST AND SAFEST WAY TO SEND MONEY IS BY TELEGRAPH OR CABLE

WESTERN UNION CABLEGRAM

THE COMPANY WILL APPRECIATE SUGGESTIONS FROM ITS PATRONS CONCERNING ITS SERVICE   1280

CLASS OF SERVICE — This is a full-rate Cablegram unless its deferred character is indicated by a suitable symbol preceding the address.

R. B. WHITE PRESIDENT   NEWCOMB CARLTON CHAIRMAN OF THE BOARD   J. C. WILLEVER FIRST VICE-PRESIDENT

SYMBOLS — LC Deferred Cablegram / NLT Cable Night Letter / Ship Radiogram

NV15 2/59=

STOP ACTION REPORTED PLANNED FOR AUTUMN METHODS UNDER
DISCUSSION INCLUDING PRUSSIC ACID STOP WE TRANSMIT
INFORMATION WITH ALL NECESSARY RESERVATION AS EXACTITUDE
CANNOT BE CONFIRMED STOP INFORMANT STATED TO HAVE CLOSE
CONNEXIONS WITH HIGHEST GERMEN AUTHORITIES AND HIS REPORTS
GENERALLY RELIABLE STOP INFORM AND CONSULT NEWYORK STOP
FOREIGN OFFICE AS NO INFORMATION BEARING ON OR CONFIRMING
STORY=
SAMUEL SILVERMAN.

THE QUICKEST, SUREST AND SAFEST WAY TO SEND MONEY IS BY TELEGRAPH OR CABLE

In August 1942, Geneva-based World Jewish Congress representative Gerhardt Riegner cabled his New York and London offices to report the Nazi plan to murder with poison gas all the Jews in occupied Europe. Riegner's alarming report was cabled to Stephen Wise, who, in turn, alerted the State Department and other American Jewish leaders. By December of that year, when the United States and Britain publicly confirmed that mass murders of Jews were taking place, many of Europe's Jews were already dead.

"Riegner Telegram" to Stephen Wise, August 29, 1942. Courtesy of the Jacob Rader Marcus Center of the American Jewish Archives.

believe. Yet the emptying of crowded ghettos and the rolling eastward of trains packed with Jews from Western Europe provided a kind of corroboration. When the State Department finally confirmed the facts and authorized Wise to inform the public, major American newspapers did not carry the announcement on the front page. The war was not going well for the Allies in November 1942, yet the decision not to make the extermination of European Jews front-page news also reflected fears among Jewish owners of papers, such as the *New York Times,* that the full glare of publicity would harm the Jewish cause. Despite the obvious surprise attack by the Japanese, too many Americans seemed ready to blame the Jews for the United States' entry into the war. Roosevelt's statement threatening punishment for war crimes avoided explicit mention of European Jews. Since no American troops occupied European soil, punishment would have to wait until the Allies won the war.

Shocked and outraged, American Jews mourned their losses. They planned mammoth rallies to convince Roosevelt to create centers of refuge. They organized an American Jewish Conference to try to unify all American Jews behind a program of rescue. They staged a dramatic pageant paying tribute to the beauty of Jewish culture and the courage of European Jews. Though the audience was moved to tears, though the rally at Madison Square Garden did warrant a banner headline, though the Conference, after much wrangling, brought diametrically opposed Jews into one meeting hall, these efforts yielded few concrete results. In April 1943 the Warsaw Ghetto erupted in revolt. It was a daring and hopeless last stand against the Nazis. But it inspired some American Jews to enlist. They would fight on behalf of the United States and European Jews against their common enemy, Nazi Germany.

Over half a million American Jews, including Lillian's son, did end up wearing Uncle Sam's uniforms. They served in all branches of the armed forces and on all fronts of the war. Military service transformed them. Integrated into their units, Jewish soldiers and sailors discovered how different Americans were from expectations based on movies and civics books. They learned that many Americans had never met a Jew before and often held stereotypes about them. Yet as the military taught them how to fight to defend their country, it gave them lessons on how to defend their religion, Judaism, and their people, Jews. And despite the deep-seated bias against Jews held by many in the regular Army and Navy, the armed forces adjusted to their diverse civilian recruits. Recognizing Judaism as one of the official religions of democracy, the military enabled the emergence of a new faith for Americans: "the Judeo-Christian tradition." The tragic deaths at sea of four chaplains—a Catholic, a Jew, and two Protestants—exemplified its hallmark of brotherhood. The commitment of Americans to the Judeo-Christian tradition as a democratic religion would spread widely in the postwar period during Dwight D. Eisenhower's presidency.

The discovery of the death camps in the spring of 1945 made some American Jews question the policy prioritizing victory in war over the rescue of European Jews. The Holocaust's dimensions staggered the imagination. Six million died, murdered in the most gruesome fashion. The War Refugee Board, established in January 1944 before the D-Day invasion of

Europe, failed to save the then undecimated Jewish populations of Hungary and Rumania. The decision reached by Zionists at the Biltmore Hotel in June 1942, during the dark days of the war, to support the establishment of a Jewish state also failed to produce consensus. American Jews continued to spar over Zionism. Great Britain refused to reverse its restrictive immigration policy. Jewish refugees, unwanted everywhere in the world, would have been welcomed in the Jewish homeland. Therefore relatively few were saved.

As American Jewish GIs returned to civilian life, they brought with them lessons learned in uniform. A new militancy entered American Jewish life; these men would not accept discrimination as the American way. Civil rights acquired an unexpected urgency. So did the struggle for a Jewish state. As one GI put it, the Army taught him to "push back" if someone tried to push him around. New solutions were needed for old problems.

Lillian did not have any relatives remaining in Europe. But if she had, she might have heard from one of them the accusation she leveled at her father and his friends on her first Sabbath evening in Boston in 1921. "Why are you showing off what you did in America, for whom, for us? Showing off about what you ate in restaurants, or how you spent your evenings in the theaters and at concerts? Didn't it bother you that you had families who were starving?" She had turned then to her father, "you knew that Kamen was on the front lines. Didn't you read the Yiddish papers? Or were you so sure that your families had perished that it was necessary to go to the theater in order to forget your sorrows?"[4] It was a damning indictment of America, and of Jews for becoming so American. Lillian never forgot her teenage tirade. But though she had a son in uniform and she raised money and signed petitions for European Jews, she knew that she had become American. As Nazi Germany ruthlessly murdered millions of Jews, she could only act within the bounds of ordinary life on the home front.

The two decades between the closing of the gates of immigration in 1924 and the end of World War II marked a period of radical adjustments. Second-generation Jews assumed positions of authority and set the tone for a diverse community. Comfortable in their identities as American Jews, they developed patterns of living that blended American and Jewish components into a middle-class synthesis. In religion, politics, and culture, Jews created an American Jewish heritage that could be passed on confidently to the next generation. Ideology, so important in this era, would not survive into the postwar period. Chastened by war, American Jews, who now constituted the largest, wealthiest, and most secure diaspora Jewish society, were ready to shoulder the burdens and responsibilities of leadership at the dawn of the "American century."

THEIR FIGHT IS OUR FIGHT

GIVE TODAY

UNITED JEWISH APPEAL
FOR REFUGEES, OVERSEAS NEEDS AND PALESTINE

American Jewry Since 1945

Jack Wertheimer

T he Second World War proved to be a watershed in the history of America's Jews no less than it was generally in the history of the United States. Like their neighbors, Jews participated in the booming expansion of the postwar decades. Thanks to the dynamic economic growth of those years, the children and grandchildren of East-European immigrants rapidly climbed the socioeconomic ladder, contributing to a widening circle of endeavors. American Jews also joined the urban exodus and settled on the new suburban frontiers, a process of geographic transplantation that depleted Jewish neighborhoods in many cities and challenged Jews to create new kinds of communities to replace them. Like other Americans, Jews also enjoyed a baby boom after the fallow years of economic depression and war.[1] These developments profoundly transformed the private and domestic lives of Jews and reshaped their religious and communal institutions too.

World War II itself irrevocably altered the nature of American Jewry's relationship to other Jewish communities. With the ascendance of America's military power, economic might, and cultural influence, the Jews of the United States rapidly took the lead in Jewish international affairs, buoyed by a new self-confidence born of their heightened sense of security and their country's global stature. The destruction of European Jewry created not only a leadership vacuum that American Jews filled, but also posed a new challenge to the American Jewish community, which had come to rely upon a constant inflow of new and ever larger waves of immigrants to

With the Statue of Liberty looming in the background, this poster reminds American Jews of their own immigrant roots and urges them to support the overseas needs of refugees in Europe and Palestine.

Fodor, "Their Fight Is Our Fight: Give Today!" United Jewish Appeal Poster [N.Y., 1945-1946]. From the HUC Skirball Cultural Center Museum Collection, Los Angeles, California. Photography by Susan Einstein.

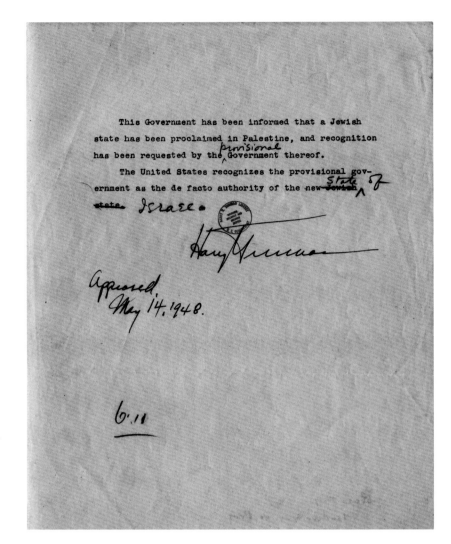

This Government has been informed that a Jewish state has been proclaimed in Palestine, and recognition has been requested by the *provisional* Government thereof.

The United States recognizes the provisional government as the de facto authority of the new *State of* ~~state.~~ *Israel.*

Harry Truman

Approved.
May 14, 1948.

6.11

Displayed here is President Truman's May 14, 1948, note recognizing the State of Israel, with his hand-written corrections.

Harry S. Truman. *Official Recognition of the State of Israel, May 14, 1948. Courtesy of the Harry S. Truman Presidential Library, National Archives and Records Administration.*

swell its ranks. In the short run, survivors of the *Shoah* brought an important infusion of traditionally leaning Jews, and particularly of Orthodox rabbinic leadership. In the longer term, however, the Holocaust meant that fewer Jews from abroad could be expected to immigrate and thereby revitalize Jewish life, as had previous waves of Jewish newcomers. The future of communities in the United States now depended almost entirely upon American Jewry's ability to renew itself and to retain the allegiance of its young.

The postwar era was also characterized by the gradual closing of the key rifts that had long divided America's Jews. At least in the immediate postwar decades, Jews enjoyed a far greater degree of communal unity than had been the case earlier in the century. The demonstrable vulnerability of European Jewry during the Holocaust, coupled with Israel's establishment in 1948, resolved the enervating battles between Zionists and anti-Zionists that for decades had riven the American Jewish community into warring ideological factions. With the exception of a tiny embattled minority, American Jews firmly identified with the Jewish state. Tensions also eased considerably by the end of World War II between the so-called Uptown and Downtown populations, the "native" Jews of German and Sephardic origin and the late-nineteenth- and early-twentieth-century immigrants from Russia, Galicia, Hungary, and Rumania. By virtue of their sheer numbers and engagement with Jewish life, the descendants of East-European Jews assumed positions of leadership in the American Jewish community after the war. The immediate postwar years also brought significant consensus on domestic and foreign policy questions across the spectrum of Jewish organizations—in marked distinction to the fractious debates that had racked the Jewish community earlier in the century and even during the war years. In short, American Jews confronted a dramatically changed environment in the aftermath of the war.

A chief characteristic of that altered landscape was the openness of American society to Jews and many other minorities. When a Jewish woman named Bess Myerson was selected as "Miss America" just a few days after Japan's surrender in September of 1945 it seemed to presage the entry of growing numbers of American Jewish men and women into mainstream society. Having grown up in a Yiddish-speaking home in the Bronx, Myerson exemplified the second-generation Jews, the children of East-European immigrants, who by virtue of sheer pluck and determination were intent on succeeding in the *Goldine Medina*, the Golden Land of America. Her selection also dramatized the openness of America to talented and energetic Jews.[2]

With the passing of each decade, ever more occupational and social barriers fell, as Jews rose to positions of prominence that had once been unthinkable: prestigious universities and colleges that had once imposed quotas on Jewish students appointed Jews to their presidencies and to positions of board leadership; major corporations that had barred Jews now hired them for key executive positions; high status civic organizations and boards of hospitals, museums, and orchestras invited Jews to assume positions of volunteer leadership; and individuals of Jewish origin achieved prominence in journalism and television, and on the stage and screen.[3] By the closing decades of the century, a Jewish woman had hurtled into space as an astronaut, Henry Kissinger had served as the chief foreign policy architect of the United States, musicians such as Neil Diamond and Billy Joel won renown as performers and composers of popular music, women such as Betty Friedan and Gloria Steinem had transformed the feminist movement, Jerry Seinfeld starred as the king of sitcom television, Rosalyn Yalow, a physicist, had won the Nobel

The crowning of Bess Myerson as Miss America in 1945 was viewed by some American Jews as marking America's new openness to its Jewish community.

"Bess Myerson seated on the Miss New York City float," Atlantic City, New Jersey, 1945. © AP/Wide World Photos. New York World-Telegram and Sun *Newspaper Photograph Collection, Prints and Photographs Division.*

presenting
Miss New York City

Prize in physiology and medicine, Steven Spielberg had garnered acclaim as a premier Holly-wood director, and Senator Joseph Lieberman had run as the nominee of the Democratic party for the vice-presidency of the United States. In contrast to American Jews of earlier eras, these individuals achieved their success even though they made no attempt to hide their identities, alter their names, or downplay their connection to the Jewish community. Like the Hall of Fame baseball player Sandy Koufax, who declined to pitch for his team when the first game of the 1965 World Series fell on Yom Kippur, these Jews understood that Americans had generally become more respectful of Jews who took a principled position of identification with their religion and people.

Impressive as were the strides taken by these and many other individuals, the overall trends attest in the aggregate to high levels of achievement and integration across the American Jewish populace. By the beginning of the twenty-first century, a quarter of all adult Jews had earned a graduate degree versus 6 percent of all Americans. And whereas 55 percent of Jewish adults had graduated from college, only 29 percent of all Americans had done so.[4] Among younger American Jews, these trends were even more pronounced. In the 1970s it was found that nearly three quarters of Jews in their thirties had attended college (but had not necessarily graduated); by the end of the century, the figure grew to 90 percent.[5]

These investments in education also yielded impressive occupational rewards. Surveys conducted in a few cities during the 1960s indicated that approximately 20 to 33 percent of Jews already worked as professionals (the numbers varied from one city to the next) and between 30 to 50 percent were managers.[6] By the beginning of the twenty-first century, over 60 percent of employed Jews were in one of the three highest status job categories: 41 percent were profes-sionals or in technical fields, 13 percent worked in management or as executives, and 7 percent in business and finance.[7] Jews were significantly represented in law firms, on Wall Street, in the medical profession, in the real estate industry, and in Silicon Valley. Their meteoric rise in the American academy was evidenced by the following gains: it was estimated in 1940 that Jews constituted 2 percent of the American professorate; thirty five years later, the figure was estimated at 10 percent overall and a quarter of the professorate teaching at Ivy League schools.[8] All of these occupational achievements translated into rising earning power: according to the most extensive study of the subject conducted in 1990, the income of American Jews exceeded that of every other American religious group.[9]

Encouraged by the feminist revolution, Jewish women kept pace with their male counter-parts.[10] By 1990, when it came to educational attainments, the gender gap between Jewish women and men had narrowed considerably, leading researchers to conclude that "the remaining differences between Jewish men and women seem well on their way to disappearing, even before the gender gap in higher education disappears in the wider population."[11] In the age group from 35 to 44, only 7 percent fewer women earned college degrees than men of the same age. Forty three percent of Jews between ages 30 to 34 who earned medical degrees were women. And even though many Jewish women took a few years off to raise their young children, they ultimately enjoyed high levels of occupational achievement and often remained in the work-force longer than Jewish men did.[12] The consequences of these changes in women's lives were, of course, far-reaching, reshaping their decision-making roles within families, their domestic arrangements, marital choices, and family size, and what they came to expect of Jewish religious and communal institutions that had previously limited their participation and leadership.[13]

As American Jewish women and men strove for ever-higher educational attainments, professional success, and social integration, they became highly mobile. Like their neighbors, postwar American Jews have been on the move. Immediately after the war, as we have noted, they relocated primarily to the suburbs, the newly constructed housing developments beyond the city limits that offered more spacious housing accommodations than urban apartment units and a patch of green lawn. Greater distances in the suburbs required parents to rethink the nature and extent of Jewish education for their children and to develop new types of communities to replace abandoned urban neighborhoods. Jewish Community Centers and synagogues, incorporating classroom and meeting room space, recreational facilities, gyms, and the like, now played the role of surrogate neighborhood on the lonely suburban frontier.[14]

Even in the immediate postwar years, not all the geographic movement was directed to the suburbs. Former GIs who had been stationed in more temperate climates during the war years moved their families to the beckoning "Golden Cities" of America's Sun Belt.[15] The Jewish population in places such as Miami and Los Angeles began to swell, the first wave of a large population shift that would redraw the map of the American Jewish community. Before World War II, an estimated 68 percent of Jews lived in the Northeast and only some 5 percent lived in the Western states.[16] And as late as 1981, it was estimated that 57 percent of Jews lived in the Northeast, 16 percent in the South, and 15 percent in the West.[17] By the beginning of the twenty-first century, Jews continued to be over-represented in the Northeast, but by a markedly lower percentage than earlier in the century (43 percent versus 19 percent of the general population); they were proportionately represented in the West (22 percent of Jews as compared

...therefore I command you saying open your hand, open it, to your brother, to your poor brother, to your needy brother in your land.
Deuteronomy 15:11

GIVE-UJA

United Jewish Appeal of Greater New York
220 West 58th Street, New York, New York 10019

This poster by artist Mark Podwal was commissioned by the United Jewish Appeal of Greater New York. It depicts a man seated on a suitcase with an image of the Kremlin in the background. Underneath are the words in Hebrew and English: "Therefore I command you saying open your hand, open it, to your brother, to your poor brother, to your needy brother in your land." (Deuteronomy 15:11)

Mark Podwal (artist), GIVE-UJA, New York, ca. 1976, Yanker Poster Collection, Prints and Photographs Division.

to 23 percent of the general populace); and they were under-represented in the Midwest (13 percent vs. 23 percent) and in the South (23 percent vs. 35 percent).[18]

The geographic and social mobility enjoyed by Jewish individuals in the postwar decades was not an unalloyed boon for the Jews as a group, for it was precisely the openness and hospitality of American society that also challenged Jews as they strove to maintain their group identity. The very social permeability that enabled individual Jews to move easily to new geographic settings and occupations also facilitated the movement of Jews away from the group. By 1990 it was estimated that more Jews were converting to other religions than Gentiles were converting to Judaism.[19] Significant percentages of Jews never affiliated with synagogues or any other Jewish organizations, with the lowest rates of affiliation evident in communities with large percentages of newcomers and transients.[20] Intermarriage between Jews and non-Jews soared after the mid-1960s, reaching 47 percent by the late 1990s; and according to the most optimistic assessments, only one third of children in such families were raised as Jews.[21] Indeed, survey research made it plain that when Jews lived at a distance from centers of large Jewish population, when they intermarried, and when they tended to have few Jewish friends they were generally unlikely to participate in organized Jewish life or to identify strongly as Jews.[22]

These losses, in turn, have been reflected in the flat population figures of the American Jewish community. According to estimates,[23] there were some 5.3 million Jews in the United States in 1957.[24] Even with the influx of a quarter of a million immigrants from the former Soviet Union, at least an equal number from Israel, and tens of thousands more from Iran, Latin America, and South Africa, estimates of the total Jewish population of the United States in the early twenty-first century ranged between 5.2 million and 6.1 million.[25] Relative to the total American populace, moreover, the Jewish population has been in free fall, dropping from a high of 3.7 percent in 1937 to barely 2 percent by the end of the twentieth century. In sum, the open society had provided manifold opportunities to individual Jews, but also had posed great challenges to their group existence.

Organized Jewish life in this period comprised an impressive assemblage of voluntary institutions. By the end of the twentieth century, American Jews supported approximately 3,700 synagogues, hundreds of Jewish day schools, summer camps, and Jewish Community Centers, dozens of museums, Jewish film festivals, and arts centers, and a wide range of other educational and cultural programs; they maintained a network of community relations organizations to combat anti-Semitism and forge intergroup alliances; and they supported a range of philanthropic groups to aid Jews abroad, particularly in Israel.[26] By the late 1990s, the combined organizations of the Jewish community raised some nine billion dollars in the form of donations, fees for service, tuition payments, state grants, and membership dues.[27] This vast enterprise, once dubbed by *Fortune* magazine "the miracle of Jewish giving,"[28] was created in the absence of state intervention that would have compelled Jews to belong to separate communities. Instead, it relied upon the willingness of Jews to establish, join, and maintain organizations. But it was a system that by virtue of its pluralism and voluntarism also encouraged the spawning of ever-new agencies and continually struggled to achieve coordination and centralization. It is all the more remarkable, therefore, that despite powerful centrifugal pressures, American Jews in the postwar decades united sufficiently to support and protect Jews at home and abroad.[29]

The glue that held this far-flung institutional structure together during the first postwar decades was a two-pronged "functional consensus," based on "assuring Israel's security and striving for a liberal America."[30] Both aims were linked to America's self-chosen role as the international guardian of democratic ideals and fair play: the American Jewish community insisted that the United States owed Israel strong support because the Jewish state was an embattled bastion of democracy surrounded by autocratic states. On the domestic front, the defense of Jews was now understood as part of a larger campaign of social action, rather than solely as a parochial cause, to insure that no group in America suffered from unfair treatment.[31]

Energized by these twin goals, American Jewish organizations achieved a high degree of common purpose in the aftermath of the Second World War. Religious groupings and defense agencies broadened their concern from the battle against anti-Semitism to support for legislation that protected all Americans: they fought for laws against housing and employment discrimination and threw their support behind labor unions, a series of campaigns that brought them into partnerships with Americans of different faiths and ethnic communities. The rationale offered by the National Jewish Community Relations Advisory Council, an umbrella agency of defense groups, was that opportunities for Jews can best "be realized in a society in which all persons are secure, whatever their religion, race or origin."[32] Not surprisingly, Jewish organizations across the religious and ideological spectrum played an active role as lobbyists during the

Abraham Joshua Heschel (on right), with (from left) Ralph Abernathy, Martin Luther King, and Ralph Bunche on the civil rights march from Selma, Alabama, to Montgomery in 1965.

Rabbi Louis Finkelstein, the president of the Jewish Theological Seminary, Conservative Judaism's central educational and theological institution, was featured on the October 15, 1951, cover of Time *magazine, signaling the coming of age of the American born and bred Conservative movement.*

"The Days of Fear Are Over," in Time: The Weekly Newsmagazine, *October 15, 1951. General Collections. Time Life Pictures/Getty Images*

legal struggles to end racial inequality, whereas others partook of the desegregation battles in the South during the civil rights struggles of the fifties and sixties. Rabbis such as Abraham Joshua Heschel literally marched arm-in-arm with Martin Luther King, Jr., in Selma. During the quarter century between World War II and the Vietnam War, Jewish and black organizations were, as one writer put it, "firmly established in the public mind as the nation's premier tribunes of conscience and voices of the downtrodden."[33]

More generally, Jews and their organizations engaged actively in intergroup activities in order to widen their circle of friends and allies. As early as 1951, *Time* magazine featured Louis Finkelstein, president of the Jewish Theological Seminary, on its cover to honor him for the pioneering role he played in the field of interfaith and intergroup relations. Finkelstein involved himself in such efforts in order to win respectability in academic and religious circles for Judaism as a significant civilization.[34] With the passage of several decades, such efforts yielded rich rewards: Judaism was increasingly regarded as not only on a par with Protestantism and Catholicism (and later in the century also with Eastern religions), as a valuable legacy for all Americans, but also as a system of thinking and culture, richly deserving of study by Americans of different back-grounds.[35] The spread of Jewish studies programs at American institutions of higher learning, the popularity of Jewish museums and also Holocaust memorials, and the incorporation of Jewish themes in serious works of fiction, poetry, art, theater, and the cinema all attested to the opening of *Jewish* life to the *American* public. These developments, so much taken for granted by the beginning of the twenty-first century, in fact, represented a major new development of the past half a century in the relationship between Jews and their neighbors. The Jewish experience had become widely accessible and respected.[36]

Even as they invested their energies in the task of mediating their religious and ethnic culture to American society at large, American Jews simultaneously attended to international matters. Indeed, the focal point of American Jewish organizational life for much of this period was to rally support for the great Jewish international causes. Central to these efforts were Israel's financial and political needs. In 1948, the year of Israel's founding, American Jews raised some $200 million, a figure that then declined to an annual fund-raising of $110 to $130 million until 1967. The Six Day War prompted donations of $318 million, and the Yom Kippur War elicited contributions of $686 million. In the ensuing years, hundreds of millions more were remitted to Israel annually, and special campaigns added to those totals, most notably the one-billion-dollar campaign in the early 1990s to help settle Jews from the former Soviet Union in Israel, and some $360 million collected during the so-called Second Intifada in the early twenty-first century.[37] On top of these sums, American Jews channeled hundreds of millions of additional dollars to Israeli institutions through various "Friends of" organizations. Equally important, Jewish organizations established an infrastructure to advocate on behalf of Israel: key Jewish organizations banded together in 1954 to found the Conference of Presidents of Major American Jewish Organizations to lobby the executive branch of the U.S. government on international matters on behalf of American Jews. And the same year witnessed the creation of the American Israel Public Affairs Committee (AIPAC), regarded by both admirers and detractors as one of the best organized and most influential political action committees, to advocate for Israel within the legislative branch. The latter was particularly effective in mobilizing its 55,000 contributors as lobbyists.[38]

During the quarter century between the emergence of the "Jews of Silence" in the mid-1960s to the fall of communism in Eastern Europe in the early 1990s, the second great cause to mobilize American Jewish organizations was the struggle to aid Soviet Jews trapped behind the Iron Curtain. The key national organizations of American Jews lobbied successive American administrations to pressure the Soviet Union to allow Jews the right of emigration. Grassroots organizations, such as the Student Struggle for Soviet Jewry and the Union of Councils for Soviet Jewry, coordinated their activities with mainstream groups, such as the National Conference on Soviet Jewry, to mobilize protest demonstrations in cities around the country. The high point of these activities were mass rallies that brought hundreds of thousands of Americans, mainly Jews, to Washington, D.C. Perhaps the greatest victory in this campaign came in the form of the Jackson-Vanik Amendment, linking American trade concessions with the Soviet Union's easing of emigration restrictions on Jews and other persecuted minorities. Although the struggles to win support from the American government on behalf of Israel and Soviet Jewry certainly were marked by fierce institutional

New York City's annual Salute to Israel parade serves as an opportunity for the Jewish community to show its solidarity with Israel and to express its own distinct ethnic identity. This poster was issued for the May 10, 1970, parade, which marked Israel's twenty-second anniversary.

Salute to Israel Parade, New York, 1970. Yanker Poster Collection, Prints and Photographs Division.

LET MY PEOPLE GO!

Student Struggle for Soviet Jewry

rivalries and policy disagreements, these causes ultimately served to unify American Jews in epic struggles to provide succor for coreligionists in need. As such, they served as major achievements of the post-Holocaust era both for the help they directed to Jews abroad and the unity of purpose they achieved for American Jews.[39]

Even as American Jewish groups strove to work in concert, counter-vailing pressures emerged in the early 1970s that weakened the "functional consensus" and fostered polarization. Borrowing from the confrontational style of sixties protest movements, youthful Jewish activists marshaled their forces at mass demonstrations and sit-ins, demanding that "the Jewish establishment" change its policies. On the right, the Jewish Defense League, headed by Rabbi Meir Kahane, emerged in the 1960s to chide communal leaders for their alleged passivity in the face of anti-Semitic provocations; on the left, groups such as Breira protested the alleged lock-step support of established organizations for the policies of Israel in the period after the Yom Kippur War of 1973. Over the next decades, critics on both ends of the spectrum developed their cases and hammered away at the twin pillars of the "functional consensus." Thinkers associated with *Commentary* maga-zine formulated a Neo-Conservative critique of the unquestioning liberal policies espoused by Jewish organizations, arguing that it was one thing to support an end to discrimination but an entirely different matter for Jews to embrace such liberal causes as affirmative action, abortion on demand, inflexible separationism between church and state, lavish government spending on welfare programs, and campaigns to weaken national defense. Focusing on a range of causes favored by the left, neo-Conservatives ques-tioned whether liberalism was congruent with Jewish values or interests. Simultaneously, Jews on the left, through their house organ *Tikkun*, ques-tioned the morality of American Jewish organizations that reflexively, in their view, sided with Israeli policies. More generally, they bemoaned the failure of Jewish leaders to "still [be] moved by the radical spirit of the Prophets."[40] With the emergence of an articulate radical left and neo-Conservative right, powerful forces were pulling the American Jewish community in polar opposite directions.

Simultaneously, Jewish communal unity was rent by heightened religious tensions. All of the religious movements of American Judaism were forced to respond to a series of new challenges emerging in the last decades of the twentieth century: the rising rate of intermarriage and the resulting question of how to integrate such families into the Jewish com-munity; the feminist and gay revolutions and the demands of women and

Opposite: From the mid-1960s until the breakup of the Soviet Union in the early 1990s, American Jews mobilized on behalf of Jews behind the iron curtain, pressuring the Soviets to allow them to emigrate. This poster shows a long line of Soviet Jews, suitcases in hand, walking towards the promised land, represented by a sun in the shape of a Star of David. The title of the poster is "Let My People Go!"

Student Struggle for Soviet Jewry, Let My People Go! *[between 1973 and 1980]. Yanker Poster Collection, Prints and Photographs Division.*

After a massive rally in 1972 on behalf of Soviet Jewry, the Greater New York Conference on Soviet Jewry publicly thanked those who attended, making the point that there is strength in numbers.

The Greater New York Conference on Soviet Jewry, "New York, you've really done it! ... 3 million Soviet Jews thank you," New York [1972]. Yanker Poster Collection, Prints and Photographs Division.

The success of efforts to win freedom for Soviet Jews, encouraged American Jewish groups to seek the right of emigration for Jews in Syria and later Ethiopia.

World Union of Jewish Students, "Freedom for Syrian Jews!" ca. 1976 Yanker Poster Collection, Prints and Photographs Division.

gay and lesbian Jews for equality in religious life; and the declining levels of synagogue affiliation and involvement among fourth- and fifth-generation Americans Jews, which forced all Jewish institutions to compete for members among the dwindling numbers of engaged Jews. The permeability of American society, the experimentation of Jews with religious syncretism, the increasing emphasis upon individual choice in religious life, and the emergence of many new types of families prompted religious groups to formulate new positions on questions of moment: What are the limits of Judaism? What is a Jewish family? What is a Jewish marriage? Who is a Jew? Given the vastly different religious outlooks of Orthodox, Conservative, Reform, Reconstructionist, Jewish Renewal, and Humanist Judaism it was perhaps inevitable that religious polarization would intensify during the last decades of the twentieth century,[41] a development that found its parallels in the conflict within other religious denominations engaged in the culture wars of the late twentieth century.

In addition to the effects of ideological and religious conflicts, Jewish communal cohesion was weakened in the late twentieth century by a powerful spirit of individualism that generally weakened group attachments within American society.[42] American Jews were no more immune from such tendencies than their neighbors. By the beginning of the twentieth century, it appeared to some observers that:

more and more, the meaning of Judaism in America transpires within the self. American Jews have drawn the activity and significance of their group identity into the subjectivity of the individual, the activities of the family, and the few institutions (primarily the synagogue) which are seen as extensions of the intimate sphere.[43]

Among younger Jews, this translated into declining levels of attachment to Israel and the peoplehood of the Jews,[44] the diminution of charitable giving to Jewish causes, and weakening levels of affiliation with Jewish institutions, a shift of enormous potential significance for the communal arrangements of American Jews.

Still, as worrisome as these trends were for the health and vitality of organized Jewish activities, they were matched by other developments over the past twenty years that reflect a new determination within the organized Jewish community to renew itself. Interest in Jewish education for people of all ages surged: more young people enrolled in all-day Jewish schools than ever before, many attending from preschool through high school; federations of Jewish philanthropy and Jewish Community Centers assumed responsibility for funding preschool, camping, and teen programs infused with Jewish content; across the country, groups stepped up their efforts to deliver Jewish adult education; philanthropists teamed with existing agencies to develop innovative educational programming on the local, national, and international level, including the Birthright Israel program, which sent young Jews between the ages of eighteen and twenty-six on a free study trip to Israel;[45] Jewish organizations across the spectrum harnessed the new medium of the Internet to deliver Jewish content; and new national initiatives were launched to provide support for the providers of Jewish education.[46] With the help of organizational and religious consultants, synagogues have engaged in self-scrutiny and a deliberate effort at "renewal"; across the Jewish denominational spectrum, congregations have introduced more accessible forms of synagogue music, provided more participatory services, upgraded opportunities for serious engagement with Jewish texts, and placed a new emphasis on petitionary, private prayers for healing—all efforts designed to make the synagogue more intimate and meaningful. Once relegated to volunteer roles, Jewish women have been serving as rabbis, cantors, principals, and congregational presidents, thereby vastly expanding and altering the pool of talented individuals assuming positions of Jewish leadership, particularly in the religious domain. And as another symptom of the serious effort to bring renewal to the community, Jewish philanthropists have forged partnerships with established agencies, challenging them to strive for excellence and to innovate new approaches.

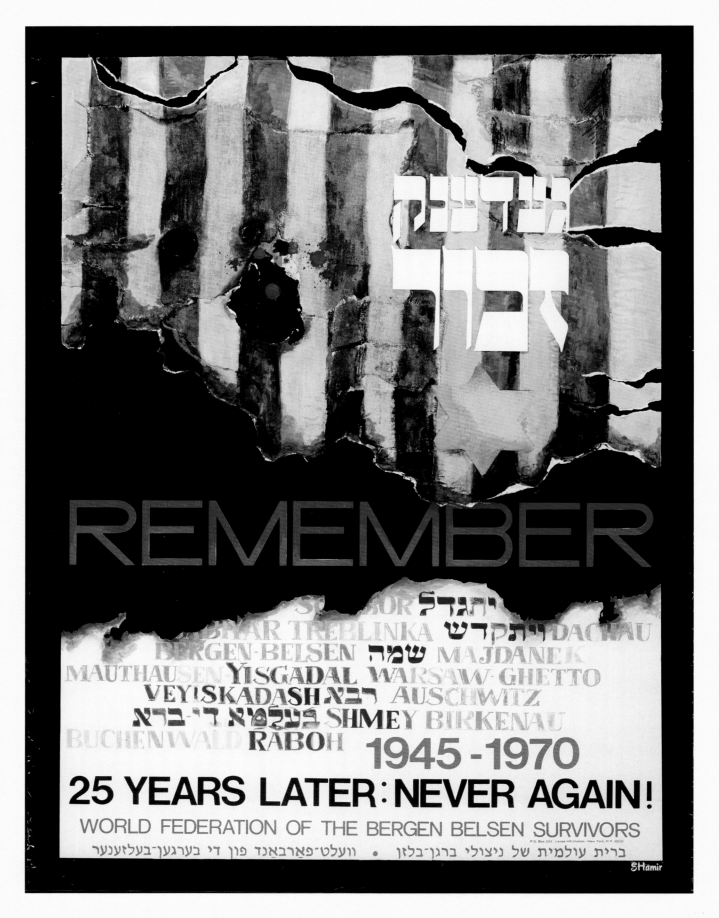

As they prepare to celebrate the 350th anniversary of Jewish life in the United States, America's Jews can look back with gratitude to a history of remarkable achievement on these shores. Jews who lived through the postwar period can marvel at how in their own lifetimes they witnessed the continuing opening of America to Jews and Jewish culture. The postwar decades brought unprecedented levels of acceptance and integration within American society; and Jews made enormous strides to strengthen their communal enterprise and raise levels of Jewish literacy, even as they launched impressive initiatives in the international arena to aid beleaguered coreligionists abroad and in the domestic arena to combat all forms of discrimination. Still, as they look forward to the next era in their history, American Jews also engage in sober and mature self-examination to address the pressing challenges to their own collective vitality in the United States.

Opposite: This Holocaust remembrance poster was issued in 1970, marking the twenty-fifth anniversary of the defeat of the Nazis. Below the word "Remember," which appears in Yiddish, Hebrew, and English on the poster, are names of notorious death camps, intertwined with the Hebrew words, in red, of the kaddish, the Jewish prayer for the dead.

World Federation of the Bergen Belsen Survivors, "Remember So[bi]bor. . . Dachau, Bergen-Belsen. . . : 1945-1970: 25 years later— never again!", New York, 1970. Yanker Poster Collection, Prints and Photographs Division.

American Judaism

Jonathan D. Sarna

T he twenty-three Jews "big as well as little" who arrived in New Amsterdam in 1654 could not have imagined that one day historians would see them as progenitors of something called "American Judaism." They had arrived in New Amsterdam as impoverished refugees and sought permission from the authorities to settle down and form a permanent Jewish community in North America, to "navigate and trade near and in New Netherland, and to live and reside there."[1] They did not fight for the right to worship in public, and for years they worshipped privately, out of public view. Only in 1685, twenty years after New Amsterdam had fallen to the British and been renamed New York, did the city's approximately twenty Jewish families petition for public worship. Their petition was denied: "publique Worship," the city's Common Council informed them, "is Tolerated...but to those that professe faith in Christ."[2]

New Amsterdam's Jews, like those of Trieste, Bordeaux, Amsterdam, London, and the Caribbean, were port Jews; they lived in societies that placed a premium on commerce and trade. The rights that these Jews battled hardest to obtain were civil and economic, not religious. Public worship, while desirable, was not an absolute Jewish religious requirement.

This Hanukkah lamp incorporates Statue of Liberty figurines as holders for the candles that are lit to mark the eight days of Hanukkah, Judaism's annual commemoration of the second century BCE victory of the Maccabees over the Syrians. In linking America's quintessential symbol of freedom and opportunity with Judaism's celebration of freedom from oppression, this menorah represents a perfect metaphor for the twin sensibilities that give American Judaism its unique character.

Manfred Anson, Statue of Liberty Hanukkah Lamp (Cast Brass), New Jersey, design 1985, fabrication 2004. Gift of Dr. Aaron J. Feingold in loving memory of his father Saul Feingold; and Peachy and Mark Levy. Hebraic Section. Photography by Susan Einstein.

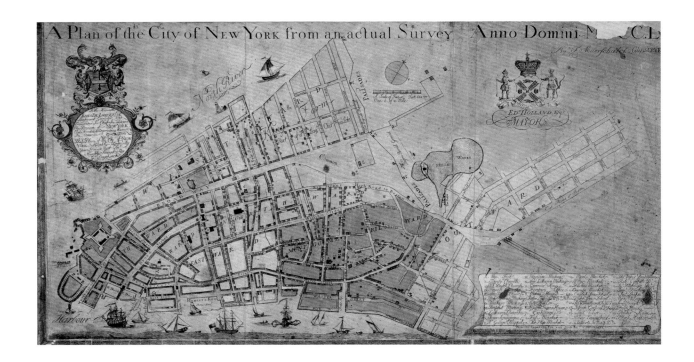

This early map of New York reflects the extraordinary diversity of the city in the eighteenth century and its hospitality to newcomers. The map provides locations for the houses of worship for Quakers, Lutherans, Catholics, Moravians, Presbyterians, Baptists, and Jews. Marked on this map (see inset) is the Mill Street location of America's first synagogue, Shearith Israel (The Remnant of Israel). Though the congregation continues to this day, neither the original synagogue building nor the street on which it was located has survived.

F. Maerschalck, A plan of the city of New York from an actual survey, anno Domini, M[D]CC,LV [[New York?] 1755?]. Geography and Map Division.

Granted the right to settle and trade openly, they conceded to worship in private, just as enterprising religious dissenters did throughout Early Modern Europe.[3]

Public worship became available to Jews without any fanfare or known change in the law around the turn of the eighteenth century, just about the time when New York's first Quaker Meeting House was erected, and before the Baptists and Catholics had opened churches in the city. For the next 125 years, the synagogue dominated Jewish religious life in New York. Indeed, the synagogue and the organized Jewish community became one and the same—a synagogue community—and as such it assumed primary responsibility for preserving and maintaining local Jewish life.[4]

The synagogue established in New York was located in a small rented house on Mill Street, today South William Street, but then popularly known as Jews' Alley. The congregation's official name became Kahal Kadosh Shearith Israel (the Holy Congregation Remnant of Israel). Like most New World synagogues of the eighteenth century its name hinted at the promise of redemption, recalling the widespread belief that the dispersion of Israel's remnant to the four corners of the world heralded the ingathering.[5]

Shearith Israel closely resembled its Old and New World counterparts in assuming responsibility for all aspects of Jewish religious life: communal worship, dietary laws, life-cycle events, education, philanthropy, ties to Jews around the world, oversight of the cemetery and the ritual bath, even the baking of matzoh and the distribution of Passover *haroset*. It saw itself and was seen by others as the representative body of the Jewish community; it acted in the name of all area Jews. It governed its members much like a church governed its parish, thereby promoting discipline while avoiding the appearance of a Jewish "state within a state." In addition, it served as a meeting and gathering place for local Jews, a venue for exchanging "news and tatle."[6]

Shearith Israel closely conformed to the traditional *minhag* (ritual) as practiced by Portuguese Jews in Europe and the West Indies. Innovations were prohibited; "our duty," Sephardic Jews in England (writing in Portuguese) once explained, is: "to imitate our forefathers." On a deeper level, Sephardic Jews believed, as did the Catholics among whom they had so long lived, that ritual could unite those whom life had dispersed. They wanted a member of their nation to feel at home in any Sephardic synagogue anywhere in the world: the same liturgy, the same customs, even the same tunes.[7]

No Jewish religious authority of any kind in colonial America possessed sufficient status to challenge the authority of the lay leadership of the synagogue community. Neither Shearith Israel, nor any of the synagogues subsequently established before the Revolution ever hired a *haham* (sage, the title given to a rabbi in the Sephardic community), nor did rabbis regularly grace American pulpits until 1840. Sermons, when they were delivered at all, were offered by visitors or by the officiating (unordained) reader. The dearth of members and funds partly explains this anomaly: as late as 1750 the city's Jewish population did not exceed three hundred (sixty families). But the practice of local churches probably explains more. Only about a fourth of the Christian congregations in the province of New York enjoyed full-time pastors in 1750, and even the Anglicans failed to appoint a bishop to oversee their flock. The absence of a professional religious authority thus did not demean Jews in the eyes of their neighbors.[8]

The two houses of worship that colonial Jews built, one in New York (1730) and the other in Newport (1763), underscored the Jewish community's values. Both favored tradition over external display. They focused on the interior of the synagogue, designed in classical Sephardic style, while keeping the exterior comparatively simple, on the scale of the modest New York churches built by the persecuted Baptists and Quakers. In this, local Jews emulated the pattern of clandestine churches in Early Modern Europe and of London's Sephardic synagogue, Bevis Marks, completed in 1701. All of these houses of worship disguised themselves as domestic structures on the outside to distinguish

The interior of Newport's Touro Synagogue is similar in design to, but smaller in size than the interiors of the large Sephardic synagogues in Amsterdam and London.

Interior, Touro Synagogue, Newport, Rhode Island, circa 1933. Historic American Buildings Survey Collection, Prints and Photographs Division.

themselves visually from established churches and avoid offending the majority faith. They projected an image of deference, offering neighbors the reassurance that Jews kept privately to themselves. In so doing, they reinforced for local Jews an important cultural lesson that centuries of diaspora experience had repeatedly taught them: to practice great discretion on the outside, not drawing excessive attention to themselves, while glorying in their faith on the inside, where tradition reigned supreme.[9]

The advantages of this all-encompassing institution were, from a Jewish point of view, considerable: the synagogue community proved an efficient means of meeting the needs of an outpost Jewish community. It promoted group solidarity and discipline; evoked a sense of tradition as well as a feeling of kinship toward similarly organized synagogue communities throughout the Jewish world; and improved the chances that even small clusters of Jews, remote from the wellsprings of Jewish learning, could survive from one generation to the next. By contrast, the right to dissent, the right to challenge the leadership in a free election, the right to secede and establish a competing congregation, the right to practice Judaism independently and on a voluntary basis—these were unknown in colonial synagogues. Jews of that time would have viewed such revolutionary ideas as dangerous to Judaism and to the welfare of the Jewish community as a whole.

Precisely these revolutionary ideas, however, were legitimated by the American Revolution. In rebelling against the British, the colonists explicitly rejected both tradition and deference, central pillars of Jewish and general society in colonial days, and they overthrew many of the established patterns of life that had previously governed their existence under the British.

Judaism too was transformed by the Revolution. Following the Revolution, in all of the communities where Jews lived, patriotic Jews returned to their synagogues and very quickly began grappling with the new situation in which they found themselves. The challenge that they faced was whether Judaism, as they knew it, could be reconciled with freedom and democracy. Could Jews maintain the traditional synagogue community structure that bound them together and promoted group survival and at the same time also accommodate new political and cultural realities?

In an initial effort to meet this challenge, each of America's synagogues rewrote its constitution (in fact they wrote constitutions for the first time; previously they had called their governing documents 'askamot or haskamot—agreements or covenants). These documents broke from the old Sephardic model, incorporated large dollops of republican rhetoric, and provided for a great deal more freedom and democracy—at least on paper.[10]

In reality, however, the age-old values of the synagogue community and the new values of the fledgling republic proved hard to reconcile. The strategy that called for promoting Judaism through tradition and a single overarching institution that would unify all Jews was crumbling under the weight of demands for more freedom and democracy. Among Jews, as among many Protestants of the day, the immediate post-Revolutionary decades were characterized by burgeoning religious ferment, challenges from below to established communal authority, and appeals to American values to legitimate expressions of Jewish religious dissent.[11]

All of this set the stage for the religious revolution that transformed Judaism in the 1820s, paving the way for a Judaism that would become distinctive to America, different from both the old synagogue community model of Western Sephardic Jews and from Judaism as it developed in Europe and the Middle East. The 1820s were a remarkable era in American history, the period of the Second Great Awakening and the beginning of the Jacksonian age. For Jews, it was also a period when they became seriously alarmed about ritual laxity and evident religious indifference. The real question, not quite articulated, was whether the existing system of Judaism left over from colonial days could adequately meet the needs of young Jews, born after the Revolution, living in the heady early-nineteenth-century atmosphere of freedom, democracy, and religious ferment. It was in response to this larger challenge that young Jews in the two largest American Jewish communities of that time, New York and Charleston, moved to transform and revitalize their faith.[12]

In New York, in 1825, a group of ambitious young Jews, mostly from non-Sephardic families (the majority of Shearith Israel had been Ashkenazi since the 1740s, at least), undertook to establish their own early worship service on Sabbath morning, run much less formally than the synagogue's, with time out for explanations and instruction, without a formal leader, and—revealingly—treating rich and poor alike. Here we see all of the themes familiar to us from the general history of American religion in this era: challenge to authority, a new form of organization, anti-elitism, and radical democratization. Shearith Israel made no effort to accommodate the concerns of these young people, fearing that their plan would "destroy the well-known and established rules and customs of our ancestors as have been practised . . . for upwards of one hundred years past." As a result, the young people withdrew and formed a new congregation, B'nai Jeshurun, New York's first Ashkenazic synagogue.[13]

Young Jews in Charleston in the mid 1820s posed a parallel challenge to their synagogue. For the most part, they were native born, dissatisfied with synagogue life, heavily influenced by Unitarianism, and yet still deeply concerned about Jewish survival. They sought much more radical changes than those sought by the young Jews of New York, including an abbreviated service, vernacular prayers, a weekly sermon, and an end to traditional freewill offerings in the synagogue. When their petition was dismissed out of hand, they too seceded in 1825 to form what they called in their constitution, The Reformed Society of Israelites for Promoting True Principles of Judaism According to Its Purity and Spirit.[14]

Looking back, the strategies proposed for revitalizing American Judaism differed in New York and Charleston. The New Yorkers, influenced by contemporary revivalism, worked within the framework of Jewish law, stressing education as well as changes in the organization and aesthetics of Jewish religious life. The Charlestonites, influenced by Unitarianism, believed that Judaism itself needed to be reformed in order to bring Jews back to the synagogue. The former adumbrated Modern Orthodox Judaism; the latter, Reform Judaism. Both explicitly rejected the traditionalist strategy of the "established" Sephardic congregations, but also challenged the authority of the synagogue community, insisting that America recognize their right to withdraw

The article accompanying these portraits is titled "Eminent Hebrew Clergymen" and includes brief biographies of each of the rabbis pictured here.

"Eminent American Clergy," in The American Phrenological Journal, *April 1868. General Collections.*

and worship as they saw fit. All over the United States in the early decades of the nineteenth century, Protestant Americans were abandoning "established" denominations in which they had been raised for ones that seemed to them more democratic, inspiring, and authentic; moving, for example, from Congregational, Presbyterian, and Episcopal churches to those of the Methodists, Baptists, and Disciples of Christ.[15] Jews now followed the same pattern.

Henceforward, in larger communities, dissenters no longer sought to compromise their principles for the sake of consensus: instead, they felt free to withdraw and start their own synagogues, which they did time and time again. In New York, there were two synagogues in 1825, four in 1835, ten in 1845, and over twenty in 1855. By the Civil War, every major American Jewish community had at least two synagogues, and larger ones like Philadelphia, Baltimore, or Cincinnati had four or more. These were not satellite congregations, created to meet the needs of dispersed or immigrant Jews, nor were they sanctioned by any central Jewish authority. That continued to be the Western-European pattern where church and synagogue hierarchies persisted. By contrast, in free and democratic America, congregational autonomy was now largely the rule—in Judaism as in Protestantism. Indeed, new congregations arose largely through a replication of the divisive process that had created B'nai Jeshurun and the Reform Society of Israelites. Members who were dissatisfied for some reason with their home congregations resigned and created new ones more suited to their needs and desires. That became the American Jewish religious pattern.[16]

The result was a new *American* Judaism—one that was diverse and pluralistic, whereas before it had been designedly monolithic. For the first time, American Jews could now choose from a number of congregations—most of them Ashkenazic in one form or another—reflecting a range of different rites, ideologies, and regions of origin. Inevitably, these synagogues competed with one another for members and for status. As a result they had a new interest in minimizing dissent and keeping members satisfied. Indeed, more than anybody realized at the time, synagogue pluralism changed the balance of power between the synagogue and its members. Before, when there was but one synagogue in every community, it could take members for granted and discipline them; they had little option but to obey. Now, American Jews did have an option; in fact, synagogues needed them more than they needed any particular synagogue. This led to the rapid demise of the whole system of disciplining congregants with fines and sanctions. Congregations became much more concerned with attracting congregants than with keeping them in line.[17]

Finally, synagogue pluralism brought to an end the intimate coupling of synagogue and community. In every major city where Jews lived, the synagogue community was replaced by a community of synagogues. No single synagogue was able any longer to represent the community as a whole. In fact, synagogues came increasingly to represent *diversity* in American Jewish life—they symbolized and promoted fragmentation. To bind the Jewish community together and carry out functions that the now privatized and functionally delimited synagogues could no longer handle required new community-wide organizations capable of transcending religious differences. Charitable organizations like the Hebrew Benevolent Society (incorporated in 1832) and fraternal organizations like B'nai B'rith (literally, "sons of the covenant," founded in 1843) soon moved in to fill the void.

By the 1840s, the structure of the American Jewish community mirrored in organization the federalist pattern of the nation as a whole, balanced precariously between unity and diversity. American Judaism had likewise come to resemble the American religious pattern. Jews, many of them young, dissatisfied with the American Jewish "establishment," influenced by the world around them, and fearful that Judaism would not continue unless it changed, had produced a religious revolution that overthrew the synagogue communities and replaced a monolithic Judaism with one that was much more democratic, free, diverse, and competitive. American Judaism, as later generations knew it, was shaped by this revolution.

Even while this was taking place, however, a different kind of revolution was brewing that would transform American Jewish life: massive immigration from Central Europe. Between 1820 and 1880, according to inexact estimates, America's Jewish population increased from 3,000 to about 250,000, and spread throughout the country, pursuing opportunities wherever it found them. The question, especially for isolated Jews, was whether they would remain Jewish. Could Judaism survive in a free and open society?[18]

Mid-nineteenth-century American Jews pursued three different strategies to try to ensure that it would. The first, perhaps best articulated by the great Orthodox Jewish leader Isaac Leeser, advocated tradition in an American key. He called for greater emphasis on Jewish education, decorum, and aesthetics, as well as a regular English-language sermon, but nothing that deviated from Jewish law. A later generation would call this Modern Orthodoxy, the term reflecting the quest to be modern and traditional at the same time.[19]

A second strategy, made famous by the great Reform Jewish leader Isaac Mayer Wise, presumed that Judaism itself needed to change in order for it to survive. Reformers urged Jews to abandon rituals that seemed incompatible

Isaac Leeser was the architect of American Jewish life. A traditionalist Hazzan-Minister (i.e., rabbi), he was editor of America's first general Jewish periodical, originator of the first Jewish publication society, and a founder of the nation's first rabbinical college. As a liturgist, he translated both the Sefardi and the Ashkenazi prayer books. Leeser also translated the entire Bible into English, editions that served English-speaking Jews for many decades. His collected essays fill ten volumes, and they cover the gamut of Jewish religious thought and communal enterprise.

Engraving, published by I. Goldman, Isaac Leeser, 1868. Prints and Photographs Division.

A pioneer of Reform Judaism in America, Isaac Mayer Wise became its acknowledged leader and its institutional architect, organizing the Union of American Hebrew Congregations (1873), the Hebrew Union College (1878), and the Central Conference of American Rabbis (1889). The reforms that he instituted were in response to modernity and Americanization, adapting to the rapid integration of American Jews into the social and cultural life of post Civil War America. This frontispiece portrait faces the title page of Isaac Mayer Wise's The Cosmic God. *It portrays Wise at age fifty-six, the year after he opened the rabbinical seminary he founded and headed till the end of his life, the Hebrew Union College in Cincinnati, Ohio.*

Isaac M. Wise, The Cosmic God, *Cincinnati, 1876. General Collections.*

A member of B'nai B'rith, America's oldest and largest Jewish fraternal order, could proudly display his membership certificate, whose illustrations would remind all of the Order's mission, and its threefold devotion: to country—the American eagle and shield; to faith—Abraham and Isaac, and Moses at Sinai; and to fraternal benevolence—visiting the sick, consoling the bereaved, caring for orphans.

Membership Certificate, B'nai B'rith, *Milwaukee, 1876. Prints and Photographs Division.*

with modernity and to adopt innovations that promised to make Judaism more appealing and spiritually uplifting, like shorter services, vernacular prayers, organ music, and mixed seating. "We hold that all such Mosaic and rabbinical laws as regulate diet, priestly purity, and dress originated in ages and under the influence of ideas entirely foreign to our present mental and spiritual state," the famed 1885 Pittsburgh Platform of Reform Judaism declared. "Their observance in our days," it continued, "is apt rather to obstruct than to further modern spiritual elevation." Reformers advocated thoroughgoing reforms—the removal of what they saw as Judaism's accumulated "defects and deformities"—to keep Judaism alive and lure young Jews back to the synagogue.[20]

A third strategy aimed at preserving Judaism in America rejected the synagogue altogether and focused on ties of peoplehood as the unifying element in Jewish life. This idea found its most important institutional expression in the Jewish fraternal organization B'nai B'rith. The preamble to the order's original constitution carefully avoided any mention of God, Torah, ritual commandments, or religious faith, but stressed the importance of Jewish unity: "B'nai B'rith has taken upon itself the mission of uniting Israelites in the work of promoting their highest interests and those of humanity." While synagogues divided Jews and alienated some of them altogether, B'nai B'rith argued that fraternal ties—the covenant (*b'rith*) that bound Jews one to another regardless of religious ideology—could bring about "union and harmony."[21]

The three strategies put forth to save American Judaism, in addition to being three means of achieving a common preservationist end, also reflected deep uncertainty surrounding the central priorities of American Jewish religious life. Which of their core values, Jews wondered, should be priority number one: (1) to uphold and maintain Judaism's sacred religious traditions, (2) to adapt Judaism to new conditions of life in a new land, or (3) to preserve above all a strong sense of Jewish peoplehood and communal unity? Many Jews, traditionalists and reformers alike, actually cherished all three of these values. The history of American Judaism is replete with oscillations back and forth among these priorities, a reflection of tensions, deeply rooted within Judaism itself, between the forces of tradition and the forces of change, between those who supported compromise for the sake of unity and those who insisted upon firmness for the sake of principle. Looking back historically, these tensions may be seen to have been highly beneficial. Proponents of different strategies and priorities in American Jewish life checked each other's excesses. Together they accomplished what none might have accomplished separately: they kept American Judaism going. But it is important to recognize, at the same time, that this benefit came at a steep price. Often, American Jewish religious life seethed with acrimonious contention, the unseemly specter of Jews battling Jews.

The arrival of German-trained, highly articulate, and ideologically passionate rabbis, beginning in the 1840s, only heightened internal battles within the American Jewish community. Rabbi Abraham Rice, an Orthodox rabbi seeking to establish "pure Orthodox belief in this land," was the first properly ordained rabbi to arrive in the country; he settled in Baltimore in 1840.[22] Subsequently, a series of other ordained (or in some cases, not-quite-ordained) rabbis migrated to the United States: at least eleven in the 1840s alone. These rabbis disagreed among themselves as to how to preserve Judaism in America: some sought to strengthen tradition, others promoted change. Together they helped to define a full spectrum of religious options that became available to American Jews during the mid-nineteenth century, a spectrum that extended from fervent Orthodoxy to radical Reform.[23]

With so many different kinds of Jews, so many ways of practicing Judaism, so many competing synagogues and strategies, and even a burgeoning number of contending rabbis, calls for peace and unity among American Jews rang out from many quarters. Indeed, Jewish leaders in America proposed a whole series of plans aimed at regulating American Jewish life by imposing some form of ecclesiastical authority and promoting communal unity. During the two decades before the Civil War, these sparked a significant communal debate over "union" that in many respects echoed the increasingly strident national debate over "The Union" taking place at the same time. One proposal called for the creation of a central religious council and a union of congregations. Another advocated the establishment of a chief rabbinate, modeled on that of England. Still a third called for a synod of rabbis, a common liturgy, and joint efforts to promote Jewish education. In the end, though, all of these efforts came to naught. Since there was no parallel Christian religious authority in America—no central Protestant council, no bishop or cardinal with nationwide jurisdiction, no synod with any real power—it was easy for opponents to dismiss any Jewish effort to create such institutions as "ridiculous" and antithetical to American ideals. Rather than compromising with their fellow Jews for the sake of communal unity, many Jews advocated firmness in defense of cherished principles. The result was an American Judaism that differed markedly from its more centrally organized and directed European counterparts.[24]

Observers at this time predicted that Reform Judaism, with its strategy of changing Judaism in order to preserve it, would triumph in America. Indeed, Rabbi Isaac Mayer Wise entitled his Reform liturgy *Minhag Amerika,* the American rite, as if to imply that more tradi-tional rites were foreign to the American temper. To further their popularity, Reform synagogues, particu-larly after the Civil War, introduced organ music into their worship, replaced gender-separated seating with mixed ("family") seating, abolished the second ("extra") day of Jewish festivals, abbreviated the Torah reading, adopted shorter non-Orthodox liturgies, and discarded the requirement that men wear prayer shawls and cover their heads during worship. Some of these changes were demanded by congregants, others were inspired by rabbis, but all of them had the same four basic aims: (1) to attract younger, Americanized Jews into the syna-gogue; (2) to make non-Jewish friends and visitors feel welcome; (3) to improve Judaism's public image; and (4) to create the kind of solemn, formal, awe-inspiring atmosphere that high-minded Jews and Christians alike, during this period, considered conducive to moral reflection and effective devotional prayer.[25]

For a brief period, in the 1870s, it appeared that this strategy had paid off. Reform Jewish leaders in Cincinnati established both a nationwide congregational union—the Union of American Hebrew Congregations (1873)—and a rabbinical seminary—the Hebrew Union College (1875)—that promised to bind Jews together and lead them forward. But the pluralism and divisiveness that had for so long been characteristic of American Judaism soon returned. Fears of assimilation, heightened anti-Semitism, and the beginnings of what became the

Isaac Mayer Wise's literary output was prodigious and included a moderate reform prayer book, Minhag Amerika; *a weekly newspaper which he edited; and works on history and theology as well as historical novels.* Minhag Amerika, *which means the "American Rite," was intended to serve all of America's Jews. A passionate patriot of his adopted country, he believed that an Americanized, liberal form of Judaism would become predomi-nant in America.*

Isaac Mayer Wise, ...Minhag Amerika, The Divine Service of American Israelites for the New Year. Cincinnati, 1872. General Collections.

mass immigration of Jews from Eastern Europe created a new mood within the American Jewish community, resulting in what was seen at the time as a dramatic Jewish awakening. Young people, concerned about the viability of Judaism and persuaded that its post-Civil War assumptions and directions had been wrong, promoted a new communal agenda in place of what Reform had offered. They advocated a return to religion, a heightened sense of Jewish peoplehood and particularism, new opportunities and responsibilities for women, and a renewed community-wide emphasis on education and culture.[26]

Finding itself suddenly on the defensive, and shaken by the same crisis of confidence that transformed so much of American Jewish life during this period, the Reform movement struggled to redefine itself. At a three-day conference called by Rabbi Kaufmann Kohler and held in Allegheny City's Concordia Hall just outside of Pittsburgh (November 16-18, 1885), eighteen rabbis, including Isaac Mayer Wise, attempted to formulate a "common platform" for Reform Judaism: a set of guiding principles that "in view of the wide divergence of opinions and the conflicting ideas prevailing in Judaism to-day," would "declare before the world what Judaism is and what Reform Judaism means and aims at." The result, known as the "Pittsburgh Platform," served for half a century as a concise summary of Reform Jewish beliefs. Among other things, it clarified that Reform Jews rejected ceremonies "not adapted to the views and habits of modern civilization," considered themselves "no longer a nation, but a religious community," expected "neither a return to Palestine, nor a sacrificial worship under the sons of Aaron," and associated Judaism with "the great task of modern times, to solve, on the basis of justice and righteousness, the problems presented by the contrasts and evils of the present organization of society."[27]

During the decades that followed, often known as the era of "Classical Reform," modernity dominated Reform Judaism's agenda. Its rabbis, like their liberal Protestant counterparts, gloried in Western culture and accepted the optimistic premises of evolutionary thought. They argued that the essence of Judaism lay in moral conduct and social justice, rather than in faith, laws, and ritual practices.[28]

While these efforts worked to strengthen and redefine Judaism among native-born and assimilating Jews, American Judaism was again being drastically transformed, this time by the immigration of some two million East-European Jews from Russia, Romania, and Austria-Hungary (largely Galicia), victims of persecution and privation. Upon arrival, they had to contend with a religious world radically different from the one they had known across the ocean. In Eastern Europe, Jews understood that, for all of the difficulties that they faced, religion defined them; it was an inescapable element of their personhood. Those who sought to observe Jewish laws and customs faced almost no difficulty in doing so, while those who sought to cast off Jewish identity entirely could not do so unless they converted.

The situation in the United States was entirely different. Indeed, what made immigration so dangerous, from the perspective of traditional European Judaism, was that religion in America was a purely private and voluntary affair, totally outside of the state's purview. As a result, Judaism proved easy enough to abandon, but, in the absence of state support, it was difficult to observe scrupulously. With the six-day work week commonplace and Sunday closing laws strictly enforced, the Sabbath proved particularly difficult for immigrants to keep. Unsympathetic employers warned newcomers that "if you don't come in on Saturday, don't bother coming in on Monday."[29]

This prayer book, prepared for and published by Temple Emanu-El in New York City, has the outline of the temple embossed in gold on its cover.

Seder Tefillah, The Order of Prayer for Divine Service, *revised by Dr. L. Merzbacher, Rabbi of the Temple Emanu-El, 1855, revised by Dr. S. Adler, New York, 1863. Hebraic Section.*

Fearing that East-European Jewish immigrants would abandon their faith altogether, religious leaders struggled to find ways to adapt traditional Judaism to America. In the mid 1880s, a few wealthy East-European congregations moved into enormous new showpiece synagogues that emphasized decorum, refinement, and high- church aesthetics, in the hope that these would prove attractive to successful East-European immigrants. There was also an ill-conceived effort to create a European-style chief rabbinate in New York. The most successful strategies, however, focused on training rabbis in America who could shape an Americanized traditional Judaism. This was the aim of the Jewish Theological Seminary, founded in 1887 to serve the needs of "Jews of America faithful to Mosaic law and ancestral tradition." Under the presidency of Solomon Schechter, whose well-publicized arrival on America's shores on April 17, 1902, was heralded as the beginning of a new era in American Jewish religious life, the Seminary became an academically rigorous "scientific" institution committed to the vigorous pursuit of Jewish scholarship. It sought to fashion a broadly inclusive American brand of non-Reform Judaism, traditional enough to satisfy Jewish law and modern enough to attract young Jews of East-European descent back to the synagogue. In time, to distinguish itself from the liberal Judaism of

ACADEMY OF MUSIC TUESDAY MARCH 15th 1881
PURIM ASSOCIATION
FANCY DRESS BALL
IN AID OF THE BUILDING FUND OF THE HEBREW BENEVOLENT AND ORPHAN ASYLUM SOCIETY.

Lavish philanthropic masquerade balls were sponsored by New York's Purim Association in the latter half of the nineteenth century. In addition to raising considerable funds for a variety of local communal organizations, these events were high points on New York Jewry's social calendar. Shown here is the announcement for the Purim Ball in support of the Hebrew Benevolent and Orphan Asylum's building fund.

Purim Association Fancy Dress Ball, March 15, 1881. Courtesy of the American Jewish Historical Society, New York, NY and Newton Centre, MA.

the Reform movement, this form of Judaism became known as "Conservative Judaism."[30]

East-European-trained rabbis who propounded a more exclusive definition of Orthodoxy opposed Schechter and the Seminary. Their solution to the problems faced by East-European Jewish immigrants in America was to reinvigorate the authority of rabbis like themselves, who would work to solve problems collectively through an organization called the Agudath ha-Rabbanim, a union of Orthodox rabbis trained in East-European Talmudical academies (*yeshivot*) and personally ordained by an East-European rabbinic luminary. The organization's exclusive definition of what constituted an Orthodox rabbi, its resistance to Americanization, and its desire to build, metaphorically, a protective wall around the Torah, an enclave where traditional Judaism would be safe from encroachments, laid the foundation upon which later rabbis built Fervent or *Haredi* Orthodoxy, the movement's right-most wing. In place of the Jewish Theological Seminary, which Agudath ha-Rabbanim criticized for its modernity and especially its critical approach to Jewish texts, it promoted Rabbi Isaac Elchanan Theological Seminary (RIETS), founded in 1897 on the model of an East-European yeshiva. There students studied traditional texts in a traditional way and in traditional Jewish languages; neither practical rabbinical training nor any significant concessions to the American environment were permitted. Only after World War I, under the leadership of Rabbi Bernard Revel, would RIETS be reorganized, modernized, and incorporated (in 1928) into Yeshiva College (later University). By then, the differences between Orthodox Judaism and Conservative Judaism were becoming clearer.[31]

During the interwar years, Orthodox Judaism and Conservative Judaism parted ways. Their rabbis, trained in different seminaries, joined different rabbinical associations. Their synagogues subscribed to different congregational unions. Their leaders clashed over issues of rabbinic authority, notably the effort to resolve the plight of the *agunah,* the deserted wife who was prevented by Jewish law from remarrying. The two movements also clashed over the ever-volatile issue of whether men and women might sit together in mixed pews as a concession to modernity, or whether the traditional separation of the sexes had to be maintained. In time, seating—separate or mixed—became a visible boundary differentiating the two movements from one another.[32]

Even as Conservative Judaism gained an identity separate from Orthodoxy, the nature of Conservative Judaism and its strategy for luring Jews back to the synagogue were thrown into flux. At one extreme stood those who believed that Conservative Jews should "conserve" tradition to the fullest extent possible; they approached all changes with skepticism, especially those that seemed incompatible with Jewish legal codes. At the other extreme stood those who insisted that the only way to "conserve" Judaism at all was to "reconstruct" it, in the hope that by harmonizing Judaism and modernity young people would find it more compelling.[33]

Rabbi Mordecai Kaplan stood at the apex of these debates, advocating what he called "A Program for the Reconstruction of Judaism." Seeking to win back to Judaism those who had become disaffected with the synagogue, he tried to reshape Judaism into a naturalistic and dynamic faith—without fixed beliefs, divine revelations, or commandments—with the Jewish people, rather than God, at its center. Kaplan's central ideas—particularly his denial of supernaturalism, his negation of Jewish chosenness, his doctrinal latitudinarianism, and his willingness to alter or discard Jewish practices that had "outlived their usefulness"—all proved highly controversial. But many found his emphases—community, modernity, Zionism, freedom—to be "extraordinarily liberating." In time, Reconstructionism became a separate movement within American Judaism, establishing a seminary of its own in 1968.[34]

Kaplan was among the first Jewish leaders to discern a change in the mood of American Jews during the 1930s, coincident with the rise of Hitlerism. "Jews . . . who had abandoned their people" were "returning like prodigal sons," he reported in 1934. "Because of the threat of annihilation," he hypothesized, the Jew was "impelled to rise to new heights of spiritual achievement." Jewish education, Jewish publishing, Jewish educational camping, and other dimensions of American Jewish life strengthened in response to the Nazi threat. This revival represented both a defensive response to adversity and a form of cultural resistance, a resolve to maintain Judaism in the face of opposition and danger. It promised to prepare the community for the new responsibilities that it faced in the Holocaust's wake.[35]

By the end of World War II, with European Jewry decimated, the major part of the world's Jewish population resided for the first time on the North American continent. Judaism strengthened during the years that followed,

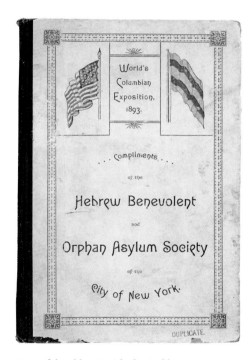

One of the oldest Jewish charitable associations in the United States— the Hebrew Benevolent and Orphan Asylum Society—prepared this special edition of its 1893 annual report in honor of the World's Columbian Exposition. In that year, the society reported that it sheltered almost 650 indigent children, with more than 2,500 individuals donating funds towards their support.

Proceedings of the Seventieth Annual Meeting of the Hebrew Benevolent and Orphan Asylum Society, *New York, 1893. General Collections.*

Festooned with Judaic, patriotic, and masonic symbols, this mizrah was hung on the eastern wall, towards Jerusalem, the direction to which prayer is oriented. The legend at the top reads, "If I forget thee o Jerusalem, let my right hand wither." (Psalms 137:5) Incorporated on the borders of this mizrah is an omer calendar, marking the seven weeks between the holidays of Passover and Shavu'ot.

Moses M. Henry, Printer, Mizrah/Omer Calendar, Cincinnati, 1850. From the HUC Skirball Cultural Center Museum Collection, Los Angeles, California (Gift of Mrs. Jacob Goldsmith). Photography by Marvin Rand.

benefiting from a strong "back-to-the-faith" movement throughout the United States—a response, some believed, to wartime horrors and to the postwar threat from "godless" Communism. As anti-Semitism declined, the religion of American Jews gained widespread recognition as America's "third faith," alongside Protestantism and Catholicism. Judaism also strengthened institutionally through the building of new synagogues and religious schools and the development of new communal institutions. In addition, Judaism began to adapt to new environments, accompanying Jews out to the suburbs and then beyond to Sun Belt cities like Miami and Los Angeles. Less noticeably but no less significantly, Holocaust-era immigrants impacted upon American Judaism during these years. Their memories, commitments, and collective sense of obligation to those who had not survived set the stage for developments that would transform all of American Judaism, Orthodoxy in particular, for decades to come— evidenced by the rise of Lubavitch and other Hasidic courts, the development of advanced Talmudic academies (*yeshivot* and *kollelim*), and the perceived inward and rightward turns in American Jewish religious life.

The early postwar decades saw universal issues like civil rights, interfaith relations, church-state separation, and the Vietnam War dominating the American Jewish agenda. Particularly in the wake of the 1967 Six Day War, the community's priorities changed, focusing more on Israel, the plight of Soviet Jewry, and remembrance of the Holocaust. Fearing once again that Judaism would not survive unless it changed, Jews also moved to revitalize their faith, developing bold new initiatives, like the communitarian *havurah* movement, to show that Judaism could be timely, meaningful, and in harmony with the counter-cultural ideas of the day. The widespread return to ritual that soon became evident across the spectrum of American Jewish life, the renewed interest throughout the community in neglected forms of Jewish music and art, the awakening of record numbers of Jews to the wellsprings of their tradition, the rise of feminism, the growth of Jewish spirituality—these and other manifestations of Jewish religious revival in America all became increasingly evident as the twentieth century wound down.[36]

Notwithstanding this evident revival, all was not well with American Judaism. Signs of assimilation abounded, reflected in a much-publicized report that more than half of all American Jews were intermarrying. Yet, at the same time, the community, we have seen, also displayed strong elements of revitalization and renewal, particularly in the area of Jewish education. The question, as Jews witnessed these two contradictory trends operating simultaneously —assimilation and revitalization—was, which one would turn out to be the dominant trend? The answer, at this point, is that nobody knows. That is still being decided day by day in the hearts and minds of contemporary American Jews.

15 CENTS A COPY

"THE NATIONAL JEWISH HOME MAGAZINE"

סענט א קאפיע 15

דער אידישער

פרויען זשורנאל

The Jewish Woman's Home Journal

AUGUST, 1922.

אויגוסט, 1922

SUBSCRIPTION PRICE
$1.50 A YEAR

סובסקריפשאן פרייז
א יאהר $1.50

America's Jewish Women

Pamela S. Nadell

A rich tapestry of diverse colors woven across time and space—that is the history of America's Jewish women. Its boldly colored images, stitched over 350 years of American Jewish history, depict these women sailing with furniture and featherbeds to land in America with their husbands, fathers, mothers, daughters, and sons. Its designs portray them planning weddings, preparing Sabbath meals over colonial hearths and in microwave ovens, bearing children and driving them to Hebrew school and Little League. They envision them praying in the women's balcony and leading the service as rabbis. They discover them in classrooms studying sacred Jewish texts and teaching American history. They find them scribbling away at their writing tables, ciphering from behind the counters of general stores, hunching over sewing machines, and dancing in front of the mirror. Bright colors burst forth as America's Jewish women cared for the orphan, welcomed the "huddled masses yearning to breathe free," marched on picket lines, and voted in Congress. Over time, as colorful new threads emerged in the canvas, strands woven earlier faded away. No matter when and where they lived—in colonial New York, in the antebellum South, in California during the Gold Rush, on Hester Street among the immigrant hordes, in New Orleans as Holocaust refugees, or in postmodern America as feminists—America's Jewish women have embroidered the tapestry that is their history. Its brightest colors reveal a

---

An editorial in the inaugural issue of this monthly illustrated magazine stated that the journal's focus would be on the "Americanization of the immigrant as well as on the Americanization of the parent." Through the journal's retention of the Yiddish language to interpret the modern culture, the editors hoped to acquaint young East-European women and their mothers with their newly adopted land and the spirit of their institutions.

Der Idisher Froyen Zshurnal *(The Jewish Woman's Home Journal), New York, August 1922. Hebraic Section.*

history of constructing, building, influencing, defining, and redefining their lives, their Judaism, and their wider communities.

1654-1880

In the autumn of 1654, shortly before the Jewish new year, twenty-three Jewish "souls, big as well as little," fleeing the long arm of the Inquisition, landed in New Amsterdam. By one account, females outnumbered males, six to four; the rest were children and young people. Of the women, two, the only ones whose names we know, were most likely widowed female heads of households. In this manner they, Ricke Nunes and Judith Mercado, claiming their place among the "Jewish Pilgrim Fathers," stitched the first skeins into the tapestry of America's Jewish women.[1]

This silver mustard pot was transformed by New York's Gomez family into a Jewish ceremonial object when they used it to store the etrog *(citron), a central component in the celebration of the fall holiday of Sukkot.*

Gomez Family, Silver Etrog Holder, circa eighteenth century. Courtesy of the American Jewish Historical Society, New York, NY and Newton Centre, MA.

Traveling with their furniture as well as their families suggests they planned to set up Jewish households. The Jewish new year 5415 fell on September 12th, within days of their landing. Most likely the men gathered to worship,[2] while the women began, as best they could, their customary tasks of preparing for the holiday and its meals. The place was new, but the rules were not. In colonial America, as wherever Jews have lived, the rhythms of Jewish life, its daily, weekly, and yearly cycles of religious services and holidays, as lived out in the home and in the synagogue, compelled women to take up their time-honored tasks. As they cleaned homes, prepared meals, and cared for their children, they set about constructing for themselves, their families, and their communities a Jewish place in this New World. Governed by the cadences of Judaism, by its Sabbaths and festivals, its dietary laws, and its laws of family life, America's early Jewish women would simultaneously integrate into the wider culture even as they lived out Jewish lives. Often they did so ingeniously, adjusting, adapting, and reinterpreting American forms to serve their Jewish purposes.

Quickly, most became respectable matrons, managing their households, which, in the case of Rebecca Machado Phillips who bore twenty-one children, could be quite large. Others certainly had smaller families. Whether or not they honored Jewish laws restricting sexual relations between husband and wife to certain weeks in a woman's monthly cycle is unclear, but, in 1786, the Jews of Philadelphia did build a *mikvah*, the ritual bathhouse essential for women's proper observance of these laws.[3]

The tapestry woven by America's early Jewish wives and mothers shows lives circum-scribed by the mundane responsibilities of housewifery, childbearing, and child raising, not easy tasks in colonial America. Housewifery meant keeping a kosher home. When, in 1774, Hetty Hays suspected that she had bought meat that was not properly koshered, she was ordered to "do Cassarar [kasher], or properly Clense, all her Spoons, plates and all other utensall, used in her House."[4] Children fell ill and died, yet a majority of Rebecca Phillips's children survived into adulthood. But among the mundane tasks of the household, "religion permeated [its] daily life."[5]

In these households objects could stand as keepers of Jewish memory. In the late eigh-teenth century, the New York Gomez family took a silver mustard pot and put in it an *etrog*, the citron used during the fall holiday of Sukkot, thereby transforming a condiment holder into a ceremonial object. When Rebecca Hendricks, a colonial young lady of breeding, practiced her needlework, she embroidered biblical verse as did other young colonial ladies of her class. But for her sampler she chose *Psalms* 78:1-14, recounting the wonders God had wrought for his chosen people and urging their children, sons and daughters, to keep the commandments.[6]

Those commandments were of the utmost concern to Abigail Franks, the great letter writer of colonial Jewry. She honored the Sabbath and holidays and kept kosher. She told her son Naphtali to "Never Eat Anything" at her brother's because she knew his household did not observe the dietary laws. She saw to it that her daughters as well as her sons learned Hebrew. But, in the open air of colonial America, she displayed an independence of mind that would come to characterize other American Jewish women. Yearning for a modernized Judaism, long before others would start constructing one, she wrote in 1739: "I Must Own I cant help Con-demning the Many Superstions wee are Clog'd with & hartly wish a Calvin or Luther would rise amongst Us[.] I Answer for my Self...I don't think religeon Consist in Idle Cerimonies[.]"[7]

The costs of the open society and such impulses were high. When her daughter Phila married outside the faith, Abigail's spirit was crushed. Of Abigail's two dozen grandchildren, not one seems to have passed on Judaism to the next generation.[8] This falling away from Judaism and the Jewish people emerges as another skein tightly woven into this tapestry of America's Jewish women.

In the tiny world of colonial Jewry, Rebecca Hendricks and Abigail Franks were not alone in weaving Judaism into their lives. On Sabbaths and festivals, Jewish women joined their fathers and brothers, husbands and sons in worship. They sat in the women's galleries built in the seaport synagogues where America's early Jews lived. Raised above the men and gazing below—their vision no longer blocked by a screen as it still was in European synagogues[9]—America's Jewish women prayed, surely gossiped, and sometimes argued. On the eve of Yom Kippur in 1755, Gitlah Hays and her Gentile guest were soaked by a sudden thunderstorm pouring in through a window which had been taken off its sashes because other ladies had complained that the gallery was too hot. When Gitlah demanded that the window be put back, the dispute drew in the men of the congregation.[10]

Rebecca Gratz (1781-1869) was the premier builder of Jewish benevolent and voluntary organizations in her native Philadelphia. In 1819, she was instrumental in founding the Female Hebrew Benevolent Society, and, in 1838, the Hebrew Sunday School.

Photoprint by Broadbent & Co., Portrait of Rebecca Gratz [Philadelphia], circa 1860. Prints and Photographs Division.

That Christian neighbors were close friends and welcome at Jewish services in early America is not surprising. The Jewish community was tiny, not even three thousand souls big and little by 1820, and its Jews lived out their lives among their neighbors and represented Judaism to them. Jewish women, as Gitlah Hays did, displayed their Judaism, so deeply woven into their lives, to Christian friends and invited these friends to celebrate with them at their weddings and circumcisions.[11]

Emulating the biblical woman of valor who "opens her hand to the poor" (*Proverbs* 31:20), early America's Jewish women joined these Christian friends and neighbors to aid others. In 1801, Rebecca Machado Phillips and some twenty other Philadelphia women, Christians and Jews, including Rebecca Gratz, founded the Female Association for the Relief of Women and Children in Reduced Circumstances.[12] But Rebecca Phillips was no less concerned with caring for her narrower Jewish community. When, in 1782, Philadelphia's Jews built a new synagogue, she and Grace Nathan raised funds to purchase its ritual objects.

In fact, for many of early America's Jewish women, their voluntarism and impulses to charity would always center, as a distinct expression of their personal piety, on their Jewish communities. Ultimately, by the early twentieth century, such voluntarism, spawning a large network of American Jewish women's organizations both within the synagogue and without, would cover large sections of this growing tapestry. But, in the nineteenth century the pioneering figure most closely associated with Jewish women's American-style voluntarism was Rebecca Gratz. Also a founder of Philadelphia's Orphan Asylum, she is best remembered for her endeavors on behalf of the Jewish people. Noting that Christian women evangelized while they aided the poor, Gratz realized Jewish women must organize to aid the Jewish poor and protect them from Christian missionizing. In 1819, she founded the Female Hebrew Benevolent Society to do just that. In 1838, when she established the first Hebrew Sunday School in America, she both launched the prototype of a new educational setting for America's Jewish children and opened a new avenue for Jewish women's communal activism as teachers.[13]

In the years of increasing immigration to America from German-speaking lands—between 1820 and 1880 America's Jews grew to a quarter of a million—eleven women from New York's Temple Emanu-El founded, in 1846, the Unabhängiger Orden Treuer Schwestern.

The only independent female fraternal order then in America, it eventually sparked a web of lodges offering these new American Jewish women mutual aid in times of emergency and sickness and guaranteeing sisters decent burial.[14]

Communal activism offered one important public avenue for Jewish women's piety in the nineteenth century. Another, perhaps surprisingly, was writing. These writers simultaneously celebrated an American genteel ideal historians call the Cult of True Womanhood, with its emphasis upon woman's innate purity and piety, and exalted Judaism's Mother in Israel, the mother of her nation and people. Charleston, South Carolina's hymnist Penina Moise called upon: "Daughters of Israel, arise!/The Sabbath-morn to greet." Baltimore's Henrietta Szold, who never married, described the ideal Jewish woman: "She teaches the children, speeds the husband to the place of worship and instruction, welcomes him when he returns, keeps the house godly and pure, and God's blessings rest upon all these things."[15]

Surely, the best-known of America's nineteenth-century Jewish female writers was poet Emma Lazarus. In the early 1880s, deeply disturbed by "The Jewish Problem" (1883) evident in the Russian pogroms, whose refugees she met through her work with the Hebrew Emigrant Aid Society, she called for founding a Jewish state in Palestine. Her magnum opus, "The New Colossus" (1883), inscribed on the pedestal of the Statue of Liberty, shows America as the "Mother of Exiles" welcoming "the huddled masses yearning to breathe free."[16] The East-European Jewish women who journeyed to America among those "huddled masses" would in the span of a few decades weave bold new colors into the tapestry of Jewish women in America.

1881-1945

Between 1881 and 1924, some two million East-European Jews streamed to America. Propelled by grinding poverty, violent pogroms, and the dislocations of revolutionary turmoil and war, theirs was overwhelmingly a migration of families. When the male head of the household journeyed ahead, as Israel Antin did in 1891, he spent the next years scrimping and saving to buy ships' tickets to bring over his wife and children. This migration utterly transformed American Jewry. By 1930 the 4.4 million American Jews, 3.6 percent of the U.S. population, comprised nearly a third of world Jewry. Many would, in time, come to call America, as did Israel's daughter Mary, *The Promised Land*.[17]

As with the history of America's earlier Jewish women, domestic concerns continue to stand out in the tapestry of the East-European Jewish immigrant women and their daughters as they made their way into America. But now these concerns were lived out in the crowded tenements of immigrant enclaves—New York's Lower East Side, Boston's North End,

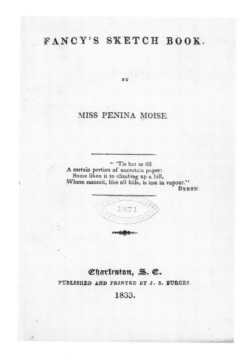

Born in Charleston, South Carolina, in 1797, Penina Moise became a widely published author and poet. A deeply religious woman, she composed hymns for use in the prayer service as well as this book of poetry, which includes poems on biblical themes and on contemporary Jewish life.

Penina Moise, Fancy's Sketch Book, Charleston, South Carolina, 1833. Rare Book and Special Collections Division.

Emma Lazarus.

1

Sonnets.

I.

The New Colossus.

Not like the brazen giant of Greek fame,
With conquering limbs astride from land to land
Here at our sea-washed, sunset gates shall stand
A mighty woman with a torch, whose flame
Is the imprisoned lightning, and her name
Mother of Exiles. From her beacon-hand
Glows world-wide welcome; her mild eyes command
The air-bridged harbor that twin cities frame.

"Keep, ancient lands, your storied pomp!" cries she
With silent lips. "Give me your tired, your poor,
Your huddled masses yearning to breathe free,
The wretched refuse of your teeming shore.
Send these, the homeless, tempest-tost to me,
I lift my lamp beside the golden door!"

1883.

(Written in aid of Bartholdi Pedestal Fund.)

and Chicago's West Side. Many strove to adhere to Judaism in this new promised land. When the price of kosher meat soared from twelve to eighteen cents a pound in New York in 1902, immigrant mothers broke into butcher shops, set meat afire, and shared recipes for meatless meals to influence their neighbors to honor their kosher meat boycott.[18]

With so many impoverished immigrants, caring for their own was an even greater task than ever. The National Council of Jewish Women, the first of the modern national Jewish women's organizations, was founded in 1893 by the now privileged Jewish women of the earlier migrations. Its members set out to protect Jewish immigrant girls traveling without guardians from falling into what was then called "white slavery," that is prostitution, and offered them vocational training and classes on how to live like Americans.[19] East-European Jewish immigrant women also established their own social welfare agencies. Poor immigrant women who had fallen upon hard times, like the newly widowed, and entrepreneurial women, who wanted to buy cloth to sew and coal to heat the bathhouse, could borrow money from immigrant women's credit networks operated by those just slightly better off than they were.[20]

But distinct new threads appear on the canvas of American Jewish women's history in these years. First among them are patterns of work. Even in the colonial era, married Jewish women managed family businesses while their husbands traveled, and the newly widowed kept kosher boardinghouses. In the nineteenth century, many Jewish women "helped out" in family businesses, selling clothing and canned goods, saddles and blankets from behind the counters of the dry goods stores their husbands owned in the small towns dotting the landscape of the South and the West.[21] But middle-class propriety, which in America expected women to busy themselves with their homes and families leaving the world of work to their men, eventually propelled these Jewish women out of the public sphere of business and into the private sphere of their homes.

The East-European Jewish immigrants came from a world which desperately needed and therefore valued women's economic contributions to the family economy. In Russia young Jewish women had worked primarily in the needle trades. Their mothers sold goods in the marketplace. Thus immigrant Jewish women came to America expecting to work and they, especially the not yet married, found employment in New York, Chicago, and elsewhere in the burgeoning ready-made clothing industry. There, sewing shirtwaists and dresses until their aching fingers bled, they stitched new patterns into this tapestry.[22]

But when they married, their husbands wanted them out from under the influence of some factory foreman. Hence married Jewish women contributed to the family economy in other ways. They took in piecework to sew and opened their tenement homes to boarders, giving the newest arrivals, often men from their hometowns, a place in the kitchen to sleep and meals to eat. They sold goods from pushcarts on the streets or "helped

Mother and daughter at the Williamsburg Bridge saying Tashlikh— *a prayer recited on the Jewish New Year that involves the symbolic casting away of sins into a natural body of water.*

Praying on the [Williamsburg Bridge], New Year's Day, 1909. George Grantham Bain Collection, Prints and Photographs Division.

In the description accompanying this photograph, Lewis Hine wrote: "The eleven year old girl and thirteen year old boy work on the ties every day after school. It is exceptional to find Jewish children doing home-work."

Lewis Wickes Hine, "Making neckties in the kitchen of Mrs. Rothenberg," in Tenement Homework Album, *February 1912. Prints and Photographs Division.*

Wearing "Abolish Child Slavery" banners in English and Yiddish, with one clearly carrying an American flag, these two girls were very likely participants in a labor parade held in New York City on May 1, 1909. American Jewish women fought both in the rank and file and as central figures in labor groups to eradicate a variety of social injustices through government legislation for the protection, especially, of women and children.

"Protest against child labor in a labor parade," New York [May 1, 1909]. George Grantham Bain Collection, Prints and Photographs Division.

out" in the family's five- and-dime or soda fountain. Later in the 1920s and 1930s, their daughters, aspiring to white-collar work wanted to be salesclerks and bookkeepers. Those able, taking advantage of New York's tuition-free Hunter College, would go on to teach in the city's ever-expanding public schools.[23]

But it was Jewish women's employment in the garment industry, especially in the dress and waist trade where they made up the vast majority of workers, that shaped their politics. Low wages, poor working conditions, and frequent layoffs propelled immigrant working girls into the International Ladies' Garment Workers' Union. In the "Uprising of the 20,000" the shirt-waist makers struck. Braving the cold and violence meted out by hired thugs, prostitutes, and police, young women, many still in their teens, walked the picket lines seeking a fifty-two-hour workweek and paid overtime. Their 1909 strike opened a decade of unrest in the garment industry. Less than two years later, after 146 workers at the Triangle Shirtwaist Company lost their lives in one of the worst industrial fires in the history of New York City, half a million gath-ered to mourn the victims and to protest the working conditions that had allowed the factory's owners to lock the escape exits to keep the girls in and union organizers out.[24] Labor unrest helps situate the neighborhood politics of the kosher meat boycott——the one in 1902 was by no means the last—and of the rent strikes Jewish women would stage into the 1930s within the patterns of political activism woven into the tapestry by America's Jewish women.[25] Not sur-prisingly, these same immigrant women actively campaigned for the New York State Suffrage Bill in 1917.[26]

But, as immigrant Jewish women and their American-born daughters ascended to the middle class, they were expected to acculturate to middle-class norms that presented women as wives and mothers largely uninvolved in economic endeavors and political crusades. Such middle-class norms surely masked the reality that many women continued to "help out" in their husbands' stores, businesses, and offices. And they hid women's ongoing political activities, now increasingly subsumed in the growing network of Jewish women's organizations.

Nevertheless, new-found leisure provided the opportunity for embroidering different colored threads into the lives of America's Jewish women, especially in the interwar years. Leisure meant time to stroll the streets of new middle-class urban neighborhoods, like the Grand Concourse in the Bronx, wheeling baby carriages holding "my son, the doctor; my daughter, the teacher."[27] It allowed for leisure pursuits: American Jewish women adopted the Chinese game of mah jongg; vacationed with their children in Jewish bungalow colonies in the Catskills, while their husbands spent the week at work in the city; and became consumers of culture—the theater, movies, and literature—eagerly embracing those on Jewish themes.[28] But, most impor-tantly, middle-class leisure allowed America's Jewish women to invent new spaces for them-selves in American Judaism. Their involvement in their synagogues and in a plethora of Jewish women's organizations became essential to sustaining Jewish life in America.

Synagogue sisterhoods encouraged women to be exemplary Jewish wives and mothers, to become a "force for Jewishness." Through the sisterhoods, women extended the boundaries of

their home to the synagogue, equipping its kitchens and catering its lunches. Sisterhood women celebrated the "Jewish Home Beautiful" at the 1939 New York World's Fair, literally singing the praises of tables set elegantly for the Sabbath and holidays. Reform Jewish women promoted Sisterhood Sabbath; Orthodox women published "Yes, I Keep Kosher." By 1923, women affiliated with each of the denominational synagogue movements of American Judaism—Reform, Conservative, and Orthodox—had created national organizations of temple and synagogue sisterhoods.[29]

But could they be rabbis? The question, first raised in the 1890s, swirled in American Jewish life for a century. In the interwar years, a handful of Jewish women spent enough time in rabbinical schools to keep it alive. Nevertheless, no woman would then be called rabbi in American Jewish life.[30]

But the synagogue and Judaism as religion represented only one venue for living out Jewish lives. In this era defined so deeply by the East-European Jews' journey to America, Jewish women wove yet other ideas and movements into their history. Some found places in the ladies' branches of the socialist brotherhood of the Yiddish-speaking Arbeter Ring, or Workmen's Circle.[31] Others, first exposed to modern dance in the settlement houses, like that founded by nurse Lillian Wald on Henry Street, danced their leftist politics and Jewish commitments.[32] Yet it is Zionism, the movement for a Jewish homeland in Israel, that bursts out as the brightest thread commanding American Jewish women's energies, enthusiasms, and commitments.

Opposite: A salivating demonic figure, labeled the "Triangle Waist Company," draws a long line of women into his factory. There, consumed in the fire's raging inferno, the women's faces drift upward in the smoky aftermath towards heaven.

Lola (pseudonym for Leon Israel), Triangle Shirtwaist Fire Cartoon, in Der Groyser Kundes: "The Big Stick," *New York, April 7, 1911. Hebraic Section.*

Police and fire officials place the victims of the Triangle Shirtwaist Company fire in coffins.

"Bodies from Washington Place fire," New York , March 25, 1911. George Grantham Bain Collection, Prints and Photographs Division.

Henrietta Szold's (1860-1945) lifework was bound up in building Hadassah, America's largest Jewish women's Zionist organization. Hadassah supported health, educational, and social service networks in Palestine and then, after 1948, in Israel. In 1933, Szold became director of Youth Aliyah, a program jointly supported by the Jewish Agency and Hadassah that succeeded in bringing more than 30,000 children from Nazi Germany and war-torn Europe to agricultural settlements in Palestine.

Tim Gidal, photographer, H. Szold dancing and standing with Youth Aliyah children S'de Ya'acov(?), August 1941. © The Israel Museum, Jerusalem. Courtesy of Hadassah, The Women's Zionist Organization of America, Inc.

In 1912, Henrietta Szold—organizer, administrator, writer, editor, educator extraordinaire, and icon of American Jewish womanhood even until today—transformed a small Zionist study circle into Hadassah, the Women's Zionist Organization of America. From then until her death in Jerusalem in 1945, Szold inspired tens of thousands of American Jewish women to harness their talents and efficiency to deliver health care to the women and children of Palestine. After 1933, Hadassah's Youth Aliyah resettled German Jewish refugee children fleeing the dark cloud of Nazism spreading over Europe. Eventually, Hadassah would grow into the largest women's organization in America, and through it American Jewish women would live Jewish lives and sustain their people in the State of Israel into the twenty-first century.[33]

Jewish women in America would nurture these commitments at home and abroad, even as the Great Depression strained their household economies propelling some, who years before had left it, back into the workforce for a time.[34] In these years America's Jewish women also struggled against the growing menace of Nazi persecution. In the 1930s, the women of the American Jewish Congress picketed Woolworth's to boycott the sale of German goods. They battled anti-Semitism at home, standing outside Catholic churches on Sundays to refute Father Charles Coughlin's anti-Semitic tirades. The shelters they established in the 1930s to house refugees fleeing Nazism would soon house allied soldiers as America entered World War II.[35]

Yet surely, many of America's Jewish women, if not most, experienced the crisis privately, as individuals. In East Baltimore in the 1930s, Rebbetzin (that is, the wife of a rabbi) Anna Alstadt Hertzberg raised money for the refugees who found their way to her kitchen and pleaded for signatures for the affidavits crucial to bring to America those still trapped in Europe. Only at the war's end did she learn what had happened to her European family. In 1946, on the eve of Yom Kippur, she lit thirty-six memorial candles, one each for her father, her siblings, and their children, her family that had perished in the Holocaust.[36]

To the Present

In the half century since the end of World War II, vivid new colors burst forth in the lives of America's Jewish women. Weaving them into the narrative of this gendered history of domestic lives, economic activities, political activism, and religious commitments adds new designs to this bright, multicolored tapestry of America's Jewish women.

Unquestionably, as ever, in these years America's Jewish women were devoted to their homes and families, synagogues, and Jewish organizations. Yet, in this most recent era of

America's history, they lived out these commitments in new settings, in the emerging Jewish suburbs, like those of Nassau County, New York, and in cities with growing Jewish populations, like Miami and Los Angeles.[37] Making these neighborhoods their own, they shopped at the Jewish bakeries and kosher butchers that cropped up. They helped start new synagogues, so that they could send their children to Hebrew school. They imported Chanukah lamps and candlesticks from Israel and sold them in gift shops run by the sisterhoods in their new temples.[38] With anti-Semitism waning in American life, these women, increasingly the daughters and the granddaughters of the East-European Jewish immigrants, discovered opportunities to journey ever more deeply, integrating into America's wider worlds. Hence, for many, Jewish commitments became but a single strand in the design of their lives, perhaps more intense when their children were young, and less so earlier and later.[39]

These most recent decades simultaneously opened up the possibility to trod different paths. Perhaps most striking of the new colors twisting through the tapestry of America's Jewish women in these years are those of the Holocaust survivors and Hasidic women. In Nazi-occupied Warsaw, Ruth Skorecki, her husband Mark, and their daughters Anne and Lila had fled the ghetto to pass as Christians. After the war, they were but four of the thousands of Displaced Persons finding their way to America. They were met in New Orleans, as were so many others elsewhere, by housewives from the National Council of Jewish Women who drove Ruth to shop for groceries and took Anne and Lila to the doctor.[40] Later, in the last quarter of the twentieth century, when a quarter of a million Soviet Jews would immigrate, Jewish women would yet again reach out to greet them and to help them master America.

Holocaust survivors also included the first Hasidic Jews to arrive. Creating enclaves in Brooklyn and elsewhere, their women stand out from the rest of America's Jewish women. Their community demands modest dress—women never wear pants; wigs conceal married women's hair. In their "gender-split world" marriage is too serious a concern to leave to the young. Professional matchmakers arrange dates, their sole purpose being to introduce a young woman to her future husband so that in the not-too-distant future she can begin her crucial work of bringing many children into this world. While many in the Hasidic world were born into it, increasingly some of America's Jewish women have entered this world from the outside.[41]

Hasidic daughters marry young and mostly eschew higher education. Yet, seeking higher education has come to characterize most of America's other Jewish women in the latter half of the twentieth century. A study of Newark, New Jersey's Weequahic High School's Class of 1958, which was 83 percent Jewish, found that 57 percent of its female Jewish grads went on to college compared to the then national norm for American women of 34 percent. That trend would continue and accelerate. By 1990, over 85 percent of Jewish women aged 30 to 39 had gone to college; of these, a remarkable 30 percent had gone on to graduate school.[42]

Not surprisingly, changing educational patterns produced changing occupational patterns. Half of the mothers of the students in Weequahic's Class of 1958 worked outside the home. Yet, much of that work, like "helping out" in the family grocery, keeping the books for the family

This woman's place is in the House...
the House of Representatives!

Bella Abzug
for Congress.

A leading American feminist and human rights activist, Bella Abzug (1920-1988) served in Congress from 1970 to 1976. In the years that followed, she headed the National Advisory Committee on Women, founded Women, USA, and cofounded the Women's Environment and Development Organization.

"This woman's place is in the house—the House of Representatives!" [New York], [between 1971 and 1976]. Yanker Poster Collection, Prints and Photographs Division.

shoe store, or running their husbands' medical offices, rendered their workforce participation largely invisible, feeding into the 1950s mythology that America's women, including its Jewish women, were mostly housewives. But by 1990, three-quarters of Jewish women aged 25 to 44 and two-thirds of those aged 45 to 64 showed up in the labor force. Moreover, an increasing number, many surely propelled by the crashing of the barriers to the professional schools in the wake of the feminist demands of the 1960s, had entered the professions.[43]

Joining the women who now became "my daughter, the doctor" was the first generation of women to become rabbis. In 1972, Sally Priesand closed, with her ordination, Reform Judaism's long debate over a woman's right to become a rabbi. Thirteen years later, Conservative Judaism ordained its first female rabbi.[44]

Occupying a historic place in the annals of Judaism, these first female rabbis have sought to open it to women's particular concerns. Their astonishing creativity, part of the emergence of feminist Judaism, has produced new prayers and ceremonials for conception, pregnancy, and childbirth; for those grieving infertility, suffering stillbirth, and turning to adoption; for the onset of menses and the completion of menopause; and for healing after rape, remaining single, and acknowledging marital separation. Furthermore, they have demanded that their congregations and communities see the new colors spreading across the tapestry of America's Jewish women; for, by the late twentieth century, it has come to include more single women, more divorced women, and more lesbians than ever before.[45]

Such demands are part of the long history of political activism of America's Jewish women. The kosher meat boycotts and labor strikes of the immigrant era gave way to new political activities in the years after World War II. In the 1960s Jewish women joining the civil rights movement put their bodies and their lives on the line as they went South with the Freedom Riders.[46] Jewish women, like Betty Friedan, author of the ground-breaking *Feminine Mystique*, stood out among the leaders of the new wave of American feminism as it burst forth.[47] Jewish women's organizations expanded their political involvements. Hadassah's Washington Action Office enabled it to champion in the nation's capital an agenda that now included ending violence against women. At the same time, individual Jewish women carved out personal places in American political life. Congresswoman Bella Abzug, Supreme Court Justice Ruth Bader Ginsburg, and U.S. Senators Barbara Boxer and Dianne Feinstein—-both from California—-stand among them. And down in New Orleans Holocaust survivor Anne Skorecki Levy's passionate quest to expose the neo-Nazism of Louisiana's politician David Duke led to his resounding defeat. Collectively, these American Jewish women embroidered politics into the canvas of their history.

Weaving a brilliant tapestry across time and space, America's Jewish women have stitched their history. Threads of different colors highlighted continuities, but their shades varied and some faded over time, even as new colors burst forth on the canvas. One brightly colored thread traces domestic lives linking the Jewish women who baked challah in their colonial hearths, the young bride crossing the continent in a covered wagon bound for Timbuktu,[48] and mothers raising their suburban children. A vivid skein tracks diverse economic activities—the women who kept colonial boarding houses, who sold miners dry goods, who stitched in tenement sweatshops, who taught in the public schools, who "helped out" in family businesses, and who invented the Barbie doll.[49] Yet, another strand colors in their religious lives. It portrays Jewish women

Sponsored by the North American Jewish Students' Network, this poster advertising a 1973 conference for Jewish women in New York City featured a photo montage with a cross-section of Jewish women and asked the questions: "Where have we come from? And where are we going?"

Barbara Gingold, photographer, "A National Conference of Jewish Women" [New York], 1973. Yanker Poster Collection, Prints and Photographs Division.

teaching Sunday school, coming down from the women's balcony to sit in family pews, sewing for the poor, celebrating bat mitzvahs, visiting the sick, leading services in summer camp, and becoming rabbis. A particularly bold hue is used for their political crusades as they marched on picket lines, voted, championed Zionism, and paraded for women's rights. Using brilliant and variegated colors, America's Jewish women have woven the rich tapestry of their history over 350 years, and we unfurl it to celebrate this landmark anniversary in the history of the Jewish people and America.

A History of American Anti-Semitism

Leonard Dinnerstein

nti-Semitism, prejudice towards a Jew or Jews as a group, because of religious heritage, is an ancient hostility propagated primarily by European Christians for the past two thousand years. This noxious bias came to the New World with the colonists and received continual reinforcement from successive waves of European immigrants. At no time, however, has anti-Semitism ever been as venomous in the colonies or in the United States as it has been in Europe. Save for voting restrictions on people who did not accept the divinity of Jesus Christ (the last remaining law on this topic was eliminated by New Hampshire in 1877), legal barriers circumscribing the rights of American Jews never developed. That does not mean, of course, that intolerance did not exist or that Christians were warm and friendly toward Jews.

Cultural stereotypes of Jews being responsible for the death of the Savior and/or engaging in unsavory economic activities remained. In times of personal or national stress or crisis, in fact, expressions of anti-Semitism intensified. Even the word "Jew" had negative connotations. On different occasions it could mean "Christ-killer," "rogue," "mean," "cold hearted," "swindler," or "selfish." Nonetheless Jews in the United States never had to contend with legal battles to engage in any social, economic, or political endeavor that they sought, although they would later use the law to curtail the rights of those who wished to circumscribe theirs. In this regard

---

In April 1913, the murdered body of a thirteen-year-old girl was found in the basement of an Atlanta pencil factory, and the factory's manager, Leo Frank, was accused of the murder. After a sensational and flawed trial which helped stoke a firestorm of hysteria and prejudice against Frank, he was sentenced to death. When Georgia's governor commuted Frank's sentence to life imprisonment, Frank was kidnapped from jail by an outraged mob and lynched.

The Lynching of Leo Frank, August 15, 1915 [Postcard]. Prints and Photographs Division.

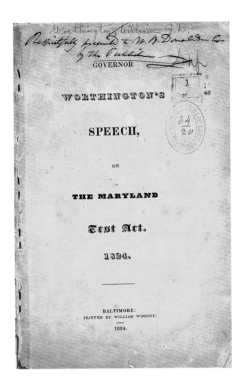

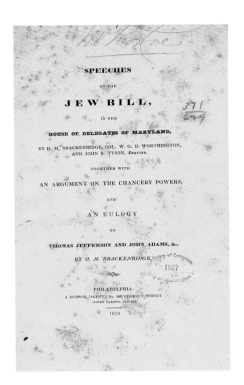

In arguing for passage of a bill to enable Jews to hold public office, Governor Worthington cited George Washington's letter to the Newport Hebrew Congregation to prove that religious freedom was mandated by the founders of the republic.

Governor Worthington's Speech on the Maryland Test Act, 1824, Baltimore, 1824. General Collections.

In this compilation of pro-Jew Bill speeches, H. M. Brackenridge notes that his speech was at the time, in 1818, "published by the Jews of Baltimore, and widely circulated." This is the most direct statement that we have of the involvement of the Maryland Jewish community in the promotion of the Jew Bill, which began in 1818 and was successfully concluded after eight years of persistent advocacy in 1826.

H. M. Brackenridge, Speeches on the Jew Bill, *Philadelphia, 1829. General Collections.*

the United States and, earlier, the thirteen colonies have always been a land of opportunity where individuals of Jewish heritage could follow their goals and make their marks according to their labor and their abilities. Moreover, never have their synagogues or temples been outlawed, although at times in American history vandals have attacked and destroyed them.

The United States has a tradition of openness and has always been a haven for white immigrants who sought a home in this country. During the colonial era white labor was always needed and settlers were encouraged to come. To be sure, many Jews stuck to themselves and, except for business activities, had little to do with Christians. But this varied from locale to locale. In South Carolina, for example, Jews not only constituted 5 percent of the white population in 1830, but they occupied several important posts within the state government. Such recognition, however, was not universal and did not prevail in the other states.

Hostility toward Jews may be seen in attitudes during the colonial period and after regarding non-Christians. Christianity (i.e., Protestantism) was considered the "true faith" and those who worshipped differently, including Catholics, were scorned and sometimes attacked. Newcomers, or even white people whose forebears arrived earlier and embraced some Protestant denomination, were acceptable, but those who chose not to make the values of the dominant culture their own were openly derided. All good Christians felt the need to proselytize and make Jews see the "error of their ways"; some Jews, especially in the eighteenth and nineteenth centuries, succumbed. In textbooks and children's street talk, rhymes often propagated the ideas that adults wanted their children to imbibe. One "Mother Goose" ditty went

Jack sold his egg
To a rogue of a Jew
Who cheated him out
Of half of his due.[1]

Another book informed children that: "the Jews are to be seen in every land. What is the reason for this? Why do they not live in a country of their own as we do? The reason is that they were disobedient to God."[2] It is because they did not accept the "true faith" that voting restrictions remained in several states well into the nineteenth century. Most Americans generally equated Protestant thought with American virtue.

Some of the more prominent Jews of antebellum America, like New York City Sheriff Mordecai Noah (who was also a playwright, newspaper editor, and former American consul in Tunis) and Uriah P. Levy, who spent most of his adult life in the Navy, were singled out by their fellows for acrimonious taunts. Abolitionist leader William Lloyd Garrison denounced Noah, who supported the institution of slavery, as: "the lineal descendant of the mobsters who nailed Jesus to the cross.... Shylock will have his flesh at any cost."[3] Levy often sailed with fellow officers who would not speak to a Jew. As readers of *Niles' Weekly Register*, the closest the nation had to a national newspaper in the Jacksonian era (circa 1820s-1840s), learned, Jews were: "everywhere despised and maltreated."[4]

Major Jewish immigration did not occur until the 1840s when waves of Central Europeans, mostly Germans, arrived in the United States. By 1880 they numbered approximately 250,000 and were generally self-employed as merchants and bankers. That they did well in the United States can be attested to by the fact that in 1890 more than 7,000 of the 10,000 Jews in New York City employed servants.[5] Many of the Central-European Jews also changed the nature of their worshipping practices to minimize anti-Semitic behavior from others. They altered the language of the weekly services from either Spanish (which the Sephardim, who had come from Spain via Holland and South America in the seventeenth century, originally preferred) or Yiddish (which the Europeans spoke) to English. Those who wanted to "Americanize" their religious services also abandoned traditional religious garb, such as prayer shawls and head coverings while worshipping, and allowed men and women to sit next to each other in the temple. Such choices and behavior were forbidden amongst Orthodox Jews. The Reform Jews, as those who Americanized their practices were called, wanted their temples to resemble churches hoping that by so doing Protestants would think of them as being part of a different denomination.

Those who wished to reform Jewish religious behavior, however, had their plans for greater acceptance by other Americans thwarted. From the 1880s through the 1920s, over two million

East-European Jews, almost all originally orthodox religiously, arrived in the United States. The Jews who had adapted to American ways feared that the male newcomers, who wore long black coats and black hats, sported unkempt beards, and prayed according to ancient traditions would increase manifestations of anti-Semitism in the United States. They were correct to have such fears.

Anti-Semitic incidents and events increased rapidly in the last third of the nineteenth century, as did social discrimination. In 1877 a prominent German Jewish banker, Joseph Seligman, was prevented from registering at the Grand Union Hotel in Saratoga Springs, New York, on the grounds that he was Jewish. Although social discrimination had already begun about a decade earlier, the hotel's stance against Seligman, friend of former Presidents Abraham Lincoln and U. S. Grant, received a great deal of newspaper attention. The incident is often referred to as the first anti-Semitic episode in American history, which it clearly was not, but this myth persists. Protestant Americans regarded Jews who had arrived some decades earlier as similar to the East-European newcomers. Hotels and country clubs banned Jews, credit bureaus refused to lend them money (a practice in existence long before the Civil War), and both public and private schools continued setting the tone for Christian children's attitudes and behavior. One Jew who grew up in Syracuse, New York, remembered how in the week before Easter:

We, the undersigned, Merchants of Cincinnati, having
noticed with a deep sense of regret, the uncalled for,
and unjust discrimination, made against the Israelites
of this Country, as a class, by Judge Hilton, of New York, in
excluding them, as guests, from his hotel at Saratoga,
and realizing that such unwarranted action, is a
gross outrage upon our Natural and legal rights, as a
class, and as Americans; an insult to modern civilization, and a stigma upon Republican Institutions, and
regarding Judge Hilton as unworthy our Commercial
intercourse, and having business transactions with the house
of Judge Hilton, known as A. T. Stewart & Co. We now
declare and pledge ourselves, to cease all business relations with the house of A. T. Stewart & Company.

In response to the Seligman incident, a group of
Cincinnati businessmen circulated a petition
protesting Hilton's action as a "gross outrage upon
our natural and legal rights, as a class, and as
Americans" and pledged to no longer do business
with the Hilton companies.

Petition of the Merchants of Cincinnati, Cincinnati,
Ohio, 1877. Courtesy of the Jacob Rader Marcus
Center of the American Jewish Archives.

THE COMMERCIAL VAMPIRE.

N. B.—THIS PICTURE WILL NOT BE FOUND ON THE BARGAIN COUNTER.

This illustration shows "Greed" depicted as a bat with stereotypically "Jewish" features. The bat is seated on a nest ringed with human skulls, each skull representing a small independent business devoured by the greedy department store owner.

Leon Barritt, "The Commercial Vampire," Vim, July 20, 1898. Prints and Photographs Division.

The readings always related to the crucifixion and the teachers seemed to have the habit of intoning their readings, and especially when the word "Jew" was mentioned, in such a manner as to convey the idea not only of contempt, but also of hatred. This was always followed during the recess and for several days after by the most hostile demeanor on the part of the Christian boys and girls of the school, some of whom resorted to physical violence and most of them to the calling of names and the making of scurrilous remarks.[6]

The end of the nineteenth and beginning of the twentieth centuries also marked a noticeable increase in hostility toward Jews from both Catholic children and adults. In the urban areas Jewish men had their beards pulled by wayward youngsters, and the police, mostly of Irish background, used their clubs freely when dealing with Jews. A Catholic woman of Irish descent, who married a Jew, was told by one of her friends, "*of course*, dear, you cannot expect us to receive a Jew."[7] Middle- and upper-class Protestants were more subtle in their behavior. They hid their bigotry, for the most part, behind exquisite public behavior and worked in their neighborhoods, clubs, and businesses to keep Jews far away from them. Amongst their peers and in private, especially after they had had a few drinks, "well bred" people did not hesitate expressing their bias.

Attacks upon Jews, both at home and abroad, led to the formation of the American Jewish Committee (1906) and the Anti-Defamation League of B'nai B'rith (1913). The former began as a result of the 1903 Kishnev pogrom in Russia in which hundreds of Jews were slaughtered. The Committee, composed of self-appointed successful, wealthy, and influential Jews, used quiet and behind-the-scenes discussions with governmental officials to try to ward off anti-Semitism and its effects. The ADL, on the other hand, came into being in September 1913, a month after the occurrence of a notorious miscarriage of justice against a Jew in an Atlanta courtroom—the sentencing of Leo Frank to hang for a murder that he did not commit.

The Leo Frank case, which quickly became a cause celebre, attracted attention because some fellow Jewish Georgians, and later other Jews throughout the United States, believed that Frank was an innocent man who had been convicted of assaulting and murdering one of his thirteen-year-old female employees solely because he was a Jew. In May 1915, after the Georgia Supreme Court had thrice denied appeals for a new trial and the U.S. Supreme Court turned down the request twice, Georgia Governor John M. Slaton, after reviewing the materials presented by the petitioner, commuted his sentence to life imprisonment. Governor Slaton also believed that Frank was innocent, but a complete pardon had not been requested. The governor assumed that the truth of Frank's innocence would eventually emerge and that a future chief executive would give him the pardon that he deserved.

Slaton's action spawned the most violent incident of anti-Semitism in U.S. history. Rednecks marched on the governor's home and denounced him as "King of the Jews."[8] State police protected the governor and his mansion until his term ended a few days later, when he and his wife were escorted to the station and secluded until they boarded a train that would take them out of the state. So many anti-Semitic rallies ensued throughout Georgia that summer that other Jews feared for their lives; many of them, along with their families, fled to other states, never to return.

Almost three months after the commutation, some of Georgia's "best citizens"[9] stormed the state prison, kidnapped Frank, and then drove through the night before they hung him from an oak tree in Marietta, Georgia, the home of the murdered child, on the morning of August 16, 1915. Never again would anti-Semites in the United States carry out such a violent attack on any Jew, although many anti-Semitic incidents and events would occur during the next ninety years.

Anti-Semitism in the United States grew precipitously from the end of World War I through the end of World War II. It was during those years that America's most intense period of hostility toward Jews occurred. Bias towards them peaked in 1946 when over 60 percent of those questioned acknowledged that they had heard anti-Semitic comments within the previous six months.[10] Americans indicated that they disliked Jews and so-called Jewish characteristics. The interlude between the ends of the wars witnessed the first two major immigration restriction acts (1921 and 1924) designed to keep out groups like the Slavs, Italians, and Jews, approximately ten million of whom had arrived during the previous three decades. While no group was specifically named, Congress gave preference in the legislation to people from Western-European nations whose people had come to this country several decades earlier.

The Ford International Weekly

THE DEARBORN INDEPENDENT

By the Year **One Dollar**   Dearborn, Michigan, May 22, 1920   Single Copy **Five Cents**

The International Jew:
The World's Problem

"Among the distinguishing mental and moral traits of the Jews may be mentioned: distaste for hard or violent physical labor; a strong family sense and philoprogenitiveness; a marked religious instinct; the courage of the prophet and martyr rather than of the pioneer and soldier; remarkable power to survive in adverse environments, combined with great ability to retain racial solidarity; capacity for exploitation, both individual and social; shrewdness and astuteness in speculation and money matters generally; an Oriental love of display and a full appreciation of the power and pleasure of social position; a very high average of intellectual ability."

—The New International Encyclopedia.

THE Jew is again being singled out for critical attention throughout the world. His emergence in the financial, political and social spheres has been so complete and spectacular since the war; that his place, power and purpose in the world are being given a new scrutiny, much of it unfriendly. Persecution is not a new experience to the Jew, but intensive scrutiny of his nature and super-nationality is. He has suffered for more than 2,000 years from what may be called the instinctive anti-semitism of the other races, but this antagonism has never been intelligent nor has it been able to make itself intelligible. Nowadays, however, the Jew is being placed, as it were, under the microscope of economic observation that the reasons for his power, the reasons for his separateness, the reasons for his suffering may be defined and understood.

In Russia he is charged with being the source of Bolshevism, an accusation which is serious or not according to the circle in which it is made; we in America, hearing the fervid eloquence and perceiving the prophetic ardor of young Jewish apostles of social and industrial reform, can calmly estimate how it may be. In Germany he is charged with being the cause of the Empire's collapse and a very considerable literature has sprung up, bearing with it a mass of circumstantial evidence that gives the thinker pause. In England he is charged with being the real world ruler, who rules as a super-nation over the nations, rules by the power of gold, and who plays nation against nation for his own purposes, remaining himself discreetly in the background. In America it is pointed out to what extent the elder Jews of wealth and the younger Jews of ambition swarmed through the war organizations —principally those departments which dealt with the commercial and industrial business of war, and also the extent to which they have clung to the advantage which their experience as agents of the government gave them.

IN SIMPLE words, the question of the Jews has come to the fore, but like other questions which lend themselves to prejudice, efforts will be made to hush it up as impolitic for open discussion. If, however, experience has taught us anything it is that questions thus suppressed will sooner or later break out in undesirable and unprofitable forms.

The Jew is the world's enigma. Poor in his masses, he yet controls the world's finances. Scattered abroad without country or government, he yet presents a unity of race continuity which no other people has achieved. Living under legal disabilities in almost every land, he has become the power behind many a throne. There are

ancient prophecies to the effect that the Jew will return to his own land and from that center rule the world, though not until he has undergone an assault by the united nations of mankind.

The single description which will include a larger percentage of Jews than members of any other race is this: he is in business. It may be only gathering rags and selling them, but he is in business. From the sale of old clothes to the control of international trade and finance, the Jew is supremely gifted for business. More than any other race he exhibits a decided aversion to industrial employment, which he balances by an equally decided adaptability to trade. The Gentile boy works his way up, taking employment in the productive or technical departments; but the Jewish boy prefers to begin as messenger, salesman or clerk—anything—so long as it is connected with the commercial side of the business. An early Prussian census illustrates this characteristic: of a total population of 269,400, the Jews comprised six per cent or 16,164. Of these, 12,000 were traders and 4,164 were workmen. Of the Gentile population, the other 94 per cent, or 153,236 people, there were only 17,000 traders.

A MODERN census would show a large professional and literary class added to the traders, but no diminution of the percentage of traders and not much if any increase in the number of wage toilers. In America alone most of the big business, the trusts and the banks, the natural resources and the chief agricultural products, especially tobacco, cotton and sugar, are in the control of Jewish financiers or their agents. Jewish journalists are a large and powerful group here. "Large numbers of department stores are held by the Jewish Encyclopedia, and many if not most . . . Gentile names. Jews are the largest and m . . . residence property in the country. They are . . . world. They absolutely control the circulation . . . out the country. Fewer than any race w . . . noticeable, they receive daily an amount of . . . would be impossible did they not have the . . . distributing it themselves. Werner Sombart . . . Capitalism" says, "If the conditions in Am . . . along the same lines as in the last generatio . . . tistics and the proportion of births among . . . the same, our imagination may picture the . . . hundred years hence as a land inhabited o . . . Jews, wherein the Jews will naturally . . .

On May 22, 1920, Henry Ford launched a series of attacks on Jews based on The Protocols of the Elders of Zion, a scurrilous anti-Semitic work concocted by members of the Russian secret police in the aftermath of World War I. The series described Jews as secretly plotting world revolution and as controlling the world's financial markets. Ford's anti-Semitic tirades found a ready audience, with circulation increasing tenfold from about 70,000 in 1920 to a peak of 700,000 in 1924.

"The International Jew," in The Dearborn Independent, May 22,1920. General Collection.

A hooded Ku Klux Klansman has his arm casually and familiarly draped over Henry Ford's shoulder, suggesting a relationship between two friends sharing common anti-Semitic, nativist, and racist beliefs.

David L. Mekler, Der Emes Vegen Henri Ford [The Truth About Henry Ford], New York, 1924. Hebraic Section.

Also during the 1920s, Henry Ford's newspaper, *The Dearborn Independent*, published excerpts from *The Protocols of the Elders of Zion*, calling its own series "The International Jew." The articles purportedly documented activities that demonstrated that Jews controlled the world's finances and were planning a coup to oust, and take over, Christian governments. Ford's campaign lasted for ninety-one consecutive weeks from 1920 to 1922 and sporadically thereafter. Not until 1927, when the American Jewish Committee forced him to sign a retraction indicating that he had no prejudice toward Jews and would cease publication of these fables, did his campaign end

The prejudice that one saw in Henry Ford's diatribes also existed elsewhere in society. In a more genteel fashion, unstated quotas emerged to bar Jews from many elite colleges and residential areas. Quotas for Jewish students began at Harvard in the early 1920s and continued through the end of the 1940s when legislation passed in New York, Rhode Island, and Massachusetts barred questions regarding religion on college applications or the favoring of applicants of one religion or another. In the previous three decades, as more Russian Jews entered college, WASP officials sought ways to limit their numbers. They could not do so on the basis of academic performance, since Jews generally did well on written tests, so other devices were sought. It was in the 1920s, therefore, that the elite Northeastern private schools began evaluating "character" and including geographical diversification among the items admissions officers were to consider. Since most Jews lived in the New York and New England areas, students applying from Idaho and North Dakota often received preference for admission. As a result of the new policies, almost all of the elite private schools cut the percentage of Jews in attendance to about 3 percent or less of the student body. Finally, Jews found difficulty finding white-collar jobs. In 1930 fully 90 percent of New York City's employers would not hire Jews for professional, managerial, or clerical positions.[11]

During the 1930s, in the midst of the worst Depression in American history, a new wave of verbal anti-Semitism occurred as both Protestant fundamentalists and Catholic priests, especially William Dudley Pelley, son of a Protestant minister, and Father Charles Coughlin, railed against the evils of Jews. Coughlin, who began his campaign in 1938, was an extremely popular radio figure for the next four years as he repeated the canards that anti-Semites had spewed forth for many years: they killed Christ, they controlled the world's economy, and they ran the Communist Party in Russia and hoped to do the same in other nations as well. One might suspect that Adolf Hitler's campaigns against Jews would have aroused the non-Jews in the United States, but they did not. Some religious publications saw Hitler's behavior as God's punishment for those who had not accepted the divinity of Jesus Christ. In 1942, after the United States had entered World War II, President Franklin D. Roosevelt intervened to silence Coughlin. His bishop then gave Coughlin a choice of resigning from the priesthood or ceasing public activities; Coughlin chose the latter.

It seems remarkable that anti-Semitism intensified in the United States during World War II. Fear and anxieties often bring out the worst in people, and Americans worried about their

husbands, fathers, sons, brothers, and cousins in the armed services. Rumors abounded, however, that Jews lacked sufficient patriotic fervor, undermined the war effort by profiteering, and avoided the draft by various schemes. A professor in New York City told colleagues that: "the Battle Hymn of the Jews is 'Onward, Christian Soldiers, we'll make the uniforms.'"[12]

During the war a report from the Office of War Information indicated widespread antagonism toward Jews in half of the forty-two states it investigated and found "unreasonable hate,"[13] particularly among the middle class in Pennsylvania. One individual reported that anti-Semitism in Minneapolis, which would later be dubbed the nation's most anti-Semitic city, was: "stronger here than anywhere I have ever lived. It's so strong that people of all groups I have met make the most blatant statements against Jews with the calm assumption that they are merely stating facts with which anyone could agree."[14] A third-generation American of Irish descent in Los Angeles was appalled by the remarks fellow Americans made about Jews. He had heard that "all of the Jews stay out of the army, or, if they get in, they are given commissions—the President is a Jew—Jews own 80 percent of the nation's wealth—Jews got us into the war—the WPA [Works Progress Administration] is controlled by Jews...."[15]

This horrific evidence of increased and outspoken anti-Semitism frightened American Jewry. By the end of the 1930s, American Jewish defense and community relations organizations had increased their staffs, determined to curb existing bigotry and prevent its continued growth. Thoughtful Jews realized that governmental assistance and unity among Jewish organization—two avenues that had not succeeded in the past—would be necessary to accomplish their goals. In the early 1940s representatives of several American Jewish groups formed the National Community Relations Advisory Council (NCRAC), which began functioning in March 1944. Its goal was to use whatever legal methods were necessary to reverse the course of growing hostility toward minorities, especially Jews.

That NCRAC was quickly successful there can be no doubt. On January 1, 1945, a labor law went into effect in New York State barring discrimination in employment. Within the next five years laws in several cities and states prohibited discrimination in employment, housing, and admission to both public and private nonsectarian schools and colleges. Forty travel agents in New York City agreed not to recommend hotels and other places of recreation that barred Jews. By 1950, pollsters found that only 24 percent of Americans claimed to have heard anyone express an antisemitic remark "in the last six months." In 1946, 64 percent had responded affirmatively to the same question.[16]

The last third of the twentieth and the first years of the twenty-first centuries have been the "golden age" for Jews in America. Anti-Semitism declined during those years, although periodic incidents and eruptions convinced many, if not most, Jews that the bias was still alive and well. In the late 1980s, for example, some male college students (including Jews) started referring to female Jewish students as "JAPS" (Jewish-American Princesses) because they were stylishly dressed and wore attractive jewelry. The teasing spread to other Eastern universities and many adult Jews worried that a new anti-Semitic trend was beginning. The "trend" lasted perhaps a year or two and then vanished.

To be sure, anti-Semitism did not disappear, but when one reviews the whole period one sees such remarkable advances for Jews in a Gentile society that non-Jews considered American Jews as privileged rather than victimized. Christians regarded Jews as having "made it" in society, and polls of all types of Americans confirmed that Jews were the wealthiest and most well-educated group in the United States. In 1992, for example, 69.2 percent of Jewish Baby Boomers (those born in 1946 through 1964) had graduated from college in contrast to 24.5 percent of non-Jews . As a result, 60 percent of the Jewish "Boomers" occupied high-status positions compared with only 30 percent of non-Jews.[17] A smaller proportion of Jews were on welfare than any other group, while a larger number ranked among those who earned $75,000 a year.[18] In 1956,

This blatantly anti-Semitic flyer—with an image of a predatory Jew and an exhortation for "Christian Vigilantes [to] Arise!"— was directed at the activities of the Hollywood Anti-Nazi League, a group that campaigned against Nazism and organized a boycott of German goods.

"Boycott the Movies!" circa 1937. Courtesy of the Urban Archives, University of California, Northridge.

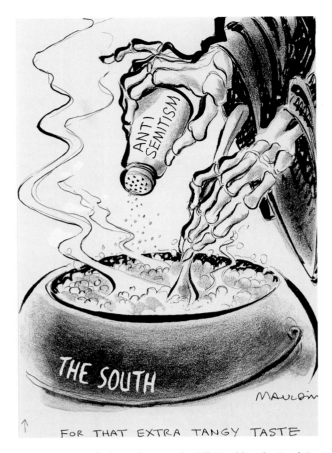

FOR THAT EXTRA TANGY TASTE

In this May 1958 editorial cartoon by Bill Mauldin, the South is depicted as a steaming cauldron, with the skeletal hands of the angel of death adding the salt of anti-Semitism to an already volatile brew. Anti-Jewish violence peaked later that year when the Reform Jewish Temple in Atlanta was dynamited by a group of extreme segregationists.

Bill Mauldin. "For that Extra Tangy Taste," in the St. Louis Post-Dispatch, *May 26, 1958. © 1958 by Bill Mauldin. reprinted Courtesy of the Mauldin Estate. Prints and Photographs Division.*

sociologist Herbert Gans noted: "organized anti-Semitism is already confined mostly to the lunatic fringe." The following year historian Oscar Handlin of Harvard University wrote that the position of Jews in the United States was far better: "than even the most optimistic individuals could have hoped for two decades earlier."[19]

Many reasons may be given for the changed situation of Jews in the United States. Certainly the effort to promote equal opportunities for all groups nears the top of those reasons. In 1954 the U.S. Supreme Court, in one of its most important decisions of the twentieth century, outlawed "separate-but-equal" education for children, and this led to a fifteen-year fight for integrated facilities in this country. Many American soldiers had returned from World War II determined to eradicate traditional, and often humiliating, ethnic and religious prejudices and they supported legal changes that would accomplish those goals. And then during the social upheavals of the 1960s Congress passed the Civil Rights Act, which outlawed discrimination by every business involved in interstate commerce. The Supreme Court interpreted the bill so widely that if a restaurant purchased napkins that were made from parts of trees cut down in another state, then that business was considered to be involved in interstate commerce.

General prosperity in the United States after World War II also loosened people's bigoted feelings, while both public and private educational institutions began teaching tolerance to the children. The fight for civil rights began wholeheartedly in 1954 and has not yet ceased. All minority groups benefited from efforts made by members of the dominant culture to focus upon equality of opportunity and to put an end to public discrimination. In that regard the civil rights movement and legislation accomplished their goals.

But at what seemed the best time for blacks in modern history, African-American hostility to Jews erupted. It was based on the same prejudices as white hostility: Christian teachings and viewing Jews as alleged economic predators. Jews were thought to have a great deal of money and to have refused to accept the true faith. Moreover, they were seen as overwhelmingly powerful. In 1859 a black slave tried to prevent her transfer to a new owner. When asked about her objections she confessed, "They tell me Miss Isaacs is a Jew; an' if the Jews kill the Lord and Master, what won't they do with a poor little nigger like me!"[20] During World War I, James

Weldon Johnson, one of the early leaders of the NAACP, wrote that three million Jews in the United States acting as a unit get results."[21] After Adolf Hitler assumed power in Germany, in 1933, W.E.B. DuBois, editor of the NAACP publication, *The Crisis*, wrote:

Nothing has filled us with such unholy glee as Hitler and the Nordics.

When the only "inferior" peoples were "niggers" it was hard to get the attention of the New York Times for little matters of race, lynchings and mobs. But now that the damned include the owner of the Times, moral indignation is perking up.[22]

Many blacks even refused to believe the news that came out of Germany. While deploring anti-Semitism, the *Philadelphia Tribune* editorialized: "It is necessary to remember, however, that perhaps most of what is told about Jewish treatment in Germany is propaganda since the Jews control to a great extent the international press."[23]

At the end of the First and Second World Wars, Jewish attitudes toward blacks were paternalistic. Blacks did not like Jews, even after receiving much assistance from them for their legal causes, schools, and hospitals. In 1945 the editor of Tennessee's *National Baptist Voice* wrote: "Negroes are filled with anti-Semitism. In any group of Negroes, if the white people are not around, the mention of the Jew calls forth bitter tirades."[24]

Tensions between blacks and Jews surfaced during a battle for control of a local school district in New York between the heavily Jewish United Federation of Teachers and the local school board which was African American. The cover story, which describes the vituperative rhetoric of the protagonists, was titled, "The Black and the Jew: A Falling Out of Allies."

"Black vs. Jew: A Tragic Confrontation," cover story in Time *magazine, January 31, 1969. Time Life Pictures/ Getty Images. General Collections.*

Blacks and Jews continued having uneasy relations with one another even though both groups were aligned during the fight for civil rights after World War II. Until the civil rights era, black views generally were ignored by the major dailies in America. Therefore the ups and downs of black and Jewish attitudes toward one another rarely received much attention. The first major episode after the passage of the Civil Rights Act in 1964 occurred in 1967 in New York City. African-American community leaders were trying to get control of their schools and hire teachers they thought would be best for their students, while members of the teachers' union opposed changing any existing rules. What essentially was a labor conflict escalated quickly into a black-Jewish situation, with the former calling the latter "racists," and the latter calling the former "anti-Semites." Thereafter there were many public situations that led to charges and countercharges between the two groups.

A major issue dividing whites and blacks, and especially Jews and blacks, in the 1970s, was "affirmative action." While blacks did not benefit economically from the civil rights legislation—in that their homes were still in slums, their schools were inferior, and their job opportunities were still limited—from the perspective of whites, African Americans were being given unprecedented assistance in trying to help them move up the socioeconomic ladder. Many whites believed that "affirmative action" would help members of minority groups. While Jews, in general, supported helping those in need, they regarded "affirmative action" as another term for "quotas," from which Jews had suffered in earlier years. American liberals split on this issue and there was no consensus on the topic. Finally, in 1977, the Supreme Court, by a vote of 5-4, stated that "affirmative action" could continue as one of the criteria in selecting people for slots at universities but it could not be the sole criterion. This opinion was reaffirmed by the Court in a 2003 decision.

But that did not end African-American attacks upon Jews. What blacks had learned from the previous two decades of conflict was that newspapers quickly reported whatever difficulties existed in the relationship between the two groups. Therefore, to get attention from white people, African Americans increased the volume of their rhetoric against Jews. Perhaps the most outspoken individual of the 1980s and 1990s was the Black Muslim minister Louis Farrakhan. Farrakhan had a broad program of activities that would help elevate African Americans in the United States. But whenever he spoke, he received hardly any newspaper coverage. Then in 1984 he proclaimed that "Hitler was a very great man"[25] and he received national attention. Farrakhan then engaged in diatribes against Jews because he was sure that his words would be heard. Although a Muslim, he often spoke in the biblical idiom that fellow blacks could understand and relate to. On one occasion he compared himself with Jesus:

Jesus had a controversy with the Jews. Farrakhan had a controversy with the Jews. Jesus was hated by the Jews. Farrakhan is hated by the Jews. Jesus was scourged by Jews in their temple. Farrakhan is scourged by Jews in their synagogues.[26]

Farrakhan continued ranting against the Jews through the 1990s and then he became ill. Since the onset of his illness, his followers have tempered their public hostility to Jews.

Another area that frightened Jews who believed that anti-Semitism was spreading again was the position some Americans took on the issue of Israeli-Palestinian relations in the Middle East. While most people in the United States still support the policies of the Israeli government, a shift has taken place. Many faculty and activists on American college campuses in 2002 to 2003 have questioned whether Israel really is seeking peace in the Middle East.

How many critics of Israeli policies are anti-Semites is impossible to know. According to Abe Foxman, head of the Anti-Defamation League, anti-Semitism declined continually over the past half century to a low of 12 percent of the American population in 1998. By 2002 that figure had risen again to about 17 percent.[27] Why has the decline reversed itself? That is difficult to say. Foxman suggested that the ADL definition of an anti-Semite might "no longer be adequate for the current situation. Much radicalism and third-worldism expresses itself against Israel in anti-Semitic ways."[28] Whether Middle-Eastern policies have affected American attitudes toward Jews may not be known for some time. One cannot measure what people think in their heads or feel in their bones. It takes time for attitudes to jell forcefully before they become part of the general public discourse; it takes even more time to see whether a phenomenon is transient or has staying power. Having said this, and having seen several other so-called eruptions of anti-Semitism wind down and vanish, it seems fair to say that anti-Semitism in the United States is weaker today than it was a decade ago and for decades before that. Despite the ADL's concern, Jerome Chanes, author of *Antisemitism in America: Exploding the Myths,* asserts that there is relatively little active anti-Semitism in this country; and what little there is has, in any case, precious little effect on the security of Jews in the United States. That security, says Chanes, is measured by the ability of Jews to participate in the society, without fear of anti-Jewish animus. On March 2, 2003, Chanes asserted: "Antisemitism in the United States continues on the decline, and the security of Jews in the U.S. is strong. Period."[29]

SECTION
3

Forward
ART SECTION
SUNDAY, NOVEMBER 1, 1936

פֿאָרווערטס

קונסט בילאגע
זונטאג, נאוועמבער 1, 1936

Forward

SECTION
3

ROOSEVELT
Labor's Choice

רוזוועלט

דעם אַרבײטערס אויסוואהל

American Jews and Politics

Stephen J. Whitfield

F rom the colonial period until the end of the nineteenth century, Jews were not
numerous enough or conspicuous enough or cohesive enough to have constituted a
singular political force. That would await two events: the mass migration from
Eastern Europe in the aftermath of Tsarist pogroms and the response of the New Deal to the
Great Depression. About a century ago, well over two million Jews arrived in the major cities of
the East Coast and the Midwest in particular; and these immigrants were mostly impoverished,
fleeing as much from the destitution that afflicted the Tsarist Empire as from its religious
persecution. At the dawn of the twentieth century, according to one government report, $9 was
the average sum in the pockets of these new Americans; and insofar as they adopted a political
stance, it was tilted further to the left than the politics of the much smaller Sephardic and
German Jewish communities that had been established earlier, and these newcomers were more
receptive to socialism than most other immigrant groups. Membership in the working and
lower classes made the Jews especially vulnerable to the crisis of capitalism that erupted in 1929,
and many businessmen and others in the middle class lost their fortunes as well. (Among
them was Isidore Miller, a New York clothier, whose son Arthur would write the most famous
dramatic critique of capitalism, *Death of a Salesman* [1949].)

The administration of Franklin D. Roosevelt promised to meet the terrible challenge of the
Great Depression; and though the shift from the Republican Party had already begun in the

This issue of the Yiddish socialist daily, the Forverts, *endorsed Roosevelt for reelection as "Labor's Choice" on
the cover of its November 1, 1936, rotogravure section. In 1936, Roosevelt garnered a whopping 85 percent of the
Jewish vote.*

"Roosevelt Labor's Choice," New York, Forverts, November 1, 1936. Serial and Government Publications Division.

This caricature of Ulysses S. Grant shows him shedding crocodile tears over the persecution of Jews in Russia, while reminding him of his infamous Order No.11 issued in 1862 that banned Jews as a class from Kentucky, Tennessee, and Mississippi. At his feet, a puddle forms bearing the legend, "Jewish vote 1884."

"Then and Now–1862 and 1882," in Puck, February 15, 1882. Prints and Photographs Division.

1920s, the elusive goals of recovery, relief, and regulatory reform that FDR formulated lured Jews into the Democratic Party in overwhelming numbers, forming a pattern that persisted for the rest of the century. The four elections that Roosevelt won set the standard against which subsequent Jewish devotion to the liberalism of the Democratic Party has come to be measured.

The depth of this fervor can be observed in microcosm with the Schechter brothers, who claimed that their kosher poultry business in Brooklyn was being badly hurt by the National Recovery Administration. The NRA was a keystone of New Deal regulation. The Schechters challenged the legality of the NRA, and the Supreme Court agreed with them in a landmark 1935 decision. The following year was a presidential election, and all sixteen votes in the Schechter family went to Roosevelt. So did the most Jewish ward in the United States, in Chicago—by a margin of 96 percent. That sort of near unanimity is only bettered in elections organized by Third World dictators, who tend to run unopposed in plebiscites. Roosevelt never again matched his 1936 electoral triumph, when he won all but two states; and even he failed to keep intact an unstable coalition that ranged all the way from white segregationists in the South to urban Negroes in the North. Other Americans were as impoverished, as crushed by the Great Depression, as were the Jews. Yet no group would cling more tenaciously to the liberal wing of the Democratic Party than would the Jews, who gave Roosevelt 90 percent of their vote in 1940 and again in 1944.

It might be contended that during the New Deal, the era that inaugurated the modern political style of the Jews, they voted to satisfy their economic interests as unhesitatingly as other disadvantaged groups. The promise of recovery from the Great Depression, so it might be conjectured, is sufficient to explain the whopping electoral majorities conferred upon Roosevelt. The New Deal was indeed resourceful and pragmatic—and moderately successful—in its effort to revise a free-enterprise system badly in need of repair. But other factors must be summoned to account for his popularity. FDR managed to symbolize the progressive spirit of communal claims against a rampant individualism. Against selfishness and greed, the New Deal pitted an ideal of solidarity toward which Jews were already sympathetic. For instance, the cartoonist William Steig was born in Brooklyn in 1907, the son of a house painter and a seamstress. "My parents didn't want their sons to become laborers, because we'd be exploited by businessmen," Steig recalled; "and they didn't want us to become businessmen, because then we'd exploit the laborers."[1] Because the family was too impoverished to enable the sons to become professionals, Steig became an artist. His success was atypical; the ethos of his family was not.

The New Deal appealed to such Jews; and in drawing upon the talent of a few conspicuous advisors, like Secretary of the Treasury Henry Morgenthau, Jr., legislative draftsman Benjamin V. Cohen, and Professor Felix Frankfurter, the president himself proved that he had triumphed over the snobbery of his patrician origins. Beginning in 1941 the commander-in-chief also embodied leadership in the Allied struggle against the Third Reich, and in the Four Freedoms offered a democratic counterweight to the nihilism of Nazism and the horror of total war. No wonder then that a Republican judge, Jonah Goldstein, famously if ruefully remarked that the Jews attached themselves to three worlds (or, in Yiddish, *velten*): *de velt* (this world), *yene velt* (the world to come), and Roosevelt.

The first test of the enduring Jewish loyalty to liberalism was not the election of 1948. The Fair Deal was after a continuation of the New Deal, and incumbent Harry Truman had recognized the state of Israel only eleven minutes after its birth. Consider the 1950s, when Jews twice had the opportunity to vote for Republican Dwight D. Eisenhower, who had been the military leader of the crusade in Europe and was thereafter first in the hearts of his countrymen. Governor Adlai Stevenson of Illinois nevertheless got almost two out of every three Jewish votes, even in 1956, when prosperity had manifestly embraced the Jewish minority, which was increasingly nestled in suburbia and in the bourgeoisie as well. A switch to the GOP may well have been in order.

By 1960 political scientists were compelled to explain why the Democratic nominee, Senator John F. Kennedy, won a higher percentage of votes among Jews than he did among his fellow Roman Catholics; or why in 1964, campaigning against the grandson of an Arizona peddler named Morris Goldwasser, incumbent Lyndon B. Johnson received proportionately as many Jewish votes as had any president since Roosevelt himself. Johnson was too cornpone a figure to remind anyone of the urbane FDR, and therefore the explanation for LBJ's appeal to Jewish voters was simple: The Great Society was designed to fulfill the unfinished pledges of the New Deal itself. In that decade Alabama's racist governor, George C. Wallace, tried to be a spoiler in

The translation of this presidential campaign pamphlet for Teddy Roosevelt into Yiddish attests to the involvement of the new immigrants in the electoral process, as well as to the efforts of the candidates to secure their vote. The pamphlet was translated into Yiddish by Simon Freed and illustrated by J. Klapp.

Byron Andrews, Di Fakten iber dem Kandidate (The Facts about the Candidate), Chicago, 1904. Courtesy of the American Jewish Historical Society, New York, NY and Newton Centre, MA.

אונזער נעקסטער קאנגרעסמאן

פֿון 12טען קאנגרעסיאנאל דיסטריקט

מאיר לאנדאן

This sample ballot in Yiddish instructs the voter as follows: "The Congressman's name appears in section number 14 of the ballot with the rest of the congressmen. To vote for Meyer London for Congress mark an X next to his name, just as it is indicated below...."

"Our Next Congressman, From the 12th Congressional District, Meyer London, sample ballot, Der Groyser Kundes: "The Big Stick," *New York, October 30, 1914. Hebraic Section.*

primaries and general elections. Jewish voters rejected his candidacy as decisively as blacks did. In 1968 the margins of Vice-President Hubert Humphrey's victories in Jewish neighborhoods closely mirrored his successes in black slums and Chicano barrios, which inspired Milton Himmelfarb of the American Jewish Committee to quip that Jews lived like Episcopalians but voted like Puerto Ricans. Soon this would not quite be true, because Jewish income levels were registering *higher* than the earnings of the Episcopalians and Congregationalists who had founded most of the New World colonies over three centuries ago. Indeed "the socioeconomic gap between Jews and Christians. . . is greater than the gap between blacks and whites," Stephan Thernstrom and Abigail Thernstrom reported in 1997. The per capita incomes of Jews was almost double the figure for Gentile Americans—a gap larger than the economic division between the two races.[2]

It was expected that 1972 would be a turning point—a dramatic shift to the Republican Party. But the point never turned. A famous news photo of Sammy Davis, Jr., embracing incumbent Richard Nixon did not prove to be prophetic of how the entertainer's coreligionists would respond to the president, who made an ethnic pitch that had all the subtlety of a recruitment poster. Such a campaign was also very effective: President Nixon secured the votes of the majority of every white ethnic group except one. As a Republican he orchestrated the customary appeals of his party to the more comfortable classes and to the residents of high socioeconomic areas, who gave the president a whopping three-fourths of their ballots. His opponent was a Methodist preacher's son from the Great Plains who was depicted as rather "soft" on the issue of Israeli security. Senator George McGovern of South Dakota sometimes seemed to be speaking to urban Jewish audiences from a different emotional area code, and he compounded a series of campaign blunders by going into the Garment District of New York to order milk with his chopped chicken liver. McGovern was the most liberal Democratic candidate in memory; no other nominee since FDR had ever tilted the party so far port side. No wonder that he managed to win less than a third of the white Gentile vote. But he got two-thirds of the Jewish vote. Indeed, so dim were the prospects of Jews abandoning their liberalism that, had the rest of the electorate voted as they did, McGovern would have buried Nixon in the greatest landslide in American history.

Or how could political scientists explain 1976? A white Southerner was much *less* likely to vote for Governor Jimmy Carter than was a Northern Jew. In fact, had it not been for the black vote, the Democratic candidate would have lost every Southern state except for his native Georgia. But Carter did attract 72 percent of Jewish ballots; and the historian may speculate that had an even more liberal Democrat been nominated—say, Senator Edward M. Kennedy of Massachusetts—the Jewish margin would have been even more enthusiastic.

Four years later Carter attracted more of the Jewish vote than did Governor Ronald Reagan of California. But for the first time since the New Deal era, a Democratic candidate could not secure a majority of that vote. Two of the polls—a CBS exit poll and a later one by the American Jewish Committee—indicated that Carter won a plurality of about 44 percent, five points ahead of Reagan. Former Congressman John Anderson of Illinois repudiated his earlier drive for a Constitutional amendment that would have declared the United States to be a Christian nation, and received about 15 percent of the Jewish vote. It is fair to assume that Anderson diverted the votes of Jews who ordinarily considered themselves Democrats and/or liberals, since the 10 percent of American Jewry that thinks of itself as Republican would have found little warrant for preferring Anderson to the conservative, equally pro-Israel Reagan. Almost 60 percent of the Jewish vote therefore remained in the Democratic and/or more liberal column in 1980. Reagan nevertheless topped even Eisenhower's percentage of the Jewish vote.

But four years later, the GOP failed to maintain its slice of the bloc that was the most reliably Democratic of the ethnic whites who once belonged to the Roosevelt coalition. The 1984 failure is remarkable. Ronald Reagan presided over a more prosperous economy than what he had inherited four years earlier. By 1984 the rate of inflation had dropped to its lowest point in twelve years; the rate of economic growth had climbed to its highest point in thirty-four years. Even the unemployment rate was skidding. Indeed, to his question, "Are you better off than you were four years ago?", most citizens (including most Jews) would have been obliged to answer in the affirmative. That, too, would have been the answer of his Democratic opponent, Walter Mondale, who had left the vice-presidency in 1981 with a net worth of only $15,000. Moreover, Reagan was on the record in opposition to interpreting affirmative action as quotas, an issue on which Jews were especially sensitive.

This photograph of Franklin Delano Roosevelt and Henry Morgenthau, Jr., features Roosevelt's personal inscription to Morgenthau, "from one of two of a kind."

Photograph of Franklin Delano Roosevelt and Henry Morgenthau, Jr., February 9, 1934. Franklin D. Roosevelt Presidential Library, National Archives and Records Administration.

This hand-drawn plaque includes dual Hebrew prayers for Winston Churchill and Franklin Roosevelt. The one for Roosevelt reads: "[May He] who gives salvation to President Roosevelt, [He] whose kingdom is everlasting, protect, and increase, and raise up all of the officials of America, and [may] the King of Kings lift them up and lengthen their days in office."

Hebrew Prayers for Roosevelt and Churchill, circa 1942. Hebraic Section.

And even though the GOP spent four times as much as did the Democrats to lure the Jewish vote, even though the incumbent did 8 percent better among the general electorate than he had done in 1980, Reagan did worse by the same percentage among Jewish voters. In getting two-thirds of the Jewish vote, former vice-president Mondale touched a more enthusiastic constituency only among blacks and the unemployed. This was so mystifying that a few neo-conservatives cried foul, charging that pollsters did not properly weigh the conservative ballots of the more pious, less chic Jewish neighborhoods. But the argument that Mondale appeared to have done better only "because poor Jews were not sufficiently sampled," sociologist Nathan Glazer concluded, still makes the Jews odd: "They are a group where you have to sample the poor in order to find Republicans."[3]

The affluence that was so evident among Jews in the decades after the Fair Deal demonstrated that pocketbook considerations would not be decisive, that Jews would not be affected as other voting blocs were. Jews have constituted an irrational number in the equation of U.S. elections, having consistently violated—since the Roosevelt era—one of the very few axioms of political science: the higher the income, the bigger the margin for the GOP. Apparently Jews have not defined their interests in the terms that others who are similarly situated have managed to do. The failure of the Republican Party to appeal to this particular minority in the era of Nixon and Reagan therefore explains why subsequent elections produced no surprises. In 1988 Governor Michael Dukakis of Massachusetts ran badly against Vice-President George H. W. Bush, losing every state in the once-solid South to the blue-blooded ex-New Englander. But Dukakis did better among Jews than even among Greek Americans. Bill Clinton's popularity among Jews need not be belabored, since it reached levels not achieved since the 1960s. His standing was not hurt by choosing only Jews as his appointees to the Supreme Court: Ruth Bader Ginsburg and Stephen G. Breyer. The greatest prosperity of the twentieth century was widely attributed to Clinton's choices to run the economy: Alan Greenspan, Robert Rubin, and Lawrence Sommers. The Democrats got 80 percent of this minority's ballots in 1992, and dropped by only two percentage points four years later, when Clinton ran for reelection against Senator Robert Dole of Kansas. Clinton's popularity among Jews held steady even during the president's impeachment ordeal of 1999. His chosen successor, Vice-President Al Gore, not only beat his opponent, Governor George W. Bush of Texas, by half a million votes in the general election, but also did much better than the Republican nominee among Jews as well, attracting 79 percent of their ballots. The historical conclusion is therefore inescapable: Democrats beat Republicans in

In 1972, Sammy Davis, Jr., endorsed Richard Nixon's reelection for president, an endorsement that did not translate into more votes for Nixon from Davis's co-religionists.

Richard M. Nixon and Sammy Davis, Jr., August 22, 1972.

Issued by the New York State Office of the Concerned Citizens for the Re-election of the President, this campaign poster for Richard Nixon emphasized the incumbent's support for Israel, as well as his efforts on behalf of Soviet Jewry. Despite these points of affinity, Jews voted overwhelmingly for George McGovern, Nixon's liberal opponent, who nevertheless lost by a landslide.

Concerned Citizens for the Re-election of the President, "Voters — if you are concerned about Israel ....," 1972. Yanker Poster Collection, Prints and Photographs Division.

Jewish precincts almost as regularly as queens beat jacks in poker.

If American Jewry is not galvanized primarily by economic concerns, then what does make its political culture distinctive? What has motivated such voters— whether casting ballots for socialist candidates earlier in the century or sustaining allegiance to Democratic Party liberalism thereafter—has been quite eccentric. It is a thirst for justice, often expressed in an idiom of moralism. Jews have envisioned politics to be the means by which unfairness, oppression, and hatred might be terminated. To offer such an interpretation hardly implies that those qualities and desires are unique to Jews, who do not hold the franchise on ethics—either in theory or in practice. But what supports such an analysis are the voting patterns and the polling data and questionnaires that admit of no other interpretation. Jews have been more susceptible than other voters to an ideal of human solidarity, to ideologies and programs that can be packaged in ethical terms, and to politicians who can present themselves as apostles of social justice. More so than other Americans, Jewish voters are inspired by appeals that can be contrived to echo the prophetic assault upon complacency and comfort.

The policies that Jews have supported and the causes that they have championed, the values they have professed to cherish and the appeals that have charmed or alarmed them have not mirrored the political profile of any other group. Arguments of immediate expediency and calls for ethnic loyalty have found them less receptive than other minorities. To be sure, when party machines and local bosses were dominant in the first third of the twentieth century in particular, Jews mostly voted for the conventional candidates. But they have differed from the Irish, the Poles, the Italians, and others in their participation in crusades designed to end the corruption that contaminated such machines. In this respect they tended to resemble patrician Protestants of respectable Anglo-Saxon stock in their Progressive hostility to the "old politics" of the bosses.

So idealistic a stance persisted, for example, at least until the outbreak of the Watergate scandal—the most notorious episode in American political history. Nearly all the president's men were convicted and sentenced to jail, or plea-bargained to avoid incarceration; and a grand jury branded Nixon himself as an unindicted co-conspirator. Well into 1974, 29 percent of Gentiles still acknowledged their approval of his administration and their regret at his resignation. For

Jews the corresponding figure almost came in under radar: 6 percent. This near-zero tolerance for the criminal abuse of power in the Nixon administration suggests something of the moralistic character of the Jewish political stance that is deeper than mere Democratic partisanship. Even though the national experiment in self-government resembles professional wrestling— with its fake pains and screams and its relative harmlessness—Jews have been conspicuously involved in seeking alternatives, in reform movements and especially in far-left ideologies that promised a cooperative commonwealth, so that the barriers of class and tribe would be transcended and so that want and poverty would be extinguished.

The demand that the world conform to standards of social justice might be contrasted with Tolstoy's summation of the Gospels into the injunction: Resist Not Evil. But the Jews who have engaged in politics seem to have been guided by a different motto: resist evil, which could be recognized and challenged through the injection of idealism in politics. Unlike African Americans, whose experience of oppression has been so direct, and whose situation has been so historically shaped by the stigma that whites have attached to skin color, Jews have constituted (in the formulation of an American historian of Zionism, Ben Halpern) an "ideological minority." Commanded to be "a kingdom of priests, a holy people," they *choose* to be different according to a particular value system, a complex of symbols and ideas that impose meaning and coherence upon their lives. Daily existence may have been reduced to pressing pants in sweatshops or delivering milk in slums. But what could give life its purpose amidst poverty, and give confidence amidst oppression, was a set of ideals that the ancient Hebrews and their descendants had developed and hoped would elevate the human condition. Those beliefs were biblical in origin; and the influence of the Hebrews' ethics has been pervasive and incalculable, defining in large measure the aspiration—if hardly the achievement—of Christians and Jews alike. There are innumerable minority groups. But neither Kurds, nor Roma, nor Sikhs, nor Mormons have been historically activated by the liberal imagination. Marginality by itself turns nobody into a reformer; to be treated differently, or shabbily, turns no one automatically into, say, a champion of civil rights or civil liberties.

In 1980, Ronald Reagan defeated Jimmy Carter, securing 39 percent of the Jewish vote to Jimmy Carter's 44 percent—the closest that a Republican has come to winning the Jewish vote since the New Deal.

Hebrew/English Ronald Reagan Campaign button, 1984. Hebraic Section.

Yet the assumption that life is given dignity insofar as it can be infused with ethical idealism has exerted a special attraction for Jews. Louis D. Brandeis noticed this in 1914, upon assuming the leadership of the Zionist movement in the United States. He acknowledged how detached he had been from Jewry and its problems and admitted his considerable ignorance of Judaism. But the Progressive attorney asserted that recent encounters with other Jews had taught him that they exhibit "those qualities which we of the twentieth century seek to develop in our struggle for justice and democracy—a deep moral feeling which makes them capable of noble acts; [and] a deep sense of [the] brotherhood of man."[4] Some of this praise can of course be discounted as self-congratulation; a fierce desire to be included in a

A successful lawyer, Louis D. Brandeis (1856-1941) became active in the nascent American Zionist movement in the early years of the twentieth century. In 1915, he became America's leading spokesman for Zionism, and his participation in the movement served to legitimize it in the eyes of American Jewry. He believed strongly that Zionism and American patriotism were compatible, a view expressed in the pamphlet displayed here. In 1916, Louis Brandeis became the Supreme Court's first Jewish justice.

Louis D. Brandeis portrait, circa 1915. Prints and Photographs Division.

Louis D. Brandeis, Zionism and Patriotism, New York, 1918. General Collections.

ZIONISM AND PATRIOTISM

BY
LOUIS D. BRANDEIS, Esq.

1918
PUBLISHED BY THE
Federation of American Zionists
44 East 23d Street
New York

movement of national restoration may have produced an excess of chauvinism. But the very fact that Brandeis approached Jewish life more or less from the outside licensed him to see more clearly than those who had absorbed its beliefs by osmosis the oddity of an emphasis upon a moralistic patrimony, which American Jews have generally translated into progressive causes and reformist methods. One downside is self-righteousness. In the Woody Allen film *Manhattan* (1979), a character with the waspish name of Yale (played by Michael Murphy) berates the neurotic Jewish seeker of integrity (played by Allen) for allegedly trying to be God. Allen exculpates himself as follows: "I—I gotta model myself after *someone!*"[5] That exchange is a clue to Jewish public culture.

Another defect of such politics is an over-investment in ideas at the expense of the concrete; the allure of rhetoric has sometimes been so seductive that mere gestures of sympathy have sufficed. Those who crafted foreign policy, for example, sometimes grasped how deftly such sentiments could be manipulated, how readily pieties could be surrogates for effective action. The ease with which FDR could get away with pretending to help alleviate the suffering of refugees in the era of the Holocaust has become a staple of the diplomatic historiography of the era of the Second World War, but a precedent can be found in the administration of his distant cousin. In 1902, after the Rumanian government intensified economic discrimination against its Jewish population, American Jewish spokesmen persuaded the Department of State to send a diplomatic note chastising such oppression as "repugnant to the moral sense of liberal modern peoples." Such notes made a hero of Secretary of State John Hay, who smirked privately about the gullibility of "the Hebrews. . . poor dears! [who] all over the country think we are bully boys."[6]

After the awful Kishinev pogrom in Tsarist-ruled Bessarabia a year later, New York's genteel "uptown" Jewish leadership—which was sensitive to what motivated the "downtown" immigrant masses—sought to deflect the outrage emanating from the Lower East Side. A petition campaign was organized. Burnished with the signatures of prestigious "allrightniks," this slow, tedious process was never expected to reach the proper address in Russia. John Hay's inspired solution, when confronted with a petition whose own promoters never intended to deliver it, was to place it in the archives of the Department of State. "In the future[,] when students of history come to peruse this document," he proclaimed during the ceremony of interment, "they will wonder how the petitioners, moved to profound indignation by intolerable wrongs perpetrated on the innocent and helpless, could have expressed themselves in a language so earnest and eloquent. . . . It is a valuable addition to public literature, and it will be sacredly cherished among the treasures of the Department."[7] How touching.

An idealism that includes the yearning to surmount parochial narrowness also explains why Jews are less impressed than other groups when their coreligionists seek or secure public office. The ethnic identity of candidates is not negligible for Jewish voters, but issues of personality and character have usually weighed more heavily. This might be contrasted with the close-as-handcuffs tribalism of Irish politics, as traditionally practiced in the major cities, or with the importance that African Americans have attached to the election of officeholders of their own race.

STOP YOUR CRUEL OPPRESSION OF THE JEWS.

Roosevelt *(to the czar)*:—"Now that you have peace without, why not remove his burden and have peace within your borders?"

In this print, a "Russian Jew" carries on his back a large bundle labeled "Oppression"; hanging from the bundle are weights labeled "Autocracy," "Robbery," "Cruelty," "Assassination," "Deception," and "Murder." In the background, on the right, a Jewish community burns, while in the upper left corner, Theodore Roosevelt asks Emperor of Russia, Nicholas II, "Now that you have peace without, why not remove his burden and have peace within your borders?"

Emil Flohri, "Stop Your Cruel Oppression of the Jews!," in Judge, *September 30, 1905. Prints and Photographs Division.*

For nearly all of the twentieth century, more Jews resided in New York than in any other city of the Diaspora. But not until 1973 did New York, with a population that was more than a quarter Jewish, elect a Jew (Abe Beame) as its mayor; and in 1982 the liberal Mario Cuomo, an Italian American, defeated Lewis Lehrman, a conservative Republican gubernatorial candidate, by two to one among New York State's Jewish voters. Perhaps what influenced them was an echo of Rabbi Stephen S. Wise's argument that the only justification for Jewish bloc voting would be to deprive unqualified Jews of public office. He counted on the fairness of his fellow citizens to elect qualified Jews. That faith has been vindicated, resulting in a national legislature in which the proportion of Jews within it is well above their 2.7 percent of the general population. The 1992 election was the first to ensure that the number of Jews serving in the U.S. Senate reached ten, the minimum necessary for a prayer quorum or *minyan*. Two of the senators were from California, the most populous state in the union, and both—Democrats Dianne Feinstein and Barbara Boxer—also happened to be members of Hadassah. Both senators from Wisconsin were Jews as well. In the 107th session of the House of Representatives, beginning in 2001, there were twenty-seven Jews, of whom twenty-three were Democrats; one, Bernie Sanders, was a Socialist who was usually aligned with the Democrats. So many Jews in Congress meant that friction was inevitable. During a House floor debate in 1991, for example, Sam Gejdenson (Democrat of Connecticut) urged his colleagues to sign a bill locating a submarine-building plant in his district, only to have Norman Sisisky (Democrat of Virginia) insist that his own district was more suitable. A third Jew, Barney Frank (Democrat of Massachusetts), told the *Washington Post* what a striking spectacle that was—"two Jews fighting over pork."[8]

When an Orthodox Jew was picked as Gore's running mate in 2000, it was the first time that a Jew had run on the ticket of a major party since the founding of the republic. But Senator Joseph Lieberman's impact on Jewish voters was slight at best, since they were very likely to be Democrats anyway. His party picked up only 1 percent of the Jewish vote from four years earlier, when both candidates on the Democratic ticket were Southern Baptists. (Nor, it should be added, was there any evidence that Lieberman's religion *hurt* the Democratic ticket.) Even when congressmen represent districts that are heavily Jewish in composition, even when senators serve states with a significant minority of Jewish voters, such politicians cannot take for granted a voting bloc signed, sealed, and delivered over to them because of a common ancestry.

Of course there have been Jews in the GOP and Jews on the right. They are more likely to be found among the very wealthy and, paradoxically, among the very poor. The Orthodox, as well as residents of the Sun Belt, are also more likely to be Republicans than their coreligionists. Neoconservatism has also exerted a special impact among the intelligentsia. The numbers are not negligible. The minimal proportion of Jews who can be relied upon to vote for the GOP in the past half century was in the range of one-fifth (a slice that doubled in 1980, when Reagan ran for the first time). The general figure of a minimum of about 20 percent can be looked at another way, however. Both political parties start out every campaign knowing that three out of every five Jews are self-designated as Democrats, and such a lead has so far been insuperable. The proportion of Jews willing to call themselves conservative (8 percent) is less than a fourth of the proportion identifying themselves to pollsters as liberals (35 percent).

That gap has been very difficult for the Republicans to narrow because of their own shift to the right, beginning with the election of Reagan in 1980. A militant, evangelical Protestantism has become a momentous engine of GOP power, a force to be reckoned with by all of the key figures within the Republican Party. Due to the Moral Majority, the Christian Coalition, and numerous other groups, progressive Republicanism has disappeared; and moderate policies and values have been discredited or at least thrown on the defensive. Such a reorientation has posed a formidable obstacle for a party hoping to compete with the opposition for Jewish voters, because they tend to be supremely modern, urban, educated, and secularized. The political culture of American Jewry collides quite directly with the objectives of the New Right.

Public opinion polls have consistently revealed a chasm on social attitudes. At least traditionally, Jews have been famous for industrial-strength families. But in the United States Jews have also tended to be more tolerant than Roman Catholics or Protestants of marital infidelity, of premarital relations, and of homosexuality. Such tolerance has clashed with what proportionately more Christians have deemed sinful in *all* circumstances. That is why Jews did not enlist in such crusades as the "Family Protection Bill" or the "Defense of Marriage Act." A political party that generally (and successfully) opposed the Equal Rights Amendment to the Constitution could not elicit much Jewish support, especially when pollsters discovered that a Jewish man was slightly more likely to favor the ERA than was a Gentile woman. Because most Jews have favored freedom of choice for pregnant women, a political party that has sought to chip away at *Roe v. Wade*—the 1973 decision that protected abortion rights—would not appeal to Jews. Puritanism is not an outgrowth of Judaism, which in the Diaspora has not promoted hedonism either but has instead championed the ideals of temperance and moderation. Jews have generally resisted the efforts of religious zealots to make personal habits the target of public policy. Nor was it coincidental that Louis Brandeis first asserted (in 1890) that privacy is the right that civilized men cherish above all others.

Evangelical Christianity has sought to lower the wall separating church and state, and to destabilize a status quo that accepted the religious neutrality of the public sector—or the equitable treatment accorded to Catholics and Jews as well as Protestants within it. Of course the First Amendment was never intended to exclude expressions of faith from public life, and the absence of an official religion must be reconciled with the protection of all forms of worship. Most Jews have claimed that a prayer recited in unison in a public school (even if no mention is made of the Savior) would violate the prohibition against the establishment of religion. Less self-evidently in friction with the First Amendment has been the ostentatious entwining by recent, "born-again" Republican presidents of politics and religion. Such professions of faith have accentuated the difference, however, between the faith of the nation's majority and the skepticism that Jews continue to harbor about the Resurrection. Thus most Jews, regardless of their prosperous condition, have remained wary of becoming Republicans.

The New Right did not directly imperil the faith of Jews, however, and has not perpetuated an earlier tradition of anti-Semitism. On the contrary, its pro-Zionism has been ardent, which has created a predicament for many Jewish voters. Because the security and welfare of Israel have been pivotal to Jewish destiny and to the future of the Jewish people everywhere else, pro-Zionism has become the prerequisite for the practice of Jewish politics in America. Not all liberals have appreciated the value of a democratic Jewish homeland, and not all champions of Israel have been liberals; hence the dilemma at the center of Jewish political culture. In 1994, for example, the Anti-Defamation League (ADL) denounced the Reverend Pat Robertson and others in a broadside entitled *The Religious Right: The Assault on Tolerance and Pluralism in America*. Eight years later, after the second *intifada* in the Holy Land, the ADL bankrolled a newspaper advertisement by Ralph Reed, Jr., once the organizational wizard behind Robertson's Christian Coalition, so that Reed could explain why his support of Israel was so fervent. Robertson and the Reverend Jerry Falwell and others on the Christian right found especially congenial the shift to the right characteristic of politics in Israel, and thus an odd alliance in the United States has been forged that may revise seven decades of Jewish liberalism.

There may be limits to this realignment, however. When the Christian Coalition met in Washington, D.C., in October 2002, the Republican whip of the House of Representatives urged the audience to support candidates who "stand unashamedly with Jesus Christ."[9] Such a list would have excluded the Democrats' vice-presidential nominee in 2000, Senator Lieberman, and suggests why the Jewish community is likely to persist in its liberalism. (Among Jews under the age of thirty-five, only a tenth call themselves Republicans.) Consciousness—if not memories—of the suffering that the ideological animus of religious majorities can inflict may keep most Jews within the ranks of the Democratic Party, which is also less white, less Protestant, and less homogeneous than its rival.

Perhaps no minority group has taken more seriously the ideal of popular sovereignty or has been more inspired by the rhetoric of democratic responsibility. Jews have been twice as likely to vote as other Americans, and have recently constituted as much as 6 percent of the electorate. Such devotion to the suffrage pays off because the Electoral College is so unrepresentative; it happens to place a heavy thumb on the scales of Jewish residential patterns. So Jewish political culture actually *matters*. To demonstrate the electoral impact of the Jewish proclivity to concentrate in states of urban density, the historian need not point only to 2000. That freakish election was decided in Palm Beach County, Florida, by several hundred elderly Jews, who got confused by the "butterfly" ballot and punched in their choice of spoiler Pat Buchanan (who gallantly acknowledged that such votes were not intended to be his). Take a more ordinary campaign, in 1976. In the state of New York, about a quarter of the voters were Jewish. They went about 80 percent for Governor Carter over President Gerald Ford, enabling the Democratic challenger to carry the state and with it the presidency. Had Carter and the incumbent evenly split the Jewish vote of New York, Carter would have *lost* the state and with it the White House. Jews happen to be massed in populous states that provide 166 electoral votes, magnifying the influence of this minority group in the winner-take-all system that was devised in 1787. That is why their attitudes have counted ever since the political alignment that was so indelibly forged in 1932, and why their public culture is not only pivotal to an understanding of their identity as Jews, but also to the evolution of American self-government itself.

A BOYCHIK UP·TO·DATE

WORDS BY
L. GILROD
MUSIC BY
D. MEYROWITZ

SONG 50.   VIOLIN 30.

New York
THEODORE LOHR
286 GRAND STREET

American Jewish Popular Culture

Jeffrey Shandler

W ere this continent's earliest Jewish settlers somehow able to return to America now, 350 years later, they might well find some of the contours of contemporary Jewish life to be familiar. Today many American Jews' lives are defined, as they were during the mid-seventeenth century, by synagogue worship, domestic ritual, devotional study, and communal philanthropy. But what would America's first Jews make of, say: the more than fifty Jewish film festivals now annually held across the United States? Jackson, Mississippi's Museum of the Southern Jewish Experience? The Jewish Sports Heroes Hall of Fame in Detroit's Jewish Community Center? The rock band Phish performing "Avinu Malkenu"? Shlock Rock? Spy novels written in Yiddish especially for ultra-Orthodox readers? Jackie Mason's *How to Talk Jewish*? Drag queens impersonating Barbra Streisand recreating Fanny Brice? Claims that Charlie Chaplin, Betty Boop, Elvis Presley, or Ali G. are Jews? T-shirts emblazoned with *"farklempt,"* "I made it to second base at Jeremy's bar mitzvah," or "Jews for Jeter"? Polo Ralph Lauren? *HEEB* magazine ("The New Jew Review")? *Maus*? *Seinfeld*? *The Hebrew Hammer*? Blueberry bagels? What would those colonial-era time travelers make of the people who engage in these diverse enterprises, especially the ones who identify themselves not as "religious" but as "cultural" Jews? And what would America's first Jews think about how the rest of the nation understands the diverse phenomena that now comprise Jewish popular culture in the United States?

The subject of this sheet music's title page is a garishly dressed dandy who is so Americanized that his Jewishnes is not outwardly apparent. The song is critical of this boychik and, through him, the American milieu that created him.

L. Gilrod and D. Meyrowitz, A Boychik Up-to-Date (An Up-to-Date Dandy), New York, n.d. Hebraic Section.

The first issue of Heeb, *which appeared in 2002, turned an ugly epithet on its head, transforming it for the magazine's intended audience into a term of pride and identity. Displayed here is the second issue, featuring a photographic essay on Jewish Bubbes (grandmothers), "the divas of South Florida.."*

Heeb: The New Jew Review, *New York, July 2002. General Collections.*

Alongside long-established modes of Jewish religious, political, and intellectual practices, another Jewish way of life has flourished in America in the past century or so, centered on an extensive array of popular culture. This includes engagement with mass media (popular fiction, periodicals, sound recordings, film, broadcasting), leisure activities (sports, games, summer camps, tourism, and attending museums, the theater, concerts, comedy clubs), and the aesthetics of daily life (taking photographs or home movies, cooking, collecting curios, surfing the Internet). The contemporary observer (to say nothing of one transported across the past three-and-a-half centuries) might be tempted to dismiss these phenomena as adventitious or trivial, deeming them irrelevant or even inimical to the essence of Jewish life in America. But to do so would overlook a significant development in American Jewry's recent history. For not only have these become some of the most commonly practiced and widely known examples of Jewish culture, but they distinguish American Jewry from other Jewish communities around the world and afford Jews a distinctive public profile in America. Moreover, these practices constitute fundamentally new ways of realizing Jewishness individually and communally.

Popular culture has provided Jews singular opportunities within the American public sphere since the turn of the twentieth century. Through their engagement in various forms of popular culture, especially those involving the mass media, Jews have become one of the most visible and most widely discussed of the nation's many minority communities. Examining American Jewish popular culture affords an opportunity to understand how this small and distinctive people, never much more than 3 percent of the nation's population, relates to what has constituted the "popular" in America over the course of the past century. Conversely, popular culture has become an important proving ground for American Jewish life, a locus of burgeoning creativity that is driven less by official agendas than by personal desires. Indeed, for some of this nation's Jews, popular culture plays a leading role in their understanding of what it means to be Jewish.

Yiddish: Immigrant Vernacular and Beyond

To a considerable degree, American Jewish popular culture is defined by the two million Jews who arrived at these shores from Eastern Europe during the period of mass immigration, lasting from the early 1880s to the start of World War I in 1914. These immigrants expanded the number of Jews in the United States exponentially, making their presence newly prominent in major American cities, especially New York. By the turn of the twentieth century, New York was home to the largest Jewish population in the world, with a concentration of Jews in one place of unprecedented number in history. The East-European immigrant community and its descendants have dominated the public profile of Jews in the United States ever since, even though there are other, much more established Jewish communities (as well as more recent ones) in America. Consequently, the public identity of future generations of American Jews has continued to be measured against these immigrants from Eastern Europe and their experiences.

This dynamic is perhaps best revealed in the changing role of Yiddish in American Jewish popular culture. The traditional language of daily life spoken by the great majority of Jews from Eastern Europe, Yiddish was at the center of an extensive immigrant popular culture that included press, literature, theater, and music. These practices flourished immediately upon the immigrants' arrival in the late nineteenth century, in response to their urgent need to negotiate the great disparities between their "Old World" past and "New World" present.[1]

These new arrivals to America confronted an unknown political, economic, and social order, as well as an unfamiliar national language. They also encountered an array of new forms of popular culture: cabarets, cafes, dance halls, nickelodeons, amusement parks, Victrolas, public libraries, and newspaper features, such as advice columns and political cartoons. America presented these Jewish immigrants, most of whom had left behind the repressive regime of the Russian Empire, with unprecedented freedoms of speech and association. At the same time, the burgeoning economy of the United States introduced them to a consumer culture that they themselves were helping to transform.[2]

Some forms of Yiddish popular culture, especially theater (itself a novelty among Jews in late-nineteenth-century Eastern Europe), thrived in America more readily than on the other side of the Atlantic Ocean. Yiddish theater soon became the focus of intense public debates about the moral, political, and esthetic implications of popular culture.[3] Even as it provided entertainment, the Yiddish stage was a powerful modernizing force in immigrant Jewish life and an important public venue for enacting a new immigrant sensibility. In addition to presenting the works of Jewish playwrights—which ranged from sentimental or sensational crowd-pleasers to historical dramas and realist social-problem plays—the Yiddish stage introduced its audiences to European drama. Immigrant Jews attended Yiddish-language performances of pioneering works of modern drama by the likes of Henrik Ibsen, Gerhardt Hauptmann, and Maxim Gorky, as well as such classic authors as Schiller, Molière, and Shakespeare (productions of whose works were occasionally touted as "*fartaytsht un farbesert*"—translated and improved.)[4]

Following World War I and the restrictive immigration quotas enacted by the U.S. Congress in the early 1920s, the scope of Jewish immigration from Eastern Europe was severely limited. Increasingly, the American-born children of immigrants defined the public profile of the nation's Jews. While many of them spoke or at least understood Yiddish, English was, as a rule, their primary language. Nevertheless, novel forms of Yiddish popular culture flourished in the decades following World War I, especially in the new venues of radio and "talking" motion pictures. At the same time that network radiocasts and Hollywood films established a national (Anglophone) mainstream culture of unprecedented scope, Yiddish radio and film emerged as alternative media for Jewish immigrants and their children. Whether bringing to the screen literary classics set in the Old World (such as *Grine felder* [Green Fields, 1937], *Tevye der milkhiker* [Tevye the Milkman, 1939]) or contemporary melodramas of urban American life (*Vu iz mayn kind?* [Where Is My Child?, 1937], *Hayntike mames* [Mothers of Today, 1939]), the several dozen Yiddish films made in the United States during the 1930s presented audiences a virtual realm in which Yiddish was the reigning language—spoken not only by Jewish characters, but also by Ukrainian peasants, African-American servants, Anglo-Saxon Protestant judges, and even German anti-Semites.[5]

In its heyday, American Yiddish radio programming was heard in New York, Chicago, Los Angeles, and other cities with large Jewish populations. Beginning in the late 1920s, these broadcasts—soap operas, news reports, musical variety programs, interview programs—were, in fact, often bilingual; the programming freely mixed English and Yiddish, sometimes within the same sentence. This language play epitomized the intergenerational negotiation of immigrant parents' sensibilities with those of their American-born children.

After World War II—which witnessed the murder of half of the world's Yiddish speakers and the destruction of their centuries-old cultural heartland in Eastern Europe, all within less than a decade—the significance of Yiddish in American Jewish life changed rapidly. On one hand, growing numbers of American Jews abandoned Yiddish as a vernacular; on the other hand, Yiddish gained new importance as a symbolic language for memorializing the victims of Nazism and recalling the East-European heritage of the immigrant generations. Yiddish informed a number of key works of "popular ethnography" of this vanished world, culminating in the hit Broadway musical of 1964, *Fiddler on the Roof*, based on the fiction of Yiddish writer Sholem Aleichem.[6]

At the same time, Yiddish became a fragmented code of Jewish ethnicity, stubbornly defying assimilationist tendencies and challenging established cultural boundaries. While many American Jews ceased speaking Yiddish as a language of daily life, the nation's non-Jewish population avidly adopted a handful of Yiddishisms. A series of mock dictionaries—including *Yiddish for Yankees*, *Every Goy's Guide to Common Jewish Expressions*, and *Drek! The REAL Yiddish Your Bubbe Never Taught You*—offers comic explanations of Yiddish

Based on the stories of Yiddish writer Sholem Aleichem, Fiddler on the Roof *resonated for second-generation American Jews because it recalled an idealized collective memory of an Eastern Europe that was no more.*

United Artists Corporation, Fiddler on the Roof *[Poster], 1971. Prints and Photographs Division.*

terms for food, sex, elimination, and states of emotional extreme, thereby presenting Yiddish as the language of a raucous, appetitive, subversive Jewish carnivalesque. Despite these developments, some Americans maintain a commitment to Yiddish as a language of daily life, which they sometimes demonstrate through the idioms of popular culture, such as translating classics of children's literature—*Winnie the Pooh* (as *Vini-der-Pu*) and *The Cat in the Hat* (as *Di kats der payats*)—into Yiddish.[7] For both Jews and non-Jews, the language marks telling developments in the meaning of ethnic difference in America. As a fragment of a language embedded in American popular culture, Yiddish has become emblematic of Jewish identity's tenacity as well as its mutability, epitomizing the ambivalent feelings of many Jews—and, more generally, of many Americans—about ethnicity.[8]

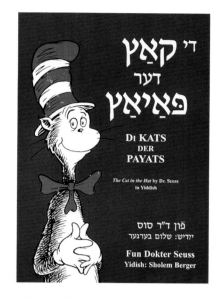

The text of this classic children's book was translated into Yiddish by Sholem Berger and was "sponsored in part by Yugentruf, an organization of young people of every ideology and background dedicated to Yiddish as a living language."

Dr. Seuss, Di Kats der Payats, The Cat in the Hat, *translated into Yiddish by Sholem Berger, New York, 2003. TM & © 1957 Dr. Seuss Enterprises, L.P. All Rights Reserved. Hebraic Section.*

At-Homeness in America's Public Sphere

For over a century, popular culture has provided Jews with singular venues for presenting themselves (and for being presented by others) to the rest of America—and to fellow Jews. Given their small number and concentration in and around major urban centers, Jews have become most widely familiar to their Gentile neighbors through representations in popular literature, live performances, film, sound recordings, and broadcasting. Consequently, seeing oneself in the imagined gaze of others has become an important component of self-realization for many American Jews.

At the turn of the twentieth century, Jewish characters—portrayed as often by Gentiles as by Jews—were but one part of the great mix of ethnic, racial, religious, and regional "types" presented in newspaper cartoons, joke books, vaudeville routines, early silent films, and comedic sound recordings. This panoply of "types" in American popular culture of the period evinced the conceptual challenge that the nation's public faced in coming to terms with its rapidly expanding, diversifying population. These representations, which could be offensively caricaturist, often provided immigrants and members of other minority communities with a daunting point of entry into the American public sphere. At the same time, they prompted new ways of thinking about racial, ethnic, religious, and regional identities. In particular, the nature of popular culture's production and reception implied that these identities might be constructed, rather than innate, fostering a distinctively plastic approach to understanding the nature of identity in America.[9]

Thus, while the images of Jews in early twentieth-century American popular culture were often crude and unflattering, they also offered a diversity of representations that suggested multiple possibilities for conceptualizing Jews within the American dramatis personae. Portrayals of Jews in short silent movies shown in nickelodeons, for example, range from the

comic stereotyping of scheming merchants in Thomas Edison's production of *Cohen's Fire Sale* (1907) to the beautiful, albeit doomed, daughter of a stern, "Old World" patriarch in *Romance of a Jewess* (1908), directed by D.W. Griffith. Among the few surviving films produced by Siegmund Lubin, a pioneering Jewish filmmaker based in Philadelphia, is *The Yiddisher Boy* (1908), in which immigrant Jewish family values, as portrayed in the celebration of the Sabbath (one of the earliest such representations of Jewish ritual on film), help establish the hero's moral worthiness.[10]

Jewish characters continued to figure occasionally in early Hollywood narratives about recent immigrants and their American-born children. These films culminate with the Warner Bros. 1927 feature, *The Jazz Singer*. Best remembered today as marking the beginning of "talking pictures," this film relates the story of a son of Jewish immigrants as he struggles between the forces of tradition versus modernity, familial and communal religious obligation versus personal artistic self-realization. Although it was inspired by the biography of its star, Al Jolson, the story told in *The Jazz Singer* has become a definitional American Jewish myth, revisited over the course of the twentieth century in Hollywood remakes, Yiddish adaptations, radio and television versions, and comic parodies. The story's repeated retellings demonstrate how its central conflicts continue to resonate with the dynamics of American Jewish life over three generations.[11]

During the middle decades of the twentieth century, the children of immigrants increasingly turned to mainstream popular culture as a forum for enacting their sense of at-homeness in America.[12] Emerging from among this generation are prominent figures in popular fiction (e.g., Edna Ferber), theater (George S. Kaufman), songwriting (Irving Berlin), vaudeville (Fanny Brice), cartoon animation (Max Fleischer), and radio comedy (Jack Benny). Some American-Jewish artists of this period were at the vanguard of a national popular culture that strove to transcend the particulars of ethnicity, religion, class, and region as well as the conventional distinctions between high and low art. Composers George Gershwin and Aaron Copland, for example, crafted compositions that hybridized the commercial theater and the concert hall and merged a variety of folk and classical idioms. Other American Jews of this generation—including playwright Clifford Odets, composer Marc Blitzstein, songwriter Lewis Allan (pen name of Abel Meeropol)—dedicated their artistic endeavors to promoting internationalist, left-wing causes through popular culture.

For the most part, these performers, writers, and composers avoided publicly identifying themselves as Jews or dealing with Jewish subjects in their work. Seeking to address a national audience, they generally treated Jewishness as something marginal, particularist, or otherwise

---

Opposite: Hollywood's first talking picture, The Jazz Singer, *starring Al Jolson as Jack Robins, a cantor's son whose break from his religious upbringing to become a successful nightclub singer and Broadway star precipitates a painful estrangement from his strictly observant and traditional father. In the final scene of the movie, Jack returns to his dying father's synagogue to chant the Kol Nidre prayer in his father's stead. For many,* The Jazz Singer *became the quintessential metaphor for intergenerational conflict between newly arrived Jewish immigrants and their American-born children.*

The Jazz Singer *[Facsimile of Lobby Card], n.d. Motion Picture, Broadcasting, and Recorded Sound Division.*

incompatible with mainstream Americanness. These integrationist impulses did not meet with universal approval. In a 1952 essay entitled "The Vanishing Jew of Our Popular Culture," critic Henry Popkin decried "what may be called 'de-Semitization' [that] is by now a commonplace in the popular arts in America," noting examples drawn from film, fiction, and vaudeville comedy acts. Popkin characterized the phenomenon as originating "in a misguided benevolence, or fear—its name is 'sha-sha' [Yiddish for "hush, hush"]." [13] Significantly, Popkin invoked Yiddish as a double-edged sign, marking the silencing of Jewishness as a Jewish act in itself.

Yet the years following World War II also witnessed important changes in Jewish visibility in the American public sphere, especially within popular culture venues. The crowning of Bess Myerson as Miss America in 1945, amid reports that she resisted pressure to change her last name to obscure her Jewish identity, became a landmark event in postwar American Jews' dynamic sense of self. Myerson's triumph echoed the acclaim of baseball players Hank Greenberg and Sandy Koufax and their refusal to play in World Series games that coincided with Yom Kippur. [14] All three were heroes of mid-twentieth-century American popular culture who had triumphed in nationwide competitions that valorized physical superiority and talent as a public performer, contests in which their being Jewish was essentially irrelevant; however, they had done so *as Jews.* Moreover, by publicly demonstrating the limits to which they would compromise their Jewishness for the sake of competition, they presented personal profiles in which being a Jew enhanced their status as American celebrities, adding their manifest respect for ethnic and religious heritage to their roster of accomplishments.

You don't have to be Jewish

to love Levy's
real Jewish Rye

"You Don't Have to Be Jewish to Love Levy's Rye Bread" was a hugely successful advertising campaign that playfully addressed cultural and ethnic stereotyping while, at the same time, undermining its relevance.

Howard Zieff, photographer, "You don't have to be Jewish to love Levy's real Jewish Rye" [New York, 1967]. Prints and Photographs Division. Used with the permission of Arnold Products, Inc. Levy's is a registered trademark of Arnold Products, Inc. Howard Zieff's photographs are represented by G. Ray Hawkins Gallery, Los Angeles.

As the grandchildren of East European immigrants came of age in the wake of World War II, American Jewish popular culture evinced a larger signal shift in national sensibility about social diversity. Concomitant with other emerging voices, especially in the African-American community, Jews publicly addressed the challenge of negotiating difference vis-à-vis an idealized, homogenous American mainstream. In the case of American Jews, one of the first venues in which this new sensibility found public expression was comedy.

In the 1950s and early 1960s stand-up comedians, who had become popular fixtures at Jewish resort hotels in the Catskill and Pocono Mountains, began to address national audiences on television talk shows and comedy albums. Performers such as Lenny Bruce, Jackie Mason, Mike Nichols and Elaine May, and Mort Sahl exploited the "safe space to say dangerous things" that comedy traditionally provides to address, among other issues, the anxieties that at-homeness in America posed for them as Jews. In one of his most frequently cited routines, Bruce offered a provocative inventory of which elements of American life were—and weren't—Jewish:

Dig: I'm Jewish. Count Basie's Jewish. Ray Charles is Jewish. Eddie Cantor's goyish [Gentile]. B'nai B'rith is goyish; Hadassah, Jewish. If you live in New York or any other big city, you are Jewish. It doesn't matter even if you're Catholic; if you live in New York, you're Jewish. If you live in Butte, Montana, you're going to be goyish even if you're Jewish. Kool-Aid is goyish. Evaporated milk is goyish even if Jews invented it. Chocolate is Jewish and fudge is goyish. Fruit salad is Jewish. Lime jello is goyish. Lime soda is very goyish.[15]

Bruce's very act of creating and reciting this list responds to a postwar destabilization of what had once been a widely self-evident sense of Jewish otherness in America and voices a desire to reassert this sense of difference in the face of widespread, compliant assimilation. This new kind of American Jewish self-critique through caustic social satire enacted before general American

In this advertisement, the "Father of Our Country," George Washington, is pressed into service to hawk "the best cherry wine," using a phrase, "Let me make one thing perfectly clear," most often associated with yet another president, Richard Nixon.

"Let Me Make One Thing Perfectly Clear!" Mogen David Cherry Wine Advertisement, New York, circa 1970s. From the HUC Skirball Cultural Center Museum Collection, Los Angeles, California (Gift of Grace Cohen Grossman). Photography by Susan Einstein.

audiences also appeared in works of fiction (for example, in the prose of Bruce Jay Friedman, Joseph Heller, and Philip Roth) and in a spate of "Jewish New Age" films (including *The Producers* [1967], *Bye Bye Braverman* [1968], and *Take the Money and Run* [1969]).[16]

The renegotiations of American and Jewish identities in these works are often complex, contrary to conventional notions of popular culture's facility. This can be seen even in something as ostensibly slight and straightforward as an advertisement. The famous print ad campaign that told the American public, "You don't have to be Jewish" to love Levy's "real" Jewish rye bread—and featuring photos of a native American Indian, an Irish policeman, an Italian cook, and African-American and Asian-American children, all happily feasting on slices of rye bread—exploits ethnic stereotypes as it subverts them. The ads' message for Jews is especially complicated. Jewishness is not only a tempting possibility for Gentiles, it is an option for American Jews as well—*they* don't "have to" be Jewish, either. Here, the marking of Jewish identity is at play, as is the notion of Jewishness as something both indelible and consumable.

Increasingly, the ability to document and recirculate works of popular culture through new technologies—such as reissuing early television broadcasts on videotape or out-of-print sound recordings on compact discs (not to mention the reselling of vintage publications and ephemera on eBay and other Internet sites)—has enabled new valuations of phenomena heretofore thought of as being simply "of its moment." In some instances, the "rediscovery" of these works has become a touchstone of a new intergenerational cultural dynamic among American Jews. When the Marx Brothers' movies of the 1930s and 1940s came under the scrutiny of film and literary scholars in the 1960s and 1970s, the performers' Jewishness was frequently identified as key to their distinctive comedic sensibility. Similarly, a generation after *Your Show of Shows* aired on NBC (1950-1954), the pioneering comedy-variety television series was celebrated as a fountainhead of American Jewish comedic talent, having had among its sketch writers such budding talents as Mel Brooks, Carl Reiner, and Neil Simon.[17] The stigmatizing of Jewish leftists during the Red Scare of the 1930s and the McCarthy Era was revisited decades later in works of vindication (such as the 1976 film *The Front*) and even nostalgia (*The Way We Were* [1973]). The recent "revival" of klezmer by American Jewish musicians born after World War II started with their discovery of 78rpm recordings of the traditional music of East-European Jewish immigrants.[18] And in Philip Roth's 1993 novel, *Operation Shylock*, the protagonist offers this subversive disquisition on the Jewishness of some of Irving Berlin's best-known contributions to American popular song a half-century earlier:

The radio was playing "Easter Parade" and I thought, but this is Jewish genius on a par with the Ten Commandments. God gave Moses the Ten Commandments and then He gave Irving Berlin "Easter Parade" and "White Christmas." The two holidays that celebrate the divinity of Christ—the divinity that's at the very heart of the Jewish rejection of Christianity—and what does Irving Berlin brilliantly do? He de-Christs them both! Easter he turns into a fashion show and Christmas into a holiday about snow.... He turns their religion into schlock. *But nicely! Nicely! So nicely the goyim don't know what hit 'em.*[19]

Even the act of inventorying Jewish celebrities—an enduringly popular pastime among many American Jews—can reveal generational differences in Jewish at-homeness in America, as exemplified by two comedy recordings. The title song of *When You're in Love, The Whole World Is Jewish*, an album of comic sketches and songs recorded in 1966, archly proclaims that, thanks to the transformative power of love, such Gentile celebrities as performers Steve McQueen, Marlon Brando, and Harry Belafonte are, in fact, fellow Jews. A similar inventory is enumerated in generation-X comedian Adam Sandler's "Chanukah Song," recorded in 1995 (for his album, *What the Hell Happened to Me?*). Here, however, the celebrities named—including rock star David Lee Roth, actor Kirk Douglas, and advice columnist Ann Landers (pen name of Esther Pauline Friedman Lederer)—actually are Jews. The public naming of Jews, coyly subverted in the mid-1960s, becomes an act of ethnic affirmation a generation later (and is offered by Sandler as consolation to "the only kid in town without a Christmas tree"). Both songs were recorded live; whereas the adult audience for "When You're in Love…" squeals with anxious laughter, Sandler's younger audience cheers raucously, celebrating the public declaration of Jewishness as an end in itself.

Addressing Anti-Semitism

At the same time that integration characterizes so much of Jewish engagement in American popular culture, it has also long served as a prominent site for discussions of intolerance. Many of these discussions have centered on Hollywood; Jewish involvement in America's movie industry has been the subject of considerable public attention ever since Hollywood's studios emerged as the film industry's national center following World War I. The Jewishness of the majority of the studios' executives inspired a number of outspoken nativists—including, most famously, industrialist Henry Ford—to denounce Hollywood in the early 1920s as the

Within American Jewish material culture, a special place is reserved for Zionist keepsakes and mementos issued in recognition of one's support for the State of Israel. Displayed here is a "Provisional Certificate of Honor" presented to Sophie Tucker by the Jewish National Fund of America, pending receipt of her permanent certificate from Jerusalem.

"From the Golden Book of the Jewish National Fund, Provisional Certificate in Honor of Sophie Tucker," n.d. Courtesy of the Jacob Rader Marcus Center of the American Jewish Archives.

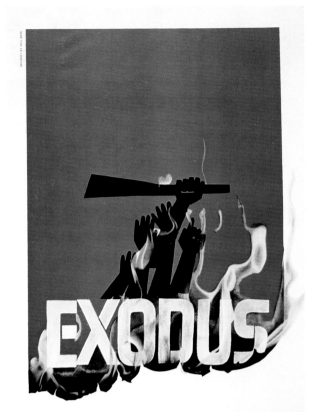

OTTO PREMINGER PRESENTS PAUL NEWMAN, EVA MARIE SAINT, RALPH RICHARDSON, PETER LAWFORD, LEE J. COBB, SAL MINEO, JOHN DEREK, HUGH GRIFFITH, GREGORY RATOFF, FELIX AYLMER, DAVID OPATOSHU, JILL HAWORTH IN "EXODUS." SCREENPLAY BY DALTON TRUMBO. BASED ON THE NOVEL BY LEON URIS. MUSIC BY ERNEST GOLD. PHOTOGRAPHED IN SUPER PANAVISION 70. TECHNICOLOR® BY SAM LEAVITT. TODD AO STEREOPHONIC SOUND. A UNITED ARTISTS RELEASE. PRODUCED AND DIRECTED BY OTTO PREMINGER.

Based on the novel by Leon Uris, Exodus *introduced America to the story of the State of Israel, turning its struggle for existence into the stuff of Hollywood legend.*

Saul Bass (designer), Exodus *[Poster], 1961. Prints and Photographs Division.*

locus of a Jewish conspiracy to debase American art, corrupt the nation's morals, and supplant its "native" (i.e., Anglo-Saxon Protestant) political and social author-ities.[20] Ford and other assailers of Hollywood's Jews conflated suspicions of Jews as racially and religiously alien with fears of Bolshevism. Anti-Communism and anti-Semitism would continue to be implicated with one another in interrogations of American popular culture through the early years of the Cold War.

Before and during World War II, American Jews tended to respond to public anti-Semitic attacks such as these with silence, preferring to treat them as beneath the dignity of a response. But postwar revelations of the Nazi-led genocide of Europe's Jews prompted new strategies, notably by organizations such as the American Jewish Committee, the American Jewish Congress, and the Anti-Defamation League of B'nai B'rith, which placed a premium on public education in combating anti-Semitism and prejudice more generally.[21]

Broadcasting served as a vehicle for some of the most ambitious efforts to address these issues under-taken by Jewish religious institutions. During the 1940s and 1950s American radio and, later, television net-works began to air ecumenical series such as *Frontiers of Faith* (NBC), *The Eternal Light* (NBC), *Lamp Unto My Feet* (CBS), *Look Up and Live* (CBS), and *Directions* (ABC) as part of fulfilling an FCC mandate to offer public service broad-casting. Conservative and Reform Jewish institutions created original dramas about Jewish ethics, history, and culture especially for these series. These radio plays presented Jewry as a dignified commu-nity, in contrast to the comical, ethnic-inflected portraits typically heard on commercial radio, and belied associations of Jews with left-wing sedition by celebrating Jewish values as compatible with American patriotism.[22] Public edification informed Hollywood features about anti-Jewish prejudice as well; among a spate of early postwar films addressing social problems ranging from alcoholism to racism were two 1947 features that addressed American anti-Semitism in popular dramatic genres: the stylish film noir *Crossfire* and the romantic intrigue (complete with disguised identities) of *Gentleman's Agreement.*

American popular culture has continued to address anti-Semitism not only in cautionary tales targeting non-Jewish audiences, but also in works that situate it as a definitional issue for American Jews themselves, especially as it relates to support for the State of Israel and remembrance of the Holocaust. Indeed, works of popular fiction, film, and broadcasting have a special primacy in establishing Israel and the Holocaust as fixtures of the civil religion of American Jews, and these issues have inspired other forms of public culture, such as Jewish museums, parades, and tourism.[23]

During the first half of the twentieth century, Zionist activists in the United States evolved an array of practices—advertising, exhibitions, pageants, summer camps—to foster support for creating a Jewish state in Palestine as a solution to modern anti-Semitism. At the same time, these endeavors provided American Jews with means of participating in the Zionist cause vicariously, through cultural activities that included acting in Zionist theatricals, singing modern Hebrew songs, and dancing to "Palestinean" folk tunes. American Zionism also developed an extensive popular culture around philanthropy, generating its own literature, performances (including concerts, dances, sporting events, and banquets), and fund-raising practices, with an elaborate material culture in the form of badges, certificates, trophies, and the like. As these activities and items concretized American Jewish connections to the remote settlements in Palestine, they established a distinctly American Zionist culture centered on community life here in the United States.[24]

Filmmaking became a prominent fixture in Zionist fund-raising efforts during the pre-state era. More vividly than any other medium, it showed diaspora Jews how settlements in Palestine were "coming alive"; the innovativeness of the medium matched the newness of the political enterprise. In the United States, such films culminated with the feature-length *Land of Promise*; produced for the Palestine Foundation Fund in 1935, it announced its "cast" as "the Jewish people rebuilding Palestine." After World War II Hollywood made several features dealing with the birth of modern Israel, including *The Juggler* (1953), *Cast a Giant Shadow* (1956), and the film that had the most extensive impact on the American public: *Exodus* (1961). Based on the eponymous novel by Leon Uris, *Exodus* presented the story of Israel's founding in the idiom of a nation-building narrative on a grand scale that was familiar to Americans from movies about their own nation's history.[25]

Popular media have figured even more extensively in situating the Holocaust as a fixture not merely of American Jewish civil religion but of the nation's ethics. Through best-selling works of fiction (e.g., *The Wall*, John Hersey's 1950 novel about the Warsaw Ghetto uprising) and nonfiction (Anne Frank's *The Diary of a Young Girl*, first published in English translation in 1952), as well as dozens of films and hundreds of broadcasts, Americans have come to feel that they are on intimate terms with this forbidding subject. Even though it is remote from the personal experience of the great majority of this nation's citizens, many acknowledge the Holocaust as an event that informs their moral consciousness. Moreover, some American films and telecasts —notably *The Diary of Anne Frank* (1959), the *Holocaust* miniseries (1978), and *Schindler's List*

In the center of this Judaica shop's window display, crowded with holy books, prayer shawls, and ritual objects, is a banner reading "God Bless America" and "It's Great to Be an American," proudly proclaiming the store owner's two war-time allegiances.

Marjory Collins, photographer, Window of a Jewish Religious Shop on Broom Street, *New York, 1942. Farm Security Administration, Office of War Information Photograph Collection, Prints and Photographs Division.*

(1993)—have had an extensive international impact, importing distinctively American visions of the Holocaust to other countries, including those where it took place. At the same time, the appearance of the Holocaust on episodes of American television series, from science fiction programs to situation comedies, has made the subject a familiar element of the nation's repertoire of moral issues. Beyond awareness of the event itself, these representations have helped establish the Holocaust as a paradigm for understanding other genocides (most recently in the Balkans and Rwanda) and other grave social problems (from the nuclear arms race to the AIDS pandemic) and have engendered an extensive public discussion of the challenges of representing history in popular culture.[26]

Popular Religion / Cult of the Popular

At the same time that popular culture has helped facilitate a new American Jewish civil religion, it has had considerable impact on the practice of Judaism. Indeed, the notion that Jewish religious life and Jewish popular entertainments are mutually exclusive has been complicated by a series of innovations conjoining the two. Beginning at the turn of the twentieth century, sound recordings of cantors excerpted liturgical performance from the context of synagogue worship. These recordings contributed to the transformation of the cantor's role from leader of communal worship to that of an artist whose musicianship could be appreciated quite apart from its spiritual role.[27] Cantors' performances on the vaudeville stage, on radio, and in early sound films elevated a handful of singers—notably Yossele Rosenblatt and Moishe Oysher—to the status of "stars" within the American Jewish community. The wide acclaim for their virtuosity and charisma was a subject of some controversy; nevertheless, it influenced the expectations for the artistry of congregational cantors generally. In addition to disturbing the conventional distinctions between sacred worship and secular art, the popularization of the cantor in early-twentieth-century America opened up the possibility for transgressing gender boundaries. A number of "lady cantors," or *khazntes*, as they were called in Yiddish, performed in live concerts, on recordings, and on the air—but not in the synagogue.

Perhaps no single topic has engendered a more complex interrelation of religion and popular culture for American Jews than the celebration of Chanukah. Its temporal proximity with Christmas elevated Chanukah's status in the traditional Jewish calendar from a minor festival to an elaborate celebration both among Jews and in the American public sphere.[28] Thus, it has become a commonplace to include the holiday's symbols, especially the *dreydl* and Chanukah

Bearing the images of great Torah sages, these cards are popular with children in Hasidic communities and represent a direct adaption of the American juvenile phenomenon of sports trading cards from an amusing and entertaining hobby to a religious and pedagogic tool.

"Rebbe" Cards, Torah Personalities, Baltimore, circa 1990. Hebraic Section.

Pictured here are the baseball cards of Sandy Koufax and Hank Greenberg, two of a new 142 card set of Jewish Major Leaguers: American Jews in America's Game *issued by the American Jewish Historical Society, in cooperation with Jewish Major Leaguers, Inc. The set is an example of another popular national Jewish pastime: inventorying Jewish celebrities.*

Jewish Major Leaguers Baseball Cards: Limited Edition Card Set, 2003. Courtesy of the American Jewish Historical Society, New York, NY and Newton Centre, MA.

menorah, in public winter holiday displays and on seasonal greeting cards. The Americanization of the holiday is epitomized by recent designs for Chanukah menorahs featuring popular cartoon characters or American sports apparatus. Since the 1980s, television series featuring Jewish characters (including *thirtysomething, Friends, South Park*) have presented episodes devoted to observing Chanukah, especially among interfaith families, for whom confronting the "December dilemma" occasions dramatic conflict. The accommodating resolutions that these broadcasts offer intimate that celebrating Chanukah, like television watching, is a practice available to all Americans.

Conversely, by the turn of the twenty-first century, American idioms of popular media and material culture have informed an Orthodox Jewish popular culture dedicated to upholding, rather than contravening, traditional religious practice. An extensive inventory of Orthodox popular music has flourished for several decades both in live performance and on recordings. Artists such as Mordechai Ben David, Avraham Fried, the Miami Boys Choir, Regesh, and many others, most of whom are based in Brooklyn, perform both traditional liturgical works and newly composed lyrics (in English, Hebrew, and Yiddish) in a range of musical styles including rock, pop, middle-of-the-road, and Middle Eastern, sometimes imbricated with traditional cantorial idioms.[29] Orthodox Jews have adapted American juvenile pastimes to suit their own sensibilities—for example, by creating board games such as *Kosherland* and *Torah Slides and Ladders*. Similarly, children of Hasidim collect cards featuring not baseball players but great Hasidic sages of the past. Most elaborate are the efforts of Lubavitcher Hasidim (also known as Chabad) to exploit a wide array of popular cultural practices as vehicles for outreach to less religiously observant Jews, epitomized by their annual telethons. Produced in Los Angeles since 1981, these broadcasts combine the protocols of the American charity telethon with the spiritual mission and aesthetic sensibility of Chabad Hasidism.

Complementing the use of popular culture to serve spiritual ends is what might be termed the "religion" of Jewish popular culture—that is, devotion to these materials and practices that in some way resembles, or even emulates, religiosity. This is readily evident in Jewish fans' dedication to favorite stars. Not only did actor John Garfield, a leading man in Hollywood films from the late 1930s until his death in 1952, attract fans who admired him especially as a fellow Jew; advertisements in Jewish publications, such as the *B'nai B'rith Messenger*, touted his appearance in films by proclaiming, "Another Jewish Actor Rises to Stardom."[30] During the 1950s Gertrude Berg, creator and star of *The Goldbergs* in its various incarnations on radio, as a stage play, a feature film, and a television series, fostered devotion to her character, family matriarch Molly Goldberg, by writing an advice column and a cookbook in Molly's name.[31]

Elevating works of American Jewish popular culture to the status of devotional objects is epitomized by movie-based tourist productions. In 1961 Israel's El Al Airline offered *Exodus* tours, during which visitors spent seventeen days traveling among sites of Jewish history, ancient and modern, as well as following in the footsteps of director Otto Preminger and the stars of his epic film about founding the State of Israel. Today, sightseers in Cracow can take *Schindler's List* tours, visiting places where the Holocaust took place alongside locations where Steven Spielberg shot his film. Blurring the boundaries between history and its representation, both of these tours conflate homage to the past with fandom in ways that can be discomforting. At the same time, they testify to the elaborate and compelling role that popular culture plays as a definitional force for many American Jews.

With the advent of the Internet, the discourse of Jewish fandom can now be archived and can bring together fellow devotees in a virtual community. Websites such as Jewhoo.com inventory famous Jews; other sites venerate—or disparage—a particular Jewish celebrity, filmmaker, or television program. These sites exemplify how American Jewish popular culture is, more than an inventory of works or practices, a matter of discussion. Indeed, discussion is key to transforming widely familiar, quotidian activities such as going to the movies, reading a book, or having a snack into Jewish cultural endeavors. The conversations that surround these activities can serve as a definitional practice for some Jews who may be seeking to address questions of personal and communal identity in cultural venues with which they are most familiar. And it is perhaps in this pursuit that America's first Jews, were they to find themselves among us today, would find common ground with Jews living in the United States at the turn of the twenty-first century, despite the great differences in how many now conceive and realize their Jewishness— in discussing their engagements with American culture as practices that inform their sense of what it means to be a Jew.

Endnotes

Prologue to American Jewish History: The Jews of America from 1654 to 1820

1   The struggle with Stuyvesant may be followed in the original sources in Morris U. Schappes, ed., *A Documentary History of the Jews in the United States, 1654-1875*, 3rd ed. (New York: Schocken Books, n.d.), pp. 1-13. For the two Jews who were already present in New Amsterdam, see Jacob Rader Marcus, *The Colonial American Jew, 1492-1776*, 3 vols. (Detroit: Wayne State University Press, 1970), vol.1, p. 216. On the cemetery, see David and Tamar De Sola Pool, *An Old Faith in the New World: Portrait of Shearith Israel, 1654-1954* (New York: Columbia University Press, 1955), pp. 31-32. For the Dutch West India Company's policy prohibiting public worship by non-Calvinists: Van Cleaf Bachman, *Peltries or Plantations: The Economic Policies of the Dutch West India Company in New Netherland 1623-1639* (Baltimore: Johns Hopkins University Press, 1969), p. 81.

2   Arnold Wiznitzer, *Jews in Colonial Brazil* (New York: Columbia University Press, 1960), pp. 69-70, 81, 130. Jews in Amsterdam who petitioned the Dutch West India Company on behalf of their coreligionists in New Amsterdam noted that Jews had gone to Martinique and to Barbados with the permission of the French and the English governments; Schappes, *Documentary History*, p. 3.

3   Oliver A. Rink, *Holland on the Hudson: An Economic and Social History of Dutch New York* (Ithaca: Cornell University Press, 1986), pp. 62, 67-68, 115-116, 134-135, 156, 158, 169, 171, 172, 175-177, 206, 212-213.

4   Jacob Barsimon joined Levy in demanding the right to serve in the guard; Schappes, *Documentary History*, p. 6. For Levy's continuing residence in the town until his death in 1683, see Leo Hershkowitz, "Original Inventories of Early New York Jews," *American Jewish History* 90 (2002): 251-252. By 1663 Jews were hardly still evident in New Amsterdam, and only Levy and Jacob de Lucena remained, the latter as late as 1678; Samuel Oppenheim, *The Early History of the Jews in New York, 1654-1664: Some New Matter on the Subject* ([New York: American Jewish Historical Society, 1909]), pp. 23, 60.

5   For efforts to settle in Curaçao in 1651, 1652, and 1659, the last successful, see Isaac S. and Suzanne A. Emmanuel, *History of the Jews of the Netherlands Antilles*, 2 vols. (Cincinnati: American Jewish Archives, 1970), vol. 1, pp. 38, 42, 45; and for attempts to settle on the Wild Coast of eastern South America in 1657 and the nearby island of Cayenne in 1659, the latter also a successful venture, see Robert Cohen, "The Egerton Manuscript," *American Jewish Historical Quarterly* 62 (1972-1973), and Simon Cohen, tr., Jacob R. Marcus and Stanley F. Chyet, eds., *Historical Essay on the Colony of*

Surinam, 1788 (Cincinnati and New York: American Jewish Archives and Ktav, 1974), pp. 183-188. For Newport: Morris A. Gutstein, *The Story of the Jews of Newport: Two and a Half Centuries of Judaism, 1658-1908* (New York: Bloch, 1936), pp. 340-342; and Leon Huhner, *The Life of Judah Touro (1775-1854)* (Philadelphia: Jewish Publication Society of America, 1946), pp. 10, 145n.5. Jacob Rader Marcus, however, doubted that Jews settled in Newport in 1658, although he did concede that it is likely some did so before 1678; *Colonial American Jew*, vol.1, pp. 314-318.

6   Schappes, *Documentary History*, pp. 12-13. George L. Smith argues "the position of the New Netherland Jews improved considerably subsequent to the pivotal citizenship [burgher rights] decision," in *Religion and Trade in New Netherland: Dutch Origins and American Development* (Ithaca: Cornell University Press, 1973), p. 218.

7   Gutstein, *Jews of Newport*, pp. 36-38, 40-43, 46, 81-82, 113-114; Emmanuel and Emmanuel, *Jews of the Netherlands Antilles*, vol. 1, p. 90. For the trade prosecution in 1685, see "Items Relating to the Jews of Newport," *Publications of the American Jewish Historical Society* 27 (1920): 175-176.

8   Eli Faber, *Jews, Slaves, and the Slave Trade: Setting the Record Straight* (New York: New York University Press, 1998), pp. 45, 49.

9   For an example of connections between Jews in New York and the Caribbean in the early 1680s and for the cemetery of 1682, see David De Sola Pool, *Portraits Etched in Stone: Early Jewish Settlers, 1682-1831* (New York: Columbia University Press, 1952), pp. 10-11, 188-189. For population data as well as Ashkenazic preponderance: Marcus, *Colonial American Jew*, vol.1, pp. 256, 258, 308, 390-391.

10   For examples of the differences between the two groups, see H. J. Zimmels, *Ashkenazim and Sephardim: Their Relations, Differences, and Problems as Reflected in Their Rabbinical Responsa* (London: Oxford University Press, 1958), pp. 188, 194, 241, 279-283.

11   Three Sephardics (Luis Moses Gomez, Mordecai Gomez, and Benjamin Mendez Pacheco) and one Ashkenazi (Jacob Franks) comprised the committee to build the synagogue. Between 1728 and 1760, Ashkenazim may have supplied as many as 54 percent of the presidents and assistants who led the congregation. "The Earliest Extant Minute Books of the Spanish and Portuguese Congregation Shearith Israel in New York, 1728-1786," *Publications of the American Jewish Historical Society* 21 (1913): 9, and passim for the officeholders.

12   Saul Jacob Rubin, *Third to None: The Saga of Savannah Jewry, 1733-1983* (n.p.: n.pub., 1983), pp. 1-3, 10.

13   Ibid., pp. 3-5. Our knowledge of the conflicts between Savannah's Sephardic and Ashkenazic components derives from the contemporary observations of the Reverend Martin Bolzius, a Lutheran minister, cited in R. D. Barnett, "Dr. Samuel Nunes Ribeiro and the Settlement of Georgia," in *Migration and Settlement: Proceedings of the Anglo-American Jewish Historical Conference Held in London Jointly by the Jewish Historical Society of England and the American Jewish Historical Society, July 1970* (London: Jewish Historical Society of England, 1971), pp. 87, 94.

14   Rubin, *Third to None*, pp. 16-21, 25.

15   Ibid., p. 16; Barnett A. Elzas, *The Jews of South Carolina from the Earliest Times to the Present Day* (Philadelphia: J. B. Lippincott Company, 1905), pp. 19-20, 23-30, 32-35, 120-121; "Earliest Extant Minute Books," p. 139; and Theodore Rosengarten and Dale Rosengarten, eds., *A Portion of the People: Three Hundred Years of Southern Jewish Life* (Columbia: University of South Carolina Press, 2002), pp. xvi, 3, 11.

16   William Vincent Byars, *B. and M. Gratz, Merchants in Philadelphia, 1754-1798* (Jefferson City, Missouri: Hugh Stephens Printing, 1916), pp. 59-60.

17   Edwin Wolf II and Maxwell Whiteman, *The History of the Jews of Philadelphia from Colonial Times to the Age of Jackson* (Philadelphia: Jewish Publication Society of America, 1965), pp. 23, 26, 30-32, 41-42, 47, 53, 58-59, 117-121.

18   Stanley F. Chyet, *Lopez of Newport: Colonial American Merchant Prince* (Detroit: Wayne State University Press, 1970), pp. 27, 42-51, 54, 56, 60, 66-73. In the early 1990s, allegations to the effect that Jews financed and controlled the Atlantic slave trade surfaced. For refutation, see Faber, *Jews, Slaves and the Slave Trade*, and Saul S. Friedman, *Jews and the American Slave Trade* (New Brunswick, New Jersey: Transaction Publishers, 1998). In Newport's case, the evidence points to participation by Jews there in thirty-four slaving ventures out of a total 930 such undertakings by Rhode Island merchants, or 3.6 percent; Faber, pp. 136-137.

19   The date of 1746 as the latest possible is known from the records of the Court of Chancery of Jamaica in a case involving Naphtali Hart; Jamaica Archives (Spanish Town, Jamaica), Records of the Court of Chancery, 1A/3/17, 30-31. For the population figure for the early 1760s: Chyet, *Lopez of Newport*, p. 52. The figures for 1774 are based upon the census conducted by the colony of Rhode Island in 1774; Faber, *Jews, Slaves, and the Slave Trade*, p. 325 n.23. For Lopez's escape from Portugal and his business enterprises in Newport, see Chyet, *Lopez of Newport*, pp. 22-23, and passim; and, for more on his slaving ventures, Virginia B. Platt, "'And Don't Forget the Guinea Voyage': The Slave Trade of Aaron Lopez of Newport," 3rd ser., *William and Mary Quarterly* 32 (1975): 601-618. Lopez's prominence in Newport is suggested by the fact that he paid by far the highest tax assessment in Newport in 1772, an amount in excess of £37, while the next highest was half that and was assessed on two men jointly; Elaine Forman Crane, *A Dependent People: Newport, Rhode Island in the Revolutionary Era* (New York: Fordham University Press, 1985), p. 25.

20   The Jewish inhabitants in these and other locations are described by Marcus in vol. 1 of *Colonial American Jew*, passim.

21   Ira Rosenwaike, *On the Edge of Greatness: A Portrait of American Jewry in the Early National Period* (Cincinnati: American Jewish Archives, 1985), p. 17; Doris Groshen Daniels, "Colonial Jewry: Religion, Domestic and Social Relations," *American Jewish Historical Quarterly* 66 (1976-1977): 380.

22   *The North-American and the West-Indian Gazetteer* (London: G. Robinson, 1776), entry for "Jamaica," for the 1776 population figure. The colony had a *haham* from Curaçao as early as 1683; M. Kayserling, "The Jews in Jamaica and Daniel Israel Lopez Laguna," orig. ser., *Jewish Quarterly Review* 12 (1900): 711.

23   Rosenwaike, *Edge of Greatness*, p. 17. For immigration from Jamaica: Maxwell Whiteman, *Copper for America: The Hendricks Family and a National Industry, 1775-1939* (New Brunswick: Rutgers University Press, 1971), pp. 69-71; from France: Zosa Szajkowski, "Jewish Emigration from Bordeaux during the Eighteenth and Nineteenth Centuries," *Jewish Social Studies* 18 (1956): 121-122; and from Holland: "Items Relating to Congregation Shearith Israel, New York," *Publications of the American Jewish Historical Society* 27 (1920): 73-78, for the marriages of three Jews from Amsterdam to New Yorkers. Jews from Holland also settled in Baltimore, along with others from England and Germany; Ira Rosenwaike, "The Jews of Baltimore to 1810," *American Jewish Historical Quarterly* 64 (1974-1975): 315-318, and Ira Rosenwaike, "The Jews of Baltimore: 1810 to 1820," *American Jewish Historical Quarterly* 67 (1977-1978): 104, 108, 114-117. For Richmond: Myron Berman, *Richmond's Jewry, 1769-1976* (Charlottesville: University Press of Virginia, 1979).

24   Samuel Reznceck, *Unrecognized Patriots: The Jews in the American Revolution* (Westport: Greenwood Press, 1975), pp. 12, 81, 84-93, 229-235.

25   For the acquisition of the right to vote and to serve in office in the original thirteen states, see Stanley F. Chyet, "The Political Rights of the Jews in the United States: 1776-1840," in *Critical Studies in American Jewish History: Selected Articles from American Jewish Archives* (Cincinnati and New York: American Jewish Archives and Ktav, 1971), vol. 2, pp. 37-62.

26   "Earliest Extant Minute Books," pp. 36-37, 51-53, 66-67, 74-75.

27 Jews in early America readily moved from one location to another. Examples are too numerous to list here fully, but they include Moses Lopez and the members of the important Rivera family, who left New York in the late 1740s and resettled in Newport (Chyet, *Lopez of Newport*, pp. 20-21); and various members of the Franks family of New York, including Coleman Solomons, a ne'er-do-well who gallivanted about between New York, Philadelphia, Charleston, and London (Eli Faber, *A Time for Planting: The First Migration, 1654-1820* [Baltimore: Johns Hopkins University Press, 1992], pp. 44-45).

28 "Earliest Extant Minute Books," pp. 49, 50-53, 57, 59, 65-66, 110-112, 115-118.

29 Examples of these extensive responsibilities occur throughout "Earliest Extant Minute Books."

30 For consultation between congregations in the English colonies and London generally, see R. D. Barnett, "The Correspondence of the Mahamad of the Spanish and Portuguese Congregation of London during the Seventeenth and Eighteenth Centuries," *Transactions of the Jewish Historical Society of England* 20 (1959-1961): 1-50. For a 1793 request for a religious ruling made by the Philadelphia congregation to London, see Jacob Rader Marcus, ed., *American Jewry—Documents—Eighteenth Century* (Cincinnati: Hebrew Union College Press, 1959), pp. 188-189.

31 Chyet, *Lopez of Newport*, p. 158; Marcus, *Colonial American Jew*, vol. 1, p. 328; Daniels, "Colonial Jewry," p. 396; Marcus, *Documents*, p. 134.

32 Peter Kalm in his visit to America in the late 1740s, cited by Hyman B. Grinstein, *The Rise of the Jewish Community of New York, 1654-1860* (Philadelphia: Jewish Publication Society of America, 1945), p. 333; and Abram Vossen Goodman, " A German Mercenary Observes American Jews During the Revolution," *American Jewish Historical Quarterly* 59 (1969-1970): 227. For the complaint to Amsterdam in 1785: Marcus, *Documents*, p. 141.

33 Goodman, "German Mercenary," p. 227. Portraits of early American Jews are abundantly accessible in Richard Brilliant, *Facing the New World: Jewish Portraits in Colonial and Federal America* (Munich and New York: Prestel, 1997).

34 Examples include Phila Franks, whose mother's anguish is discussed below; Shina Simon, in Wolf and Whiteman, *Jews of Philadelphia*, pp. 239-240; and Sarah Da Costa, the daughter of the Charleston congregation's cantor, in Malcolm Stern, "The Function of Genealogy in American Jewish History," *Essays in American Jewish History to Commemorate the Tenth Anniversary of the Founding of the American Jewish Archives Under the Direction of Jacob Rader Marcus* (Cincinnati: American Jewish Archives, 1958), p. 94.

35 Joseph L. Blau and Salo W. Baron, eds., *The Jews of the United States, 1790-1840: A Documentary History*, 3 vols. (New York: Columbia University Press, 1963), vol. 2, p. 551; Marcus, *Documents*, pp. 129, 150, 160-161, 179-180.

36 Leo Hershkowitz and Isidore S. Meyer, eds., *The Lee Max Friedman Collection of American Jewish Colonial Correspondence: Letters of the Franks Family (1733-1748)* (Waltham: American Jewish Historical Society, 1968), pp. xxi, 4-5, 7-8, 11-12, 24-26, 31, 34, 37, 40-41, 48, 52, 69, 84-85, 103-106, 116-119, 124-125, 129 n.3; and the frontispiece for her portrait.

37 Carl Bridenbaugh, *Peter Harrison: First American Architect* (Chapel Hill: University of North Carolina Press, 1949), pp. 48-52, 98-104. Unusually fine images of the exterior and interior are in *Touro Synagogue of Congregation Jeshuat Israel, Newport, Rhode Island* (Newport: Remington Ward, 1948), opposite pp. 7 and 20.

38 Nancy Halverson Schless, "Peter Harrison, the Touro Synagogue, and the Wren City Church," *Winterthur Portfolio* 8 (Charlottesville: University of Virginia Press, 1973), pp. 187-192, 195-200.

39 Images of the exterior and interior are in Rachel Wischnitzer, *Synagogue Architecture in the United States: History and Interpretation* (Philadelphia: Jewish Publication Society of America, 1955), pp. 21-22.

40 For a rendering of the synagogue, see Faber, *Time for Planting*, among the illustrations following p. 68. The drawing is derived from the 1742 Grim map of New York City, where the city's houses of worship along with other public buildings are depicted at the top. The map, "A Plan of the City and Environs of New York," is reproduced in I. N. Phelps Stokes, *The Iconography of Manhattan Island, 1498-1909*, 6 vols. (New York: Robert A. Dodd, 1915-1928), vol. 1, plate 32[a].

41 Leon A. Jick, *The Americanization of the Synagogue, 1820-1870* (Hanover: University Press of New England, 1976), p. 10; Jacob Rader Marcus, "The Handsome Young Priest in the Black Gown: The Personal World of Gershom Seixas," *Hebrew Union College Annual* 40-41 (1969-1970): 438, 445; Thomas Kessner, "Gershom Mendes Seixas: His Religious 'Calling,' Outlook, and Competence," *American Jewish Historical Quarterly* 58 (1968-1969): 468.

42 Robert J. Dinkin, *Voting in Provincial America: A Study of Elections in the Thirteen Colonies, 1689-1776* (Westport: Greenwood Press, 1977), pp. 31-32; Chyet, *Lopez of Newport*, pp. 34-40; Schappes, *Documentary History*, p. 26.

43 Leo Hershkowitz, "Some Aspects of the New York Jewish Merchant and Community, 1654-1820," *American Jewish Historical Quarterly* 66 (1976-1977): 13, 16-18; Beverly McAnear, "The Place of the Freeman in Old New York," *New York History* 21 (1940): 419, 425; Marcus, *Colonial American Jew*, vol. 3, pp. 1126-1127; Abram Vossen Goodman, *American Overture: Jewish Rights in Colonial Times* (Philadelphia: Jewish Publication Society of America, 1947), pp. 111-112, 114; *The Constitution of the State of New York* (Fishkill: n.p., 1777), pp. 17, 18, 21-22.

44 Jacob R. Marcus, "Jews and the American Revolution: A Bicentennial Documentary," *American Jewish Archives* 27 (1975): 116-119; Rezneck, *Unrecognized Patriots*, pp. 14-17, 21-66.

45 Schappes, *Documentary History*, pp. 65, 69.

46 Ibid., pp. 79-81.

47 Chyet, "Political Rights of the Jews," pp. 55-59.

48 Schappes, *Documentary History*, pp. 122-125; Blau and Baron, *Jews of the United States*, vol. 2, pp. 318-323; Jonathan D. Sarna, *Jacksonian Jew: The Two Worlds of Mordecai Noah* (New York: Holmes and Meier, 1981), pp. 27-28.

49 Chyet, "Political Rights of the Jews," pp. 54, 60.

50 For Jefferson's letters, see Abraham J. Karp, *From the Ends of the Earth: Judaic Treasures of the Library of Congress* (Washington: Library of Congress, 1991), pp. 240-245.

A Century of Migration, 1820-1924

1 Quoted in Mark Wischnitzer, *To Dwell in Safety: The Story of Jewish Migration Since 1800* (Philadelphia: Jewish Publication Society, 1948), p. 29.

2 Ibid., p. 22.

3 Arthur Ruppin, *Jews in the Modern World* (London: Macmillan and Company, 1934), p. 114.

4 Quoted in Salo W. Baron, *The Russian Jew under Tsars and Soviets* (New York: Macmillan, 1964), p. 50.

5 Emma Lazarus, *Songs of a Semite: The Dance to Death, and Other Poems* (New York: Office of *The American Hebrew*, 1882).

6   Cyrus Adler, ed., *The Voice of America on Kishineff* (Philadelphia: Jewish Publication Society of America, 1904).

7   Quoted in Hasia R. Diner, *Hungering for America: Italian, Irish, and Jewish Foodways in the Age of Migration* (Cambridge: Harvard University Press, 2002), p. 198.

8   Hinde Amchanitzky, *Lehr Bukh vie azoy tzu Kokhen un Baken* (New York: Abraham Fernberg, 1901), p. 10, 12, 13, 18-19, 33.

The Crucial Decades

1   Lillian Gorenstein, "A Memoir of the Great War, 1914-1924," *YIVO Annual* 20, ed. Deborah Dash Moore (1991):125-184, quotes from 167-170.

2   Henry L. Feingold, *A Time for Searching: Entering the Mainstream, 1920-1945* (Baltimore and London: Johns Hopkins University Press, 1992), p. 29.

3   Louis Wirth, "The Ghetto," *On Cities and Social life*, ed. Albert J. Reiss, Jr. (Chicago: University of Chicago Press, 1964), p. 94.

4   Gorenstein, p. 175.

American Jewry Since 1945

1   In fact, the Jewish baby boom began a few years before that of the general population, sometime around the year 1941, rather than 1946. On the baby boomers, see Chaim I. Waxman, *Jewish Baby Boomers: A Communal Perspective* (Albany: SUNY Press, 2001).

2   Edward S. Schapiro, *A Time for Healing: American Jewry Since World War II* (Baltimore: Johns Hopkins University Press, 1992), pp. 8-10.

3   The "American success story" of Jews who rose to positions of prominence during this period is examined in the first section of Charles E. Silberman's *A Certain People: American Jews and Their Lives Today* (New York: Summit Books, 1985), pp. 21-156.

4   *National Jewish Population Survey 2000-2001: Strength, Challenge and Diversity in the American Jewish Population*. A United Jewish Communities Report, September 2003, p. 6.

5   On the seventies, Chaim I. Waxman, *America's Jews in Transition* (Philadelphia: Temple University Press, 1983), p. 145. The late twentieth-century figure is based on the 2000 National Jewish Population Study and was graciously provided by Dr. Charles Kadushin of the North American Jewish Data Bank.

6   Marshall Sklare, *America's Jews* (New York: Random House, 1971), p. 62.

7   *National Jewish Population Survey 2000-2001*, p. 6.

8   Schapiro, *A Time for Healing*, p. 101 on the professorate; on the broader occupational success of Jews, see his entire chapter "A Tale of Two Shapiros."

9   Barry A. Kosmin and Seymour P. Lachman, *One Nation Under God: Religion in Contemporary American Society* (New York: Crown, 1993), p. 260.

10   Riv-Ellen Prell, *Fighting to Become Americans: Jews, Gender, and the Anxiety of Assimilation* (Boston: Beacon Press, 1999), pp. 202-203.

11   Moshe Hartman and Harriet Hartman, *Gender Equality and American Jews* (Albany: SUNY Press, 1996), p. 44.

12   Ibid., pp. 42, 113-114, 163-164.

13   On this theme, see Sylvia Barack Fishman, *A Breath of Life: Feminism in the American Jewish Community* (New York: The Free Press, 1993).

14   For the classic study of this process, see Marshall Sklare and Joseph Greenbaum, *Jewish Identity on the Suburban Frontier: A Study of Group Survival in the Open Society* (Chicago: University of Chicago Press, 1979).

15   The growth of these Jewish communities, which would in time become the second and third largest in the United States, is traced by Deborah Dash Moore, *To the Golden Cities: Pursuing the American Jewish Dream in Miami and L.A.* (New York: The Free Press, 1994).

16   Sidney Goldstein and Alice Goldstein, *Jews on the Move: Implications for Jewish Identity* (Albany: SUNY Press, 1996), p. 41.

17   Waxman, *America's Jews in Transition*, p. 138.

18   *National Jewish Population Survey 2000-2001*, p. 5.

19   Barry A. Kosmin et al., *Highlights of the National Jewish Population Survey* (New York: Council of Jewish Federations, 1991), p. 6.

20   Ira M. Sheshkin, *How Jewish Communities Differ: Variations in the Findings of Jewish Population Studies* (New York: North American Jewish Data Bank, 1991), p.105.

21   *National Jewish Population Survey 2000-2001*, pp. 16, 18.

22   Several of these matters are discussed in Steven M. Cohen, *Religious Stability and Ethnic Decline: Emerging Patterns of Identity in the United States* (New York: JCC Association, 1998).

23   Since the U.S. census may not include questions about religion, estimates of the Jewish population rely upon methods that periodically have been subjected to much scrutiny and criticism.

24   Sklare, *America's Jews*, p. 38.

25   See a discussion of these estimates in the *American Jewish Year Book* (New York: American Jewish Committee, 2002), pp. 612-616. The low birthrate of Jews surely contributed to this demographic decline: figures from the early twenty-first century indicate that more Jewish women than all U.S. women remain childless in every age group through the age of 44, and Jewish women have also given birth to fewer children than U.S. women. *National Jewish Population Survey 2000-2001*, p. 3. Similar patterns were observed in 1973; see Sidney Goldstein, "Jews in the United States: Perspectives from Demography," *American Jewish Year Book* (1981), p. 39.

26   On synagogues, see "Census of U.S. Synagogues, 2001," *American Jewish Year Book* (2002), pp. 112-150.

27   Jack Wertheimer, "Current Trends in American Jewish Philanthropy," *American Jewish Year Book* (1997), p. 40.

28   "The Miracle of Jewish Giving," *Fortune*, January 1966, p. 149.

29   For a more detailed analysis of these developments, see Jack Wertheimer, "Jewish Organizational Life in the United States Since 1945," *American Jewish Year Book* (1995), pp. 3-98.

30   See Arthur A. Goren, "A Golden Decade for American Jews: 1945-1955," *Studies in Contemporary Jewry* 8 (1992): 3-20.

31   The most important sociological study of this period found evidence of strong support for these twin goals among the rank and file. When the "Lakeville" study of the late 1950s questioned Jews about their "image of the good Jew," 63 percent of the sample thought it essential or desirable to be "a liberal on political and economic issues," 83 percent stated the same about the importance of working "for equality for Negroes," 68 percent deemed it essential or desirable for the good Jew to support Israel. Sklare and Greenbaum, *Jewish Identity on the Suburban Frontier*, p. 322.

32   Quoted by Peter Y. Medding, "Segmented Ethnicity and the New Jewish Politics," *Studies in Contemporary Jewry* 3 (1987): 32-33.

33   On these developments, see J. J. Goldberg, *Jewish Power: Inside the American Jewish Establishment* (Reading, Massachusetts: Addison-Wesley, 1996), pp. 312-320.

34   *Time*, Oct. 15, 1951, pp. 52-57. Finkelstein traced his efforts to the Jewish imperative to make "peace between man and his fellows."

35   The most famous mid-century expression of Judaism's parity was found in the influential work of Will Herberg, a Jew, who wrote a book tellingly entitled, *Protestant, Catholic, Jew: An Essay in American Religious Sociology* (New York: Doubleday, 1955).

36   For a rich panoramic sweep of American Jewish cultural offerings, see Stephen J. Whitfield, *In Search of American Jewish Culture* (Hanover, New Hampshire: Brandeis University Press, 1999).

37   Jack Wertheimer, "Current Trends in American Jewish Philanthropy," *American Jewish Year Book* (1997), pp. 3-92, esp. pp. 18-19.

38   Wertheimer, "Jewish Organizational Life in the United States Since 1945," pp. 54-59.

39   Ibid., pp. 59-64. American Jews also helped in the rescue of Ethiopian Jews during the 1990s.

40   Schapiro, *A Time for Healing*, pp. 217-228.

41   These divisions are explored in Jack Wertheimer, *A People Divided: Judaism in Contemporary America* (New York: Basic Books, 1993) and Samuel G. Freedman, *Jew versus Jew: The Struggle for the Soul of American Jewry* (New York: Touchstone, 2001).

42   On these trends, see Robert N. Bellah et al., *Habits of the Heart: Individualism and Commitment in American Life* (Berkeley: University of California Press, 1985) and Robert Putnam, *Bowling Alone: The Collapse and Revival of American Community* (New York: Touchstone, 2000).

43   On the role of the "sovereign self" in the making of religious decisions, see Steven M. Cohen and Arnold M. Eisen, *The Jew Within: Self, Family, and Community in America* (Bloomington: University of Indiana Press, 2000), esp. pp. 183-184.

44   Cohen, *Religious Stability and Ethnic Decline*, pp.18-20.

45   In its first four years, the program sent 30,000 young American Jews to Israel. *Jewish Week*, Nov. 14, 2003, p. 3

46   Jack Wertheimer, "Jewish Education in the United States: Recent Trends and Issues," *American Jewish Year Book* (1999), pp. 3-115.

American Judaism

The bulk of this paper is drawn from my *American Judaism: A History* (New Haven: Yale University Press, 2004), with the permission of the publisher.

1   Arnold Wiznitzer, "The Exodus from Brazil and Arrival in New Amsterdam of the Jewish Pilgrim Fathers, 1654," *Publications of the American Jewish Historical Society* 44 (1954): 80-98; the quote is from Isaac S. Emmanuel, "New Light on Early American Jewry," *American Jewish Archives* 7 (January 1955): 51.

2   Morris U. Schappes, *A Documentary History of the Jews of the United States, 1654-1875* (New York: Schocken, 1971), p. 19.

3   David Sorkin, "The Port Jew: Notes Toward a Social Type," *Journal of Jewish Studies* 50 (1999): 87-97; Benjamin J. Kaplan, "Fictions of Privacy: House Chapels and the Spatial Accommodation of Religious Dissent in Early Modern Europe," *American Historical Review* 107 (October 2002): 1031-1064.

4   Leo Hershkowitz, "The Mill Street Synagogue Reconsidered," *American Jewish Historical Quarterly* 53 (1964): 404-410; Jacob R. Marcus, *The Colonial American Jew, 1492-1776* (Detroit: Wayne State University Press, 1970), esp. p. 402.

5   Arnold Wiznitzer in *Publications of the American Jewish Historical Society* 46 (1956): 48, n. 41 suggests that the name refers to the "remnant of Israel" that survived from Recife in 1654 and points to the use of this phrase in a depiction of Recife's fall by Isaac Aboab de Fonseca. Jacob R. Marcus, however, cites documents from the early 1720s suggesting that the congregation's original name was not Shearith Israel but Shearith Yaakob (Remnant of Jacob); see Jacob R. Marcus, *Studies in American Jewish History* (Cincinnati: Hebrew Union College Press, 1969), pp. 44-45.

6   See generally, David de Sola Pool and Tamar de Sola Pool, *An Old Faith in the New World: Portrait of Shearith Israel, 1654-1954* (New York: Columbia University Press, 1955) and Marcus, *Colonial American Jew*, pp. 855-1110. Quote is from Leo Hershkowitz and Isidore S. Meyer, eds., *The Lee Max Friedman Collection of American Jewish Colonial Correspondence: Letters of the Franks Family (1733-1748)* (Waltham: American Jewish Historical Society, 1968), p. 60.

7   Lionel D. Barnett, ed. and trans., *El Libro de los Acuerdos* (Oxford: Oxford University Press, 1931), p. 3; Herman P. Salomon, "Joseph Jesurun Pinto (1729-1782): A Dutch Hazan in Colonial New York," *Studia Rosenthaliana* 13 (January 1979): 18-29.

8   Hyman B. Grinstein, *The Rise of the Jewish Community of New York* (Philadelphia: Jewish Publication Society, 1945), p. 469; Richard W. Pointer, *Protestant Pluralism and the New York Experience: A Study of Eighteenth-Century Religious Diversity* (Bloomington: Indiana University Press, 1988), pp. 13-15.

9   Jon Butler, *Awash in a Sea of Faith: Christianizing the American People* (Cambridge: Harvard University Press, 1990), pp. 113-116; Rachel Wischnitzer, *Synagogue Architecture in the United States* (Philadelphia: Jewish Publication Society, 1955), pp. 11-19; Carol Herselle Krinsky, *Synagogues of Europe: Architecture, History, Meaning* (Cambridge: MIT Press, 1985), pp. 412-415; Kaplan, "Fictions of Privacy": 1031-1064.

10 Jonathan D. Sarna, "What Is American About the Constitutional Documents of American Jewry," in *A Double Bond: The Constitutional Documents of American Jewry*, ed. Daniel J. Elazar, Jonathan D. Sarna, and Rela G. Monson (Lanham, Maryland: University Press of America, 1992), pp. 35-38.

11 See Nathan O. Hatch, *The Democratization of American Christianity* (New Haven: Yale University Press, 1989), and, for an example, Sydney M. Fish, "The Problem of Intermarriage in Early America," *Gratz College Annual of Jewish Studies* 4 (1975): 85-94.

12   Malcolm H. Stern, "The 1820s: American Jewry Comes of Age," in *A Bicentennial Festschrift for Jacob Rader Marcus,* ed. Bertram W. Korn (New York: Ktav, 1976), pp. 539-549.

13   Joseph L. Blau and Salo W. Baron, eds., *The Jews of the United States: A Documentary History, 1790-1840* (New York: Columbia University Press, 1963), p. 541; Pool, *An Old Faith in the New World,* p. 436; Grinstein, *Rise of the Jewish Community of New York,* pp. 40-49.

14   For various accounts, see James William Hagy, *This Happy Land: The Jews of Colonial and Antebellum Charleston* (Tuscaloosa: University of Alabama Press, 1993), pp. 128-160; Robert Liberles, "Conflict over Reforms: The Case of Congregation Beth Elohim, Charleston, South Carolina," in *The American Synagogue: A Sanctuary Transformed,* ed. Jack Wertheimer (New York: Cambridge University Press, 1987), pp. 274-296; Michael A. Meyer, *Response to Modernity: A History of the Reform Movement in Judaism* (New York: Oxford University Press, 1988), pp. 228-233; L. C. Moise, *Biography of Isaac Harby* (Columbia, South Carolina, 1931); Lou H. Silberman, *American Impact: Judaism in the United States in the Early Nineteenth Century,* The B.G. Rudolph Lectures in Judaic Studies (Syracuse: Syracuse University Press, 1964); Gary P. Zola, *Isaac Harby of Charleston 1788-1828* (Tuscaloosa, Alabama: University of Alabama Press, 1994), pp. 112-149.

15   Hatch, *Democratization of American Christianity,* p. 59.

16   Grinstein, *Rise of the Jewish Community of New York,* pp. 472-474; Gerard R. Wolfe, *The Synagogues of New York's Lower East Side* (New York: New York University Press, 1978), p. 37.

17   Jonathan D. Sarna, "The Evolution of the American Synagogue," in *The Americanization of the Jews,* ed. Robert M. Seltzer and Norman J. Cohen (New York: New York University Press, 1995), pp. 219-221.

18   For various accounts, see Abraham Barkai, *Branching Out: German-Jewish Immigrants to the United States, 1820-1914* (New York: Holmes & Meier, 1994); Naomi W. Cohen, *Encounter with Emancipation: The German Jews in the United States, 1830-1914* (Philadelphia: Jewish Publication Society, 1984); Hasia Diner, *A Time for Gathering: The Second Migration 1820-1880* (Baltimore: Johns Hopkins University Press, 1992); Jacob R. Marcus, *United States Jewry, 1776-1985* (Detroit: Wayne State University Press, 1991-1993), vols. 2-3. For the transformation of Judaism, see Leon Jick, *The Americanization of the Synagogue, 1820-1870* (Hanover, New Hampshire: Brandeis University Press, 1976).

19   Lance J. Sussman, *Isaac Leeser and the Making of American Jewry* (Detroit: Wayne State University Press, 1995); cf. Mordechai Breuer, *Modernity Within Tradition: The Social History of Orthodox Jewry in Imperial Germany* (New York: Columbia University Press, 1992).

20   Michael A. Meyer, *Response to Modernity: A History of the Reform Movement in Judaism* (New York: Oxford, 1988): pp. 225-270, 387-388.

21   Edward E. Grusd, *B'nai B'rith: The Story of a Covenant* (New York: Appleton, 1966): pp. 112-170, esp. p. 20; Deborah Dash Moore, *B'nai B'rith and the Challenge of Ethnic Leadership* (Albany: SUNY Press, 1981): pp. 1-34.

22   I. Harold Sharfman, *The First Rabbi: Origins of Conflict Between Orthodox and Reform: Jewish Polemic Warfare in Pre-Civil War America, A Biographical History* (Malibu, California: Pangloss Press, 1988); Moshe Davis, "Abraham I. Rice: Pioneer of Orthodoxy in America," *America and the Holy Land: With Eyes Toward Zion —IV* (Westport: Praeger, 1995), p. 100; Israel Tabak, "Rabbi Abraham Rice of Baltimore," *Tradition* 7 (Summer 1965): 100-120.

23   H. G. Reissner, "The German-American Jews (1800-1850)," *Leo Baeck Year Book* 10 (1965): 104-107.

24   Joseph Buchler, "The Struggle for Unity: Attempts at Union in American Jewish Life, 1654-1868," *American Jewish Archives* 2 (June 1949): 2-27; Jonathan D. Sarna, *American Judaism: A History* (New Haven: Yale University Press, 2004), pp. 104-105.

25   I. J. Benjamin, *Three Years in America* (Philadelphia: Jewish Publication Society, 1956), vol. 1, p. 78; Meyer, *Response to Modernity*, pp. 251-252; Michael A. Meyer, *Judaism Within Modernity: Essays on Jewish History and Religion* (Detroit: Wayne State University Press, 2001), pp. 223-238; Jonathan D. Sarna and Karla Goldman, "From Synagogue-Community to Citadel of Reform," *American Congregations*, ed. James Lewis and James Wind (Chicago: University of Chicago Press, 1994), p. 177.

26   Jonathan D. Sarna, *A Great Awakening: The Transformation That Shaped Twentieth Century American Judaism and Its Implications for Today* (New York: Council for Initiatives in Jewish Education, 1995).

27   Walter Jacob, ed., *The Changing World of Reform Judaism: The Pittsburgh Platform in Retrospect* (Pittsburgh: Rodef Shalom Congregation, 1985); the platform is reprinted in Meyer, *Response to Modernity*, pp. 387-388.

28   Meyer, *Response to Modernity*, pp. 264-295.

29   Sarna, *American Judaism*, pp. 151-163.

30   Hasia R. Diner, "Like the Antelope and the Badger: The Founding and Early Years of the Jewish Theological Seminary, 1886-1902," in *Tradition Renewed: A History of the Jewish Theological Seminary of America*, ed. Jack Wertheimer (New York: Jewish Theological Seminary, 1997): pp. 3-42; Robert E. Fierstien, *A Different Spirit: The Jewish Theological Seminary of America, 1886-1902* (New York: Jewish Theological Seminary, 1990); Abraham J. Karp, "Solomon Schechter Comes to America," *American Jewish Historical Quarterly* 53 (1963): 44-62.

31   *Sefer Ha-Yovel Shel Agudath Ha-Rabbanim* . . . [in Hebrew] (New York: 1928); Gilbert Klaperman, *The Story of Yeshiva University: The First Jewish University in America* (New York: Macmillan, 1969), pp. 48-72; Jeffrey S. Gurock, *The Men and Women of Yeshiva University: Higher Education, Orthodoxy, and American Judaism* (New York: Columbia University Press, 1988), pp. 18-42.

32   Sarna, *American Judaism*, pp. 237-242.

33   Marshall Sklare, *Conservative Judaism: An American Religious Movement* (New York: Schocken, 1972); Herman H. Rubenovitz and Mignon L. Rubenovitz, *The Waking Heart* (Cambridge, Massachusetts: Nathaniel Dame & Company, 1967), pp. 73-84.

34   Mordecai M. Kaplan, "A Program for the Reconstruction of Judaism," *Menorah Journal* 6, no. 4 (August 1920): esp. 183, 195-196; Mordecai M. Kaplan, *Judaism As a Civilization* (Philadelphia: Jewish Publication Society, 1994 [1934]); Charles S. Liebman, "Reconstructionism in American Jewish Life," *American Jewish Year Book* 71 (1970): 3-99; Mel Scult, *Judaism Faces the Twentieth Century: A Biography of Mordecai M. Kaplan* (Detroit: Wayne State University Press, 1993); Jeffrey S. Gurock and Jacob J. Schacter, *A Modern Heretic and a Traditional Community: Mordecai M. Kaplan, Orthodoxy and American Judaism* (New York: Columbia University Press, 1997).

35   Kaplan, *Judaism As a Civilization*, p. 76; Sarna, *American Judaism*, pp. 267-271.

36   For an elaboration on these two paragraphs, with full documentation, see Sarna, *American Judaism*, pp. 272-355.

America's Jewish Women

1   Arnold Witznitzer, "The Exodus from Brazil and Arrival in New Amsterdam of the Jewish Pilgrim Fathers, 1654," *Publications of the American Jewish Historical Society* 44 (December 1954): 80-97.

2   Ibid., 98.

3   Jacob Rader Marcus, ed., *The American Jewish Woman: A Documentary History* (Cincinnati: American Jewish Archives, 1981), p. 34.

4   Holly Snyder, "Queens of the Household: The Jewish Women of British America, 1700-1800," in *Women and American Judaism: Historical Perspectives*, ed. Pamela S. Nadell and Jonathan D. Sarna (Hanover, New Hampshire: Brandeis University Press, 2001), pp. 15-45, quotation, p. 25.

5   Aviva Ben-Ur, "The Exceptional and the Mundane: A Biographical Portrait of Rebecca Machado Phillips (1746-1831)," in *Women and American Judaism*, ed. Nadell and Sarna, pp. 46-80.

6   Ellen Smith, "Portraits of a Community," in *American Jewish Women's History: A Reader*, ed. Pamela S. Nadell (New York: New York University Press, 2003), pp. 13-25, quotations, pp. 13, 19.

7   Snyder, "Queens of the Household," Franks quoted, pp. 24-25.

8   Smith, "Portraits of a Community," p. 17.

9   On this critical observation, see Karla Goldman, *Beyond the Synagogue Gallery: Finding a Place for Women in American Judaism* (Cambridge: Harvard University Press, 2000), pp. 38-50.

10 Snyder, "Queens of the Household," p. 17.

11 Philadelphia's Dr. Benjamin Rush, physician to Rebecca Machado Phillips's family and signer of the Declaration of Independence, attended both a wedding and circumcision in her home; Ben-Ur, "The Exceptional and the Mundane," pp. 60-61. On Jewish population statistics, see Jonathan D. Sarna, ed., *The American Jewish Experience*, 2nd ed. (1986) (New York: Holmes & Meier, 1997), p. 359.

12 Ben-Ur, "The Exceptional and the Mundane," pp. 63-64.

13 For a brief overview of Gratz, see Dianne Ashton, "Rebecca Gratz," in *Jewish Women in America: An Historical Encyclopedia*, ed. Paula Hyman and Deborah Dash Moore (New York: Routledge, 1997), pp. 547-550. It is based on Dianne Ashton, *Rebecca Gratz: Women and Judaism in Antebellum America* (Detroit: Wayne State University Press, 1997).

14 Cornelia Wilhelm, "The Independent Order of True Sisters: Friendship, Fraternity, and a Model of Modernity for Nineteenth-Century American Jewish Womanhood," *American Jewish Archives Journal* 54, no. 1 (2002): 37-63.

15 Diane Lichtenstein, *Writing Their Nations: The Tradition of Nineteenth-Century American Jewish Women Writers* (Bloomington: Indiana University Press, 1992), Hymn 154 by Penina Moise, quoted p. 72, Szold quoted p. 83.

16 For a brief overview of Lazarus's life, see Diane Lichtenstein, "Emma Lazarus," in Hyman and Moore, *Jewish Women in America*, pp. 806-809.

17 Sarna, *The American Jewish Experience*, p. 359. See Pamela S. Nadell, "Mary Antin," in Hyman and Moore, *Jewish Women in America*, pp. 55-57.

18 Paula Hyman, "Immigrant Women and Consumer Protest: The New York City Kosher Meat Boycott of 1902," 1980; reprinted in Nadell, *American Jewish Women's History: A Reader*, 1980, pp. 116-128.

19 Faith Rogow, "National Council of Jewish Women," in Hyman and Moore, *Jewish Women in America*, pp. 968-979. This is based on her book, Faith Rogow, *Gone to Another Meeting: The National Council of Jewish Women, 1893-1993* (Tuscaloosa: University of Alabama Press, 1993).

20 Shelly Tenenbaum, "Borrowers or Lenders Be: Jewish Immigrant Women's Credit Networks," in Nadell, *American Jewish Women's History*, pp. 79-90.

21 Snyder, "Queens of the Household," pp. 18, 31. Hasia R. Diner, *A Time for Gathering: The Second Migration, 1820-1880* (Baltimore: Johns Hopkins University Press, 1992), pp. 81-84.

22   For one overview of women's work outside New York, see Linda Mack Schloff, "'We Dug More Rocks': Women and Work," in Nadell, *American Jewish Women's History*, pp. 91-99. This is excerpted from Linda Mack Schloff, *"And Prairie Dogs Weren't Kosher": Jewish Women in the Upper Midwest Since 1855* (St. Paul: Minnesota Historical Society Press, 1996). On women in the garment trades, see Susan A. Glenn, *Daughters of the Shtetl: Life and Labor in the Immigrant Generation* (Ithaca: Cornell University Press, 1990).

23   By 1960 the majority of all New York City teachers were Jewish women; Ruth Jacknow Markowitz, *My Daughter, the Teacher: Jewish Teachers in the New York City Schools* (New Brunswick: Rutgers University Press, 1993).

24   Sources on the strike include Irving Howe, *World of Our Fathers* (New York: Touchstone Books, 1976); and Glenn, *Daughters of the Shtetl*. An excellent online exhibition is *Triangle Factory Fire* ([29 October 2003]); available from http://www.ilr.cornell.edu/trianglefire/. The classic article on female union organizers is Alice Kessler-Harris, "Organizing the Unorganizable: Three Jewish Women and Their Union," 1976; reprinted in Nadell, *American Jewish Women's History*, 1976, pp. 100-115.

25   Beth S. Wenger, "Budgets, Boycotts, and Babies: Jewish Women in the Great Depression," in Nadell, *American Jewish Women's History*, pp. 185-200.

26   Elinor Lerner, "Jewish Involvement in the New York City Woman Suffrage Movement," *American Jewish History* 71 (June 1981): 442-461.

27   Markowitz opens her book with this; Markowitz, *My Daughter, the Teacher*, p. 1. On the neighborhoods of second settlement, see Deborah Dash Moore, *At Home in America: Second Generation New York Jews* (New York: Columbia University Press, 1981).

28   The growing literature on American Jews' vacation patterns includes Irwin Richman, *Borscht Belt Bungalows* (Philadelphia: Temple University Press, 1998). Jewish women's involvement in American culture is beyond the scope of this essay.

29   On the sisterhoods, see Jenna Weissman Joselit, "The Jewish Priestess and Ritual: The Sacred Life of American Orthodox Women," in Nadell, *American Jewish Women's History*, pp. 153-174, especially, pp. 161-163. This is excerpted from Jenna Weissman Joselit, *New York's Jewish Jews: The Orthodox Community in the Interwar Years* (Bloomington: Indiana University Press, 1990). Pamela S. Nadell and Rita J. Simon, "Ladies of the Sisterhood: Women in the American Reform Synagogue, 1900-1930," in *Active Voices: Women in Jewish Culture*, ed. Maurie Sacks (Urbana: University of Illinois Press, 1995), pp. 63-75. On "Jewish Home Beautiful," see Jenna Weissman Joselit, *The Wonders of America: Reinventing Jewish Culture, 1880-1950* (New York: Hill and Wang, 1994), pp. 161-162.

30   Pamela S. Nadell, *Women Who Would Be Rabbis: A History of Women's Ordination, 1889-1985* (Boston: Beacon Press, 1998).

31   Mary McCune, "Creating a Place for Women in a Socialist Brotherhood: Class and Gender Politics in the Workmen's Circle, 1892-1930," *Feminist Studies* 28, no. 3 (2002): 585-612.

32   Julia L. Foulkes, "Angels 'Rewolt!': Jewish Women in Modern Dance in the 1930s," 2000; reprinted in Nadell, *American Jewish Women's History*, pp. 210-217.

33   Joyce Antler, "Zion in Our Hearts: Henrietta Szold and the American Jewish Women's Movement," 1995; reprinted in Nadell, *American Jewish Women's History*, pp. 129-149. For a full-length biography of Szold, see Joan Dash, *Summoned to Jerusalem: The Life of Henrietta Szold* (New York: Harper & Row, 1979).

34   Wenger, "Budgets, Boycotts, and Babies."

35   Rona Sheramy, "'There Are Times When Silence Is a Sin': The Women's Division of the American Jewish Congress and the Anti-Nazi Boycott Movement," *American Jewish History* 89, no. 1 (2001): 105-121.

36 Arthur Hertzberg, *A Jew in America: My Life and a People's Struggle for Identity* (New York: Harper San Francisco, 2002), pp. 73, 142-143. On the role of the rebbetzin, see Shuly Rubin Schwartz, "'We Married What We Wanted to Be': The Rebbetzin in Twentieth Century America," *American Jewish History* 83, no. 2 (1995): 223-246.

37 Aleisa Fishman, "Keeping Up with the Goldbergs: Gender, Consumer Culture, and Jewish Identity in Suburban Nassau County, NY, 1946–1960" (Ph.D. dissertation, American University, 2004). Deborah Dash Moore, *To the Golden Cities: Pursuing the American Jewish Dream in Miami and L.A.* (New York: Free Press, 1994).

38 Joellyn Wallen Zollman, "Shopping for a Future: A History of the American Synagogue Gift Shop" (Ph.D. dissertation, Brandeis University, 2002).

39 Marshall Sklare was the first to discuss the retention of Jewish religious rituals in the suburbs in terms of their focus on the children; Marshall Sklare, *Jewish Identity on the Suburban Frontier: A Study of Group Survival in the Open Society*, 2nd ed. (Chicago: University of Chicago Press, 1967, 1979), pp. 58-59.

40 Lawrence N. Powell, *Troubled Memory: Anne Levy, the Holocaust, and David Duke's Louisiana* (Chapel Hill: University of North Carolina Press, 2000), on the NCJW, pp. 380-382.

41 Stephanie Wellen Levine, *Mystics, Mavericks, and Merrymakers: An Intimate Journey among Hasidic Girls* (New York: New York University Press, 2003), esp. pp. 34, 47-48, 54. Levine notes that the average Lubavitcher Hasidic family has eight children needing financial support, p. 54.

42 Sherry B. Ortner, *New Jersey Dreaming: Capital, Culture, and the Class of '58* (Durham: Duke University Press, 2003), p. 240. Sidney Goldstein, "Profile of American Jewry: Insights from the 1990 National Jewish Population Survey," *American Jewish Year Book* 92 (1992): 77-173, table 13.

43 Ortner, *New Jersey Dreaming*, p. 37; Goldstein, "Profile of American Jewry," pp. 115-116.

44 Nadell, *Women Who Would Be Rabbis*.

45 Pamela S. Nadell, "Original Voices: The First Generation of Female Rabbis" (paper presented at the conference on Women and American Judaism, Wayne State University, May 2003).

46 Debra L. Schultz, *Going South: Jewish Women in the Civil Rights Movement* (New York: New York University Press, 2001).

47 Joyce Antler, *The Journey Home: How Jewish Women Shaped Modern America* (New York: Schocken Books, 1997), pp. 259-284.

48 Fanny Brooks is considered the first Jewish woman to cross the plains. She sold goods to miners in Timbuktu in the 1850s; Ava F. Kahn and Marc Dollinger, eds. *California Jews* (Hanover, New Hampshire: Brandeis University Press/University Press of New England, 2003), p. 31.

49 Ruth Mosko Handler named the Barbie doll for her daughter Barbara; Julie Altman, "Ruth Mosko Handler," in *Jewish Women in America*, ed. Hyman and Moore, pp. 591-592.

A History of American Anti-Semitism

1 Quoted in Sigmund Livingstone, *Must Men Hate?* (New York: Harper and Bros., 1944), p. 4.

2 Alfred Moritz Myers, *The Young Jew* (Philadelphia: American Sunday-School Union, 1848), p. 7.

3   Quoted in Louis Ruchames, "The Abolitionists and the Jews: Some Further Thoughts," Bertram A. Korn, ed., *A Bicentennial Festschrift for Jacob Rader Marcus* (Waltham, Massachusetts: American Jewish Historical Society, 1976), pp. 509-510.

4   Quoted in Leonard Dinnerstein, *Antisemitism in America* (New York: Oxford University Press, 1994), p. 17.

5   John Higham, *Send These to Me*, rev. ed. (Baltimore: Johns Hopkins University Press, 1984), p. 124.

6   Quoted in Lloyd P. Gartner, "Temples of Liberty Unpolluted: American Jews and Public Schools, 1840-1875," in Korn, *Bicentennial*, pp. 175-176.

7   "The Experience of a Jew's Wife," *American Magazine* 78 (December 1914): 49.

8   Quoted in Leonard Dinnerstein, *The Leo Frank Case* (New York: Columbia University Press, 1968), p. 130.

9   For a description of the lynchers see Steve Oney, *And the Dead Shall Rise* (New York: Pantheon, 2003), chap. 14 *passim*.

10 Helen Gaudet Erskine, "The Polls: Religious Prejudice, Part 2: Anti-Semitism," *Public Opinion Quarterly* 29 (Winter 1965-1966): 651.

11 Heywood Broun and George Britt, *Christians Only* (New York: Vanguard Press, 1931), p. 273.

12 Morris Freedman, "The Knickerbocker Case," *Commentary* 8 (August 1949): 2.

13 Quoted in Dinnerstein, *Antisemitism in America*, p. 136.

14 Sheldon Menefee, *Assignment U.S.* (New York: Reynal and Hitchcock, Inc., 1943), p. 102.

15 Maury Paul, "Letter to the Editor," *Time* 41 (April 12, 1943): 10.

16 See note 10.

17 Chaim I. Waxman, *Jewish Baby Boomers: A Communal Perspective* (Albany: State University of New York Press, 2001), pp. 27-28, 29.

18 NJPS Review Committee, Mark A. Schulman, chair, "The National Jewish Population Survey, 2000-2001," released September 19, 2003, pp. 6, 23; Peter Novick, *The Holocaust in American Life* (Boston: Houghton Mifflin Co., 1999), pp. 183, 195.

19 Herbert J. Gans, "The Future of American Jewry," *Commentary* (June 1956): 557; Oscar Handlin, "The American Jewish Committee," *Commentary* (January 1957): 9.

20 *Harper's Magazine* 19 (1859): 859-860.

21 James Weldon Johnson, "The Negro and the Jew," *New York Age* (February 2, 1918): p. 4.

22 "As the Crow Flies," *The Crisis* 40 (September 1933): 97.

23 "Germany vs. America," *Philadelphia Tribune*, July 5, 1934, p. 4.

24 "The Jew and the Negro," *National Baptist Voice* (Nashville, Tennessee) 38 (May 15, 1945): 1.

25 Quoted in Fred Barnes, "Farrakhan Frenzy," *New Republic* 193 (October 28, 1985): 14.

26 Quoted in Julius Lester, "The Time Has Come," *New Republic* 193 (October 21, 1985): 12.

27 Jerusalem Center for Public Affairs, "The Resuscitation of Anti-Semitism, An American Perspective: An Interview with Abraham Foxman," October 1, 2003, p. 2.

28 Ibid., p. 7. The interview will be part of a forthcoming book, *Changing Jewish Attitudes and Expectations in the American Public Square*, ed. Manfred Gerstenfeld.

29 E-mail from Jerome Chanes to Leonard Dinnerstein, March 2, 2003.

American Jews and Politics

1 Quoted in Sarah Boxer, "William Steig, 95, Dies; Tough Youths and Jealous Satyrs Scowled in His Cartoons," *New York Times*, October 5, 2003, I, p. 30.

2 Stephan Thernstrom and Abigail Thernstrom, *America in Black and White: One Nation, Indivisible* (New York: Simon and Schuster, 1997), p. 541.

3 Nathan Glazer et al., "Jews and American Politics—1984. . . and After," *This World* 10 (Winter 1985): 18.

4 Quoted in Melvin I. Urofsky, *A Mind of One Piece: Brandeis and American Reform* (New York: Charles Scribner's Sons, 1971), p. 100.

5 Woody Allen, *Four Films of Woody Allen* (New York: Random House, 1982), p. 265.

6 Quoted in Henry L. Feingold, *A Midrash on American Jewish History* (Albany: State University of New York Press, 1982), p. 203.

7 Quoted in Feingold, *Midrash*, p. 204.

8 Quoted in *Jews in American Politics*, ed. L. Sandy Maisel (Lanham, Maryland: Rowman and Littlefield, 2001), p. 62.

9 Quoted in Gershom Gorenberg, "Christian-Right Zionism," *New York Times Magazine*, December 15, 2002, p. 72.

American Jewish Popular Culture

1 See Barbara Kirshenblatt-Gimblett, "The Folk Culture of Jewish Immigrant Communities: Research Paridigms and Directions," in *The Jews of North America*, ed. Moses Rischin (Detroit: Wayne State University Press, 1987), pp. 79-94.

2 See Andrew R. Heinze, *Adapting to Abundance: Jewish Immigrants, Mass Consumption, and the Search for American Identity* (New York: Columbia University Press, 1990).

3 See Nina Warnke, "Immigrant Popular Culture as Contested Sphere: Yiddish Music Halls, the Yiddish Press, and the Process of Americanization, 1900-1910," *Theatre Journal* 48 (1996): 321-335.

4 See Joel Berkowitz, *Shakespeare on the American Yiddish Stage* (Iowa City: University of Iowa Press, 2002).

5 See J. Hoberman, *Bridge of Light: Yiddish Film Between Two Worlds* (New York: Schocken, 1991).

6   See Barbara Kirshenblatt-Gimblett, "Imagining Europe: The Popular Arts of American Jewish Ethnography," in *Divergent Jewish Cultures: Israel and America*, ed. Deborah Dash Moore and S. Ilan Troen (New Haven: Yale University Press, 2001), pp. 155-191. On *Fiddler on the Roof*, see Seth Wolitz, "The Americanization of Tevye or Boarding the Jewish *Mayflower*," *American Quarterly* 49 (1988): 514-536.

7   A. A. Milne, *Vini-der-Pu*, trans. Leonard Wolf (New York: Dutton Children's Books, 2000); Dr. Seuss, *Di kats der payats*, trans. Sholem Berger (New York: Twenty-fourth Street Books, 2003).

8   See , *Adventures in Yiddishland: Postvernacular Language and Culture*, University of California Press, forthcoming.

9   See Harley Erdman, *Staging the Jew: The Performance of an American Ethnicity, 1860-1920* (New Brunswick, New Jersey: Rutgers University Press, 1997).

10 See Patricia Erens, *The Jew in American Cinema* (Bloomington: Indiana University Press, 1984).

11 See *The Jazz Singer*, ed. Robert L. Carringer (Madison: University of Wisconsin Press, 1979); Mark Slobin, "Some Intersections of Jews, Music, and Theater," in *From Hester Street to Hollywood: The Jewish-American Stage and Screen*, ed. Sarah Blacher Cohen (Bloomington: Indiana University Press, 1983), pp. 29-43; J. Hoberman, "On *The Jazz Singer* and *The Jazz Singer*: A Chronology," in *Entertaining America: Jews, Movies, and Broadcasting*, ed. J. Hoberman and Jeffrey Shander (Princeton: Princeton University Press, 2003), pp. 77-92.

12 See Deborah Dash Moore, *At Home in America: Second Generation New York Jews* (New York: Columbia University Press, 1981).

13 Henry Popkin, "The Vanishing Jew of Our Popular Culture," *Commentary* 14, no. 1 (July 1952): 46.

14 See Edward Shapiro, *A Time for Healing: American Jewry since World War II* (Baltimore: Johns Hopkins University Press, 1992), pp. 9-15.

15 William Novak and Moshe Waldoks, eds., *The Big Book of Jewish Humor* (New York: Harper and Row, 1981), p. 60.

16 See J. Hoberman, "Flaunting It: The Rise and Fall of Hollywood's 'Nice' Jewish (Bad) Boys," in Hoberman and Shandler, *Entertaining America*, pp. 220-243.

17 See J. Hoberman and , "Our *Show of Shows*" and "The Marx Brothers," in *Entertaining America*, pp. 144-149, 159-163.

18 See Mark Slobin, *Fiddler on the Move: Exploring the Klezmer World* (New York: Oxford University Press, 2002).

19 Philip Roth, *Operation Shylock: A Confession* (New York: Simon and Schuster, 1993), p. 157.

20 See Steven Carr, *Hollywood and Anti-Semitism: A Cultural History up to World War II* (Cambridge: Cambridge University Press, 2001).

21 See Stuart Svonkin, *Against Prejudice: American Jews and the Intergroup Relations Movement from World War to Cold War* (New York: Columbia University Press, 1997).

22 See Jeffrey Shandler and Elihu Katz, "Broadcasting American Judaism: The Radio and Television Department of the Jewish Theological Seminary," in *Tradition Renewed: A History of the Jewish Theological Seminary*, ed. Jack Wertheimer (New York: Jewish Theological Seminary, 1997), pp. 363-401.

23 See Jonathan S. Woocher, *Sacred Survival: The Civil Religion of American Jews* (Bloomington: Indiana University Press, 1986).

24   See Arthur A. Goren, "Celebrating Zion in America," in *Encounters with the "Holy Land": Place, Past, and Future in American Jewish Culture*, ed. and Beth S. Wenger (Hanover, New Hampshire: Brandeis University Press / Philadelphia: Center for Judaic Studies, University of Pennsylvania / Philadelphia: National Museum of American Jewish History, 1997), pp. 41-59; , "Producing the Future: The Impresario Culture of American Zionism before 1948," in *Divergent Jewish Cultures: Israel and America*, ed. Deborah Dash Moore and S. Ilan Troen (New Haven: Yale University Press, 2001), pp. 53-71.

25   See Deborah Dash Moore, *To the Golden Cities: Pursuing the American Jewish Dream in Miami and L.A.* (New York: Free Press, 1994), chap. 8.

26   See Judith Doneson, *The Holocaust in American Film*, 2nd ed. (Syracuse: Syracuse University Press, 2002); Jeffrey Shandler, *While America Watches: Televising the Holocaust* (New York: Oxford University Press, 1999); Hilene Flanzbaum, ed., *Americanization of the Holocaust* (Baltimore: Johns Hopkins University Press, 1999).

27   See Mark Slobin, *Chosen Voices: The Story of the American Cantorate* (Urbana: University of Illinois Press, 2002).

28   See Jenna Weissman Joselit, *The Wonders of America: Reinventing Jewish Culture, 1880-1950* (New York: Hill and Wang, 1994), chap. 6.

29   See Mark Kligman, "On the Creators and Consumers of Orthodox Popular Music in Brooklyn," *YIVO Annual* 23 (1996): 259-293.

30   See Samuel J. Rosenthal, "Golden 'Boychik,'" in Hoberman and Shandler, *Entertaining America*, pp. 173-175.

31   See Donald Weber, "Goldberg Variations: The Achievements of Gertrude Berg," and J. Hoberman, "*The Goldbergs*: A Chronology," in Hoberman and Shandler, *Entertaining America*, pp. 113-127.

Suggested Readings
in American Jewish History

Peggy K. Pearlstein

About the Judaica Collections of the Library of Congress

Baker, Zachary, comp. *"The Lawrence Marwick Collection of Copyrighted Yiddish Plays at the Library of Congress."* forthcoming.

Besso, Henry V. *Ladino Books in the Library of Congress: A Bibliography.* Washington: Library of Congress, 1963.

Heskes, Irene. *Yiddish American Popular Songs, 1895-1950: A Catalog Based on the Lawrence Marwick Roster of Copyright Entries.* Washington: Library of Congress, 1992.

Karp, Abraham J. *From the Ends of the Earth: Judaic Treasures of the Library of Congress.* Washington: Library of Congress, 1991.

Kohn, Gary, comp. *The Jewish Experience: A Guide to Manuscript Sources in the Library of Congress.* Cincinnati: American Jewish Archives, 1986.

Library of Congress Hebraic Collections: an Illustrated Guide. Text by Michael W. Grunberger. Washington: Library of Congress, 2001.

Marwick, Lawrence. "The Hebrew Collections in the Library of Congress," *Jewish Book Annual* 36 (1978-79).

Murphy, Ellen R. "Jewish Genealogical Materials in the Library of Congress," *Toledot: The Journal of Jewish Genealogy* 4 (1982): 3.

Pearlstein, Peggy K. and Barbara A. Tenenbaum. "Area Studies Collections," in *American Women: A Library of Congress Guide for the Study of Women's History and Culture in the United States.* Washington: Library of Congress, 2001.

Pearlstein, Peggy K. "Jewish Sources for Genealogy in the U.S. Library of Congress," *Avotaynu: The International Review of Jewish Genealogy* 10 (1994): 3.

Weinstein, Myron M., editor. *The Washington Haggadah: A Facsimile Edition of an Illuminated Fifteenth-Century Hebrew Manuscript at the Library of Congress, Signed by Joel ben Simeon.* Washington: Library of Congress, 1991.

General Reading

Diner, Hasia. *The Jews of the United States, 1654 to 2000.* Berkeley: University of California Press, 2004.

Feingold, Henry L., General Editor. *The Jewish People in America.* 5 vols. Baltimore and London: The Johns Hopkins University Press, 1992.

Fischel, Jack and Sanford Pinsker, editors. *Jewish-American History and Culture: An Encyclopedia.* New York and London: Garland Publishing Company, 1992.

Karp, Abraham J. *A History of the Jews in America.* Northvale: Jason Aronson, 1997.
Rev. edition of *Haven and Home.*

Marcus, Jacob Rader. *The American Jew, 1585-1990: A History.* Brooklyn: Carlson Publishing, 1995.

Marcus, Jacob Rader. *United States Jewry, 1776-1985.* 4 vols. Detroit: Wayne State University Press, 1985-1993.

Papo, Joseph M. *Sephardim in Twentieth Century America: In Search of Unity.* San Jose: Pele Yoetz Books; Berkeley: Judah L. Magnes Museum, 1987.

Raphael, Marc Lee, editor. *Jews and Judaism in the United States: A Documentary History.* New York: Behrman House, 1983.

Schappes, Morris U. *A Documentary History of the Jews in the United States, 1654-1875.* 3rd ed., New York: Schocken Books, [1971].

Prologue to American Jewish History: The Jews of America From 1654 to 1820

Beginnings, Early American Judaica: A Collection of Ten Publications, in Facsimile, Illustrative of the Religious, Communal, Cultural & Political Life of American Jewry, 1761-1845. Introduced by Abraham J. Karp. Philadelphia: Jewish Publication Society of America, [1975].

Blau, Joseph L. and Salo W. Baron, editors. *The Jews of the United States, 1790-1840: A Documentary History.* 3 vols. New York: Columbia University Press, 1963.

De Sola Pool, David. *Portraits Etched in Stone: Early Jewish Settlers, 1682-1831.* New York: Columbia University Press, 1952.

Faber, Eli. *A Time for Planting: The First Migration, 1654-1820.* [Baltimore: Johns Hopkins University Press, 1992]. Volume I, *The Jewish People in America.*

Marcus, Jacob Rader. *The Colonial American Jew, 1492-1776.* 3 vols. Detroit: Wayne State University Press, 1970.

Marcus, Jacob Rader. *Early American Jewry.* 2 vols. Philadelphia: Jewish Publication Society, 1951-53.

Rosenwaike, Ira. *On the Edge of Greatness: A Portrait of American Jewry in the Early National Period.* Cincinnati: American Jewish Archives, 1985.

A Century of Migration

Cohen, Naomi. *Encounter With Emancipation: German Jews in the United States, 1830-1914.* Philadelphia: Jewish Publication Society, 1984.

A Century of Migration *(continued)*

Diner, Hasia. *Hungering for America: Italian, Irish, and Jewish Foodways in the Age of Migration.* Cambridge: Harvard University Press, 2002.

Diner, Hasia. *A Time for Gathering: The Second Migration, 1820-1880.* Baltimore and London: The Johns Hopkins University Press, 1992. Vol. II, *The Jewish People in America.*

Grinstein, Hyman B. *The Rise of the Jewish Community of New York, 1654-1860.* Philadelphia: Porcupine Press, 1976. Reprint.

Higham, John. *Send These to Me: Immigrants in Urban America.* Rev. ed. Baltimore: Johns Hopkins University Press, 1984.

Howe, Irving. *World of Our Fathers,* with the assistance of Kenneth Libo. New York: Harcourt Brace Jovanovich, 1976.

Rischin, Moses. *The Promised City: New York's Jews, 1870-1914.* Cambridge: Harvard University Press, 1977.

Simon, Rita J. *In the Golden Land: A Century of Russian and Soviet Jewish Immigration in America.* Westport: Praeger, 1997.

Sorin, Gerald. *A Time for Building: The Third Migration, 1880-1920.* Baltimore and London: The Johns Hopkins University Press, 1992. Vol. III, *The Jewish People in America.*

America's Jewish Women

Antler, Joyce. *The Journey Home: Jewish Women and the American Century.* New York: The Free Press, 1997.

Antler, Joyce, editor. *Talking Back: Images of Jewish Women in American Popular Culture.* Hanover: Brandeis University Press: Published by University Press of New England, 1998.

Baum, Charlotte, Paula E. Hyman and Sonya Michel. *The Jewish Woman in America.* New York: Dial Press, 1976.

Diner, Hasia R. and Beryl Lieff Benderly. *Her Works Praise Her: A History of Jewish Women in America from Colonial Times to the Present.* New York: Basic Books, 2002.

Fishman, Sylvia Barack. *A Breath of Life: Feminism in the American Jewish Community.* Hanover: Brandeis University Press: Published by University Press of New England, 1995.

Goldman, Karla. *Beyond the Synagogue Gallery: Finding a Place for Women in American Judaism.* Cambridge: Harvard University Press, 2000.

Hyman, Paula E. *Gender and Assimilation In Modern Jewish History: the Roles and Representation of Women.* Seattle: University of Washington Press, 1995.

Hyman, Paula E. and Deborah Dash Moore. *Jewish Women in America: An Historical Encyclopedia.* 2 vols. New York: Routledge, 1997.

Marcus, Jacob Rader. *The American Jewish Woman: A Documentary History.* New York: Ktav Publishing House; Cincinnati: American Jewish Archives, 1981.

Marcus, Jacob Rader. *The American Jewish Woman, 1654-1980.* New York: Ktav Publishing House; Cincinnati: American Jewish Archives, 1981.

Nadell, Pamela S., editor. *American Jewish Women's History: A Reader*. New York: New York University Press, 2003.

Nadell, Pamela S. and Jonathan D. Sarna, editors. *Women and American Judaism: Historical Perspectives*. Hanover and London: University Press of New England, 2001.

Nadell, Pamela S. *Women Who Would Be Rabbis: A History of Women's Ordination, 1889-1985*. Boston: Beacon Press, 1998.

The War Between Jewish Brothers in America

Evans, Eli. *Judah P. Benjamin: The Jewish Confederate*. New York: Free Press, 1988.

Evans, Eli. *The Provincials: A Personal History of Jews in the South*. New York: Free Press, 1973, reissued, 1997.

Faber, Eli. *Jews, Slaves, and the Slave Trade: Setting the Record Straight*. New York: New York University Press, 1998.

Friedman, Saul S. *Jews and the American Slave Trade*. New Brunswick: Transaction Publishers, 1998.

Korn, Bertram Wallace. *American Jewry and the Civil War*. Philadelphia: Jewish Publication Society, 2001.

Rosen, Robert N. *The Jewish Confederates*. Columbia: University of South Carolina Press, 2000.

Simonhoff, Harry. *Jewish Participants in the Civil War*. New York: Arco Publishing Company [1963].

Wolf, Simon. *The American Jew as Patriot, Solder, and Citizen*. Boston, Gregg Press, 1972. [c 1895].

The Crucial Decades

Cohen, Naomi W. *The Americanization of Zionism, 1897-1948*. Hanover and London: Brandeis University Press, 2003.

Feingold, Henry L. *A Time for Searching: Entering the Mainstream, 1920-1945*. Baltimore and London: The Johns Hopkins University Press, 1992. Vol. IV, *The Jewish People in America*.

Gorenstein, Lillian. "*A Memoir of the Great War, 1914-1924,* " in Deborah Dash Moore, editor. *YIVO Annual* (1991). Vol. 20: 125-184.

Heinze, Andrew R. *Adapting to Abundance: Jewish Immigrants, Mass Consumption, and the Search for American Identity*. New York: Columbia University Press, 1990.

Joselit, Jenna Weissman. *The Wonders of America: Reinventing Jewish Culture, 1880-1950*. New York: Hill and Wang, 1994.

Moore, Deborah Dash. *At Home in America: Second Generation New York Jews*. New York: Columbia University Press, 1981.

Moore, Deborah Dash. *To the Golden Cities: Pursuing the American Jewish Dream in Miami and L.A*. New York: The Free Press, 1994.

Wenger, Beth S. *New York Jews and the Great Depression: Uncertain Promise*. Syracuse: Syracuse University Press, 1999.

Anti-Semitism

Blakeslee, Spencer. *The Death of American Antisemitism*. Westport: Praeger, 2000.

Carr, Steven. *Hollywood and Anti-Semitism: A Cultural History Up to World War II*. Cambridge: Cambridge University Press, 2001.

Chanes, Jerome, editor. *Antisemitism in America Today: Outspoken Experts Explode the Myths*. Secaucus: Carol Pub. Group, 1995.

Chanes, Jerome. *A Dark Side of History: Antisemitism Through the Ages*. [United States]: Anti-Defamation League, 2000.

Dinnerstein, Leonard. *Antisemitism in America*. New York: Oxford University Press, 1994.

Dinnerstein, Leonard. *Uneasy at Home: Antisemitism and the American Jewish Experience*. New York: Columbia University Press, 1987.

Dobkowski, Michael N. *The Tarnished Dream: the Basis of American Anti-Semitism*. Westport: Greenwood Press, 1979.

Gerber, David A., editor. *Anti-Semitism in American History*. Urbana: University of Illinois Press, 1986.

Higham, John. *Strangers in the Land: Patterns of American Nativism, 1860-1925*. New Brunswick: Rutgers University Press, [2002].

Oney, Steve. *And the Dead Shall Rise: The Murder of Mary Phagan and the Lynching of Leo Frank*. New York: Pantheon Books, 2003.

American Jewry Since 1945

Flanzbaum, Hilene, editor. *The Americanization of the Holocaust*. Baltimore: Johns Hopkins University Press, 1999.

Freedman, Samuel. *Jew vs. Jew: The Struggle for the Soul of American Jewry*. New York: Touchstone, 2001.

Goldberg, J.J. *Jewish Power: Inside the American Jewish Establishment*. Reading: Addison-Wesley, 1996.

Herberg, Will. *Protestant, Catholic, Jew: An Essay in American Religious Sociology*. New York: Doubleday, 1955.

Moore, Deborah Dash. *To the Golden Cities: Pursuing the American Jewish Dream in Miami and L.A.* New York: The Free Press, 1994.

Shapiro, Edward S. *A Time for Healing: American Jewry Since World War II*. Baltimore and London: The Johns Hopkins University Press, 1992. Vol. V, *The Jewish People in America*.

Sklare, Marshall. *America's Jews*. New York: Random House, 1971.

Sklare, Marshall. *Jewish Identity on the Suburban Frontier: A Study of Group Survival in the Open Society*. Chicago: University of Chicago Press, 1979.

Silberman, Charles E. *A Certain People: American Jews and Their Lives Today*. New York: Summit Books, 1985.

Waxman, Chaim I. *America's Jews in Transition*. Philadelphia: Temple University Press, 1983.

American Judaism

Gurock, Jeffrey S. *American Jewish Orthodoxy in Historical Perspective*. Hoboken: Ktav Pub. House, 1996.

Jick, Leon A. *The Americanization of the Synagogue, 1820-1870*. Hanover: University Press of New England for Brandeis University, 1976.

Meyer, Michael A. *Response to Modernity: A History of the Reform Movement in Judaism*. Detroit: Wayne State University Press, 1995. Previously published: New York: Oxford University Press, 1988.

Raphael, Marc Lee. *Judaism in America*. New York: Columbia University Press, 2003.

Raphael, Marc Lee. *Profiles in American Judaism: the Reform, Conservative, Orthodox, and Reconstructionist Traditions in Historical Perspective*. San Francisco: Harper & Row, 1984.

Sarna, Jonathan. *American Judaism: A History*. New Haven: Yale University Press, 2004.

Wertheimer, Jack. *A People Divided: Judaism in Contemporary America*. [Waltham, Mass.]: Brandeis University Press; Hanover: University Press of New England, 1997.

Wertheimer, Jack, editor. *Tradition Renewed: A History of the Jewish Theological Seminary*. 2 vols. New York: The Seminary, 1997. Previously published: New York: Basic Books, 1993.

Woocher, Jonathan S. *Sacred Survival: The Civil Religion of American Jews*. Bloomington & Indianapolis: Indiana University Press, 1986.

American Jews and Politics

Dollinger, Marc. *Quest for Inclusion: Jews and Liberalism in Modern America*. Princeton: Princeton University Press, 2000.

Feingold, Henry L. *Lest Memory Cease: Finding Meaning in the American Jewish Past*. Syracuse: Syracuse University Press, 1996.

Forman, Seth. *Blacks in the Jewish Mind; A Crisis of Liberalism*. New York: New York University Press, 1998.

Friedman, Murray. *What Went Wrong?: The Creation and Collapse of the Black-Jewish Alliance*. New York: The Free Press, 1995.

Fuchs, Lawrence H. *The Political Behavior of American Jews*. Westport: Greenwood Press, 1980, c 1956.

Goren, Arthur A. *The Politics and Public Culture of American Jews*. Bloomington: Indiana University Press, 1999.

Halpern, Ben. *Jews and Blacks; the Classic American Minorities*. [New York]: Herder and Herder, [1971].

Isaacs, Stephen D. *Jews and American Politics*. Garden City: Doubleday, 1974.

Liebman, Arthur. *Jews and the Left*. New York: Wiley, 1979.

Maisel, L. Sandy, editor. *Jews in American Politics*. Lanham: Rowman & Littlefield, 2001.

Medoff, Rafael. *Jewish Americans and Political Participation*. Santa Barbara: ABC Clio, 2002.

Staub, Michael E. *Torn at the Roots: The Crisis of Jewish Liberalism in Postwar America*. New York: Columbia University Press, 2002.

American Jewish Popular Culture

Brook, Vincent. *Something Ain't Kosher Here*. New Brunswick: Rutgers University Press, 2002.

Cohen, Sarah Blacher, editor. *From Hester Street to Hollywood: the Jewish-American State and Screen*. Bloomington: Indiana University Press, 1983.

Doneson, Judith E. *The Holocaust in American Film*. Syracuse: Syracuse University Press, 2002.

Erdman, Harley. *Staging the Jew: the Performance of an American Ethnicity, 1860-1920*. New Brunswick: Rutgers University Press, 1997.

Erens, Patricia. *The Jew in American Cinema*. Bloomington: Indiana University Press, 1984.

Gertel, Elliot. *Over the Top Judaism: Precedents and Trends in the Depiction of Jewish Beliefs and Observances in Film and Television*. Lanham: University Press of America, 2003.

Goldman, Eric A. *Visions, Images, and Dreams: Yiddish Film Past and Present*. Teaneck: Ergo Media, 1988.

Gottlieb, Jack. *Funny, It Doesn't Sound Jewish: How Yiddish Songs and Synagogue Melodies Influenced Tin Pan Alley, Broadway, and Hollywood*. Albany: State University of New York, in association with the Library of Congress, 2004.

Heinze, Andrew R. *Adapting to Abundance: Jewish Immigrants, Mass Consumption, and the Search for American Identity*. New York: Columbia University Press, 1990.

Hoberman, J. *Bridge of Light: Yiddish Film Between Two Worlds*. New York: Museum of Modern Art, 1991.

Pearl, Jonathan and Judith Pearl. *The Chosen Image: Television's Portrayal of Jewish Themes and Characters*. Jefferson: McFarland, 1999.

Shandler, Jeffrey. *While America Watches: Televising the Holocaust*. New York: Oxford University Press, 1999.

Whitfield, Stephen J. *In Search of American Jewish Culture*. Hanover: Brandeis University Press, 1999.

Zurawik, David. *The Jews of Prime Time*. Hanover: University Press of New England, 2003.

About the Contributors

Hasia Diner is the Paul and Sylvia Steinberg Professor of American Jewish History and Director of the Goldstein-Goren Center for American Jewish History. She is the author of numerous books, including *Lower East Side Memories: The Jewish Place in America, Hungering for America: Italian, Irish, and Jewish Foodways in the Age of Migration*, and, with Beryl Lief Benderly, *Her Works Praise Her: A History of Jewish Women in America from Colonial Times to the Present*, and, most recently, *A History of the Jews of the United States, 1654–2000.*

Leonard Dinnerstein is Professor Emeritus of History at the University of Arizona, where he taught from 1970–2004. He is the author of *The Leo Frank Case, America and the Survivors of the Holocaust*, and *Anti-semitism in America*, which won the National Jewish Book Award in History for 1993–1994.

Eli N. Evans is the author of *The Provincials: A Personal History of the Jews of the South, Judah P. Benjamin: The Jewish Confederate*, and *The Lonely Days were Sundays: Reflections of a Jewish Southerner.*

Eli Faber is Professor of History at the City University of New York, at both John Jay College of Criminal Justice and the University Graduate Center. He is the author of *A Time for Planting: The First Migration, 1654–1820*, which is the first volume of *The Jewish People in America*, as well as of *Jews, Slaves, and the Slave Trade: Setting the Record Straight.*

Michael W. Grunberger is Head of the Hebraic Section in the Library of Congress and curator of the Library of Congress's exhibition, *From Haven to Home: 350 Years of Jewish Life in America*. In recent years, he has served as the Library of Congress curator for *Zion's Call: A Library of Congress Exhibition Marking Israel's Fiftieth Year* and *Scrolls from the Dead Sea: The Ancient Library of Qumran and Modern Scholarship.*

Deborah Dash Moore is the William R. Kenan, Jr. Professor of Religion at Vassar College and director of the Jewish Studies Program. She has written widely on American Jewish history in the twentieth century. Her books include *To the Golden Cities: Pursuing the American Jewish Dream in Miami and LA* and *At Home in America: Second Generation New York Jews*. Her most recent book is *GI Jews: How World War II Changed a Generation.*

Pamela S. Nadell is Professor of History and Director of the Jewish Studies Program at American University. She is the author of *Women Who Would Be Rabbis: A History of Women's Ordination*, editor of *American Jewish Women's History*, and co-editor, with Jonathan D. Sarna, of *Women and American Judaism: Historical Perspectives*.

Peggy K. Pearlstein is the Area Specialist in the Hebraic Section of the Library of Congress. President of the Research and Special Libraries Division of the Association of Jewish Libraries, she has written on American Jewish history and Jewish genealogy.

Jonathan D. Sarna is the Joseph H. & Belle R. Braun Professor of American Jewish History at Brandeis University and chairs the Academic and Editorial Board of the Jacob Rader Marcus Center of the American Jewish Archives. He also serves as chief historian of the National Museum of American Jewish History and of Celebrate 350 and most recently is the author of *American Judaism: A History*.

Jeffrey Shandler is an Assistant Professor in the Department of Jewish Studies at Rutgers University. He is the author of *While America Watches: Televising the Holocaust*, coauthor (with J. Hoberman) of *Entertaining America: Jews, Movies, and Broadcasting*, and co-editor (with Hasia Diner and Beth S. Wenger) of *Remembering the Lower East Side: American Jewish Reflections*.

Jack Wertheimer is Provost and the Joseph and Martha Mendelson Professor of American Jewish History at the Jewish Theological Seminary of America. He is the author of *A People Divided: Judaism in Contemporary America* and a series of studies on the changing institutional life of American Jewry in the postwar era.

Stephen J. Whitfield is the Max Richter Professor of American Civilization at Brandeis University. He has served as visiting professor at the Hebrew University of Jerusalem, the Catholic University of Leuven (Belgium), and twice at the Sorbonne. He is the author of eight books, most recently *In Search of American Jewish Culture*, and is the editor of *A Companion to 20th-Century America*.

Index

Page numbers in italics refer to illustrations.

Rosen, Robert, 51, 53
Rosenblatt, Yossele, 209
Roth, Philip, 203, 204
Rothschild, Salomon de, 56
Rubin, Robert, 185
Russia
    Jewish emigrants from, 73, 81, 84, 84–85
    oppression of Jews in, *190*
    pogroms in, 85–86, *189*
    See also Soviet Jewry

S

Sahl, Mort, 203
Salomon, Haym, 30–31
Salute to Israel parade, *121*
Sanders, Bernie, 190
Sandler, Adam, 204–205
Sarna, Jonathan D., 18
Savannah, Georgia, 27, *44*
Schechter, Solomon, 141, 142
Schiff, Jacob H., 16
Schindler's List, 207, 211
Schurz, Carl, 56
Schwarz, Julius, *81*
Seddon, James A., 49
Seinfeld, Jerry, 115
Seixas, Gershom Mendes, *38*, 38
Seixas, Moses, 23
Seixas family, 30
Seligman, Joseph, 77–78, *166*, 166, *167*
Sephardic Jews, 26–27, 38, 74, 131, 133–134
The Settlement Cookbook, 92
Seuss, Dr., *199*
Shandler, Jeffrey, 18
Shearith Israel (New York), 31–32, *38*, *130*, 130–131, 133
Sherman, William Tecumseh, 56, 63
Sholem Aleichem, 198
Simon, Joseph, *33*, 34
Sisisky, Norman, 191
Six Day War, 121
Skorecki, Anne, 159, *161*
Skorecki, Lila, 159
Skorecki, Mark, 159
Skorecki, Ruth, 159
Slaton, John M., 169
slavery, *48*, 49
Smith, John Rubens, 37
Solomon, Edward, 56
Sommers, Lawrence, 185
Soviet Jewry, 121–123, *123*
Soviet Union, German invasion of, 108
Spielberg, Steven, 116
Spinoza, Baruch, 16
Statue of Liberty, 85, *92*, *97*, *113*, *129*, *151*, *152*
Steig, William, 180
Steinem, Gloria, 115

Stevenson, Adlai, 181
Stieglitz, Alfred, *79*
Stiles, Ezra, 39
Straus, Lazarus, 75–76
Student Struggle for Soviet Jewry, 121, *123*
Stuyvesant, Peter, 23, 24, 25, 26
Sukkot, *148*, 149
Synagogues
    architecture of, 36–38, *37*
    autonomy of, 134–135
    as community, 130–133
    sermons preached in, *36*
    sisterhoods, 155–157
    transformation of, 133–135
Szold, Henrietta, 151, *158*, 158
Szyk, Arthur, *9*

T

Tashlikh, *153*
Temple Emanu-El (New York), *141*, 150
Thalia Theatre, *90*
Thernstrom, Abigail, 182
Thernstrom, Stephan, 182
Tikkun, 123
Time magazine, *175*
Torah ark lintel, *33*
Torah scroll, *25*
Touro Synagogue (Newport), *37*, *131*
"Trefa Banquet," *140*
Triangle Shirtwaist Company, 157
Truman, Harry, *37*, *114*, 181
Tucker, Sophie, *205*

U

Unabhängiger Orden Treuer Schwestern, 150
Uncle Sam, *77*
Union of American Hebrew Congregations, *136*
Union of Councils for Soviet Jewry, 121
United Federation of Teachers, *175*
United Jewish Appeal, *113*, *117*
United States of America
    Jewish communities in, 86–93
    Yiddish map of, *70*
    See also Jewish immigrants to the United States
Urbansky, David, 54
Uris, Leon, *206*, 207

V

volunteer organizations, 100–101, 118–119

W

Wald, Lillian, 157

The Wall (Hersey), 207
Wallace, George C., 181–182
War Refugee Board, 110–111
Warsaw Ghetto uprising, 110, 207
Washington, George, *23*, 40–41, 42, *92*, *164*, 203
Wertheimer, Jack, 17
"When You're in Love, The Whole World Is Jewish," 204, 205
Whiston, William, 15
Whitehurst, Jesse, 47
Whitfield, Stephen J., 18
Wirth, Louis, 98
Wise, Isaac Mayer, 63, 65, *136*, 136–137, *139*, 140
Wise, Stephen S., *101*, 101, 108, *109*, 110, 190
Wolf, Simon, 49–50, 54, 55, 56
Workmen's Circle, 100
World Federation of the Bergen Belsen Survivors, *127*
World Union of Jewish Students, *124*
World War I poster, *97*
World War II, 107–111, *208*
    aftermath of, 113–115, 127, 143, 145
WPA Adult Education Program, *99*

Y

Yalow, Rosalyn, 115–116
Yeshiva College, 102, 142
Yiddish culture, 104
    films, 197–198
    as influence on American popular culture, 196–199
    play scripts, 16
    radio programming, 198
    theater, 16, 90, *90*, 104, 197
Yiddish dictionaries, 198–199
The Yiddisher Boy, 201
Yiddish language cookbook, 89–90, *90*
Yiddish press, 89–90
Yom Kippur War, 121, 123
Your Show of Shows, 204
Youth Aliyah, 100, *158*
Yulee, David (Levy), 58–59

Z

Zacharie, Isachar, 17, 59–63, *61*
Zionism, 100, 101, 157–158, 187, *188*, 192, *205*, 207